MW01630191

Voice
Lessons

Voice Lessons

ALICE EMBREE

BRISCOE CENTER
FOR AMERICAN HISTORY
THE UNIVERSITY OF TEXAS AT AUSTIN

DISTRIBUTED BY TOWER BOOKS, AN IMPRINT
OF THE UNIVERSITY OF TEXAS PRESS

Requests for permission to reproduce material from
this work should be sent to:
Office of the Director
Dolph Briscoe Center for American History
University of Texas at Austin
2300 Red River Stop D1100
Austin, TX 78712-1426

♾ The paper used in this book meets the minimum
requirements of ANSI/NISO z39.48-1992 (r1997)
(Permanence of Paper).

ISBN 978-0-9997318-6-4 (hardcover)
ISBN 978-1-953480-04-0 (library ebook)
ISBN 978-1-953480-05-7 (nonlibrary ebook)

Library of Congress Control Number: 2021931677

Frontispiece:
Alice Embree speaking at a University Freedom
Movement rally in April 1967, after being put on
disciplinary probation by the University of Texas
for an antiwar speech. *Photo by John Avant,
John Avant Photographic Archive, Briscoe Center
for American History.*

Unless otherwise noted, illustrations are from the
Alice Embree Papers, Briscoe Center for American
History, University of Texas at Austin.

Contents

Foreword

IT'S HARD TO BELIEVE THAT I'VE ONLY KNOWN ALICE EMBREE for five years. Trying to reconstruct how our relationship came about, I found an email she sent me in April of 2015 telling me about herself and asking if I would like to meet. "I was active in SDS and early Women's Liberation in Austin," she wrote, "and put on disciplinary probation by UT for an antiwar speech. My father was on the faculty at UT so I was hardly an outside agitator." The background was unnecessary. I already knew about Alice from one of my favorite books about the 1960s, *The Politics of Authenticity*, by Doug Rossinow, a book that uses Austin as a case study for exploring the New Left's origins, ideology, and impact. Alice also contributed to the landmark 1970 collection *Sisterhood Is Powerful*. As an American studies professor in Texas who teaches about the 1960s, it would be embarrassing for me not to know who she was. Now I know that such a lack of presumptuousness is typical Alice. And it's part of why I love the title of her memoir, *Voice Lessons*. For most of her life, beginning in high school, when she refused to accept that her African American classmate could not eat with her in a restaurant, Alice Embree has been an outspoken advocate for justice. Ironically, however, all these years she's struggled to find her voice.

Besides being far too modest about her own accomplishments, Alice is generous: with her time, with her knowledge, and with the incredible archive of materials she collected, organized, and then donated to the Briscoe Center for American History. Alice's archive is a great boon for researchers, but those interested in the many struggles, projects, and movements in which Alice has participated can gain intimate and personal insights into this history from reading Alice's memoir. Firsthand, we learn about integrating the dorms at the University of Texas. We learn what it was like to launch and operate *The Rag*, one of the earliest, most influential, and longest-running underground newspapers. We get an inside view of Students for a Democratic Society and the experience of participating in some of their most important actions, from organizing the university's version of the free speech movement to marching against the Vietnam War to leading efforts to bring controversial speakers to campus. Alice recounts the devastating aftermath of the University of Texas Tower shooting in 1966 as well as efforts by survivors to deal with its legacy decades later. We hear about how regent Frank Erwin summarily canceled a university exchange with Chile upon discovering that the "Embree girl" had gone on the exchange (in 1967) after having been on disciplinary probation for her outspoken criticism of the war in Vietnam. We even get an inside view of the Columbia University takeover in 1968, for Alice was there, on leave from the University of Texas and living in New York City.

If women's liberation told us that "the personal is political," Alice's own experience proves it. In the late 1960s Alice was part of what Rossinow describes as "the ultimate movement couple." But she and Jeff Shero (fellow SDS activist and founder of the movement newspaper *Rat*) parted ways because of how he responded to the now famous women's takeover of *Rat*. *Rat*'s evolution from an underground newspaper touting its boldness by way of a "naked chick" on its cover to one reclaimed by pissed-off feminists marked a major transition for Alice as well. Her memoir reveals how personal *and* political it felt when she heard and saw the man she loved dismissing women's frustration with the paper's sexism, which, while not unusual for its time, was also striking.

Although Alice recounts how frustrating it was to be treated, again and again, as an accessory or a secondary player by men in the movement (why, for instance, did so many of the women on *The Rag* start out as typists rather than writers?), we see that Shero's dismissal of women's concerns was probably most responsible for Alice's embrace of women's liberation. Her involvement in that movement is instructive for a younger generation of feminists, giving lie to the notion that white activists in women's liberation were naïve about or willfully ignorant of what the Black feminist scholar Kimberlé Crenshaw called "intersectionality," which holds that no single form of oppression (sexism, racism) can be understood in isolation. Alice has always been thinking intersectionally. But she also continues to grow and learn. She was involved with some of the most well-known struggles of the '60s and '70s as well as some lesser known. After participating in the Chile exchange, she became involved with the North American Congress on Latin America and the Austin Committee for Human Rights in Chile. She has remained an activist, involving herself in movements and groups from feminist publishing to Democratic Socialism to protests at our US senators' Austin offices (where I've run into her). She writes for, appears on, and works behind the scenes at progressive media outlets.

In the years since Alice introduced herself to me, I think it's fair to say that we've become friends. She's been a guest speaker for several of my classes and even came to the Briscoe Center while I had students doing research on the 1960s, just to act as a consultant on anything they might uncover. A few years ago, I asked Alice if she'd considered writing a memoir about her experiences. Few memoirs of 1960s activism are by women or by Texans, and despite Rossinow's important book, many people associate '60s activism with places like New York City, Berkeley, and Chicago, forgetting about Austin's defining role. *Voice Lessons* thus fills an important gap. While I can't take credit for convincing Alice to write her memoir, I'm so glad it's finally coming out. Alice has found her voice, and now many of us can learn from what she has to tell us.

Julia Mickenberg
Professor, American Studies
The University of Texas at Austin

Preface

When Alice Embree entered the University of Texas as a freshman in 1963, she quickly demonstrated her interest in politics by joining the campus affiliate of the national Young Democrats. Deeply affected by the growing antiwar and social justice protest movements of the 1960s, Alice's political world view took a turn farther to the left, and she eventually joined Students for a Democratic Society (SDS). She walked a picket line to oppose segregated dorms on campus, marched in protests against the Vietnam War, helped start Austin's legendary underground newspaper *The Rag*, and was put on disciplinary probation after an unauthorized antiwar speech on the West Mall that drew the ire of none other than Frank Erwin, the powerful chairman of the UT Board of Regents and political confidant of President Lyndon B. Johnson.

Soon after being placed on disciplinary probation, Alice dropped out of school to focus her attention on the dominant causes of the 1960s and 1970s: the struggle for civil rights, the anti-Vietnam war movement, women's liberation, and other social justice efforts. At one point she moved to New York to serve as one of the original staffers at the New York underground newspaper *Rat*. When Alice eventually returned to

Austin, she moved to the forefront of the women's liberation movement, running a women's press and continuing to participate in protests. She eventually returned to school and earned a master's degree in community and regional planning. Alice has continued to be deeply involved in a wide array of grassroots political, economic, social, and cultural causes, including regularly speaking to classes at the University of Texas about the women's liberation movement. Much as she found her place as an activist, she wants other women to find their voices too.

In 2015 Alice Embree generously donated to the Briscoe Center the papers documenting her work for the causes that she has supported nearly all her adult life. Her papers include correspondence, photographs, and miscellaneous documents, records (including a copy of her FBI file), and ephemera related to her activism. The collection also includes miscellaneous published material, including copies of underground publications such as the *Rat* and *Off Our Backs*. Alice has now added her insightful memoir to this historical documentation. *Voice Lessons* is one of a series of books the Briscoe Center has produced that preserve the historically important memoirs of individuals whose papers and oral histories are at the center or whose lives are closely connected to the center's collections. The Briscoe Center only publishes books that are based largely on the center's collections. Alice's papers certainly meet that criterion.

In *Voice Lessons* Alice discusses growing up in Austin and her days at the university, as well as her involvement in a variety of causes, including organizing SDS chapters in the western United States, participating in a student exchange program in Chile (with future congressman Lloyd Doggett), traveling covertly to Cuba, attending the Woodstock music festival, and protesting at the 1968 Democratic National Convention in Chicago. Alice's memoir is significant, not only because she has led an extraordinary life, but also because it adds another female voice to the effort to tell the story of the activist movements of the 1960s and 1970s. Alice provides a valuable perspective on the history of these movements that, among other things, addresses the issues of access to birth control, who does the typing and who does the writing, and, most importantly, who has a voice in the story of the movement. Her thoughtful memoir opens our eyes to what it was like to be an active participant in causes that continue to affect us all. I'm pleased that Alice has decided to share her recollections of these experiences with a wider audience, and I'm proud that the Briscoe Center is making that possible.

Alice was the speaker at a Briscoe Center event in March 2020 celebrating the opening of "On with the Fight!," an exhibit based on the rich women's history archives in our collections, including examples from her papers. A week later the university (and most of the country) shut down. Most of this manuscript was written before the coronavirus pandemic, but all of the work to produce the book has been done remotely. Accordingly, I want to thank the center's talented book editor, Dr. Holly Taylor, for her skillful work with Alice on the text and her management of the project during this difficult time. Alison Beck, the Briscoe Center's director of special projects, made an important contribution as well, especially in working with the book's photographs.

And, of course, I thank Alice Embree for honoring the center by entrusting her memorabilia and papers to our care.

Don Carleton
Executive Director
Briscoe Center for American History

Voice Lessons

Introduction

I WAS A SHY THIRTEEN-YEAR-OLD IN 1959, ALL EYES UPON ME as I walked down a chapel aisle in New York's Cathedral of St. John the Divine. I wore white gloves and a pale-beige dress as my sister's maid of honor. There wasn't much time to learn the halting processional gait. I was terrified that I would trip with everyone watching. My older sister was marrying a New York attorney.

That memory clashes with one in 1971. I was dressed in flowing garb and bangles, my hair ratted out, on the grounds of the soon-to-be-dedicated Lyndon Baines Johnson Presidential Library. I was part of a different kind of sisterhood by then. As self-styled witches, we circled the fountain and placed a hex upon those halls—"The blood of the Vietnamese people will haunt you forever."

Twelve years had passed in my transformation from self-conscious young teenager to angry activist. Still, the shyness lingered. In 1968, my friend Mariann Wizard described me in a poem: "shy Alice with an air of good-girl going bad." She nailed it.

Throughout my life, the shy teenager danced with the audacious witch. I have always been drawn to the women like Mariann who could turn the

Southern belle stereotype on its head with brazen belly laughs and wicked snark delivered with a Texas drawl.

My story is of tumultuous decades and lessons learned. I first gained a voice as an activist against the vestiges of Jim Crow and a raging war, then raised that voice as part of a women's movement. Women traveled a long distance in those decades as we left our assigned roles in the dustbin of history.

Memory is mutable. Neuroscientists say you can change memory as you recall it. I suppose you can tone the memory muscle with practice and research. With that in mind, I've worked on the chronology of events that shaped me. But memories don't imprint upon your brain in equal measure according to chronology. A day can leave the mark of a lightning strike and be replayed in slow motion over the course of a lifetime. A decade may leave faint traces—a run-on sentence of daily routine— making you wonder later how you got breakfast on the table and the kids to school on time.

I was the quintessential homegrown radical. That was particularly disturbing to the university administrators who put me on disciplinary probation in 1967. Hardly an outside agitator, I grew up in Austin, my father a professor on the campus where I was a member of the Students for a Democratic Society. Austin was a small college town then. Now it's bursting at the seams and mired in traffic, with a population that has grown fivefold since 1960.

At my sixth-grade graduation, I won a Bible for writing the best essay about "what America means to me." I recall walking down that aisle at All Saints' Church when my name was announced. I remember how much I was a believer, grateful to live in the world's model for democracy. I had extolled American virtues to the best of my sixth-grade ability. I had learned the elementary lessons of American exceptionalism quite well.

Segregation loosened the outer membrane of my belief that everything was well. My grade-school certainty began to come apart in my hands, brittle as an onion's skin. The Episcopal school that had bestowed the Bible was segregated. My junior high wasn't integrated until the ninth grade; my high school had only a handful of Black students. The university where I landed as a freshman had segregated dorms, and Black students were excluded from collegiate sports. The more I looked, the more other fault lines were exposed.

When Vietnam entered my field of vision in 1963, the official layers of justification began to give way as well. "Stopping communism" was the reason we were given for the war. My generation couldn't stop picking at that thin, translucent cover story. It didn't stand up to scrutiny as the whole truth.

Why didn't those in power tell us that Vietnam had been a French colony, that Vietnamese liberation forces had fought the French to a humiliating defeat in 1954, that the country had been only temporarily partitioned? The papery Cold War rationale crumbled in my hands as I turned my attention to Southeast Asia.

Then, in late 1969, another layer pulled away. I was visiting Jeff Shero, a man I had been involved with for five years. He had started an underground newspaper in New York City and was taking a break to work on a book in Mississippi. The guy he had left in charge of the newspaper called from New York. Women had taken over the paper.

I could only hear one side of the conversation as Jeff became more animated and angry, dismissing women activists we both knew as "bourgeois bitches." The personal became wrenchingly political.

The women's seizure of power was taking place 1,200 miles away from the phone conversation I could overhear, but those women might as well have tossed a Molotov cocktail into the Greenville, Mississippi, room where I was listening. I returned to Austin by myself with the aftershock still reverberating.

My relationship with Jeff did not survive my embrace of the women's liberation movement. I found a home in an audacious women's community. I helped start a women's press, sang in a women's band, and organized International Women's Day events. I wouldn't have written this account if I had not experienced the sisterhood and solidarity of women's liberation.

•   •   •   •   •

That groundbreaking creativity referred to as "seminal" derives, of course, from semen. As in, *The Rag* was "a seminal influence in the national underground press movement."[1]

When I hear the word "seminal" used as a descriptor, I counter with "ovular," just to make a point about the point we are referencing. Of course that's not even the whole point. Men of a certain age stake their claim to history and proclaim their significance. They usually begin with the pronoun "I" to discuss shared work.

The women's liberation movement used the pronoun "we" to reference our collective effort. We have done this so well that we have sometimes erased our individual agency in events and dissipated our collective impact on history. We've become an ethereal and unspecific "we" that can't be searched for on the World Wide Web.

Men who were leaders in the 1960s remember a time when their voices were the loudest in the meetings. They drowned out the voices of women and never realized that leadership should be shared across gender lines. The bedrock of organizing is sharing responsibility and expanding leadership skills. Male leaders at that time never encountered meeting facilitators who instructed them not to speak again until someone who hadn't spoken had stepped up.

So here's another point, which I heard from Texas governor Ann Richards: "The rooster crows; the hen delivers."

Too many guys who were active in the '60s think that if they had one quarter of a teaspoon of creative juice in a project, it trumped any amount of quiet sustaining energy to make sure the baby survived and thrived.

I still get angry when I hear the claim to importance for the first year (of eleven) in the history of the underground newspaper *The Rag*. Comments about the "slow death" and "über" democracy of the newspaper's latter years set me on simmer. The intent is to diminish the many years that followed.

In the beginning, in 1966, *The Rag* had a Funnel and a Funnella—a man and a woman acting as nonhierarchical editors. "Ahead of the times," it is said. But the bylines don't spell out gender parity. While there were exceptions, men wrote most of the articles and determined most of the content until 1969.

I typed rather than wrote that first year because I had a skill that was needed. My writing was never requested or cultivated or mentored in that first year at *The Rag*. It took a dose of anger to get my voice on paper.

Antiwar march in front of the Texas state capitol. From left, Jeff Shero, me, and Grace Cleaver in foreground, 1964 or 1965. *UT Texas Student Publications photo, Briscoe Center for American History.*

It took a women's liberation movement to get women's leadership and content into the paper.

My narrative is born out of personal necessity. It is a way to untie a knot, the one I get tied into when the narrative of women is minimized. Memoirs by men have claimed and shaped the history of the movements that straddled the '60s and '70s. There are exceptions—but let there be two, three, many exceptions, many descriptions by women, about women, about men and women, about the '60s and about the '70s.

•　•　•　•　•

My journey through the 1960s and 1970s veered sharply off course from the one my parents intended for me. My sister, nine years my senior, graduated from the University of Texas in 1958 with exemplary grades. I made my way instead to civil rights demonstrations, then to the Students for a Democratic Society, then to disciplinary hearings for giving a speech in an unauthorized campus location. I dropped out of college in 1967, relocating to New York City. With an East Coast vantage point, I found myself on barricades in New York and Chicago. I was among the throng of young people at Woodstock.

What distinguished my experience from my older sister's was historical timing. In February 1960, Black students, most too young to vote, sat down at a lunch counter in Greensboro, North Carolina, asking to be served. That direct action was an adrenaline shot to the sluggish American heart, a profound demonstration of participatory democracy. It ushered in a decade of student activism.

How could you ignore the black-and-white images on network news that followed? White people used billy clubs, dogs, and fire hoses against nonviolent Black protesters. White mobs taunted young Black children as they solemnly entered schools. Once seen, the Jim Crow laws of segregation, poll taxes, and voter intimidation could not be easily unseen.

Sometimes the signs separating races were explicit. "Colored" designated the lesser drinking fountains. Sometimes the signs were coded: "We reserve the right to refuse service." In the banks where mortgage loans were negotiated, the red lines were silent dividers, almost impossible to decode.

My generation, the bulging demographic of post–World War II, hit universities like a tidal wave. We were the offspring of a growing national prosperity. The world war had reduced many nations to rubble. The United States emerged, largely unscathed, with industrial momentum and little international competition. The nation's deferred sexual energy, interrupted by wartime deployments, soon made its appearance in hospital maternity wards with wall-to-wall babies.

My parents came of age in a starkly different time, the Great Depression. Their lives were shaped by economic uncertainty in a way that mine was not.

Shenandoah to Austin

MY PARENTS MET AT SHENANDOAH COLLEGE IN DAYTON, VIR-ginia, in the early years of the Great Depression. Economic turmoil roiled the country.

My father, Royal Embree Jr., was the eldest son in a family of five children and the first among his siblings to go to college. He received a BA from Washington and Lee University in Lexington, Virginia. The university was close to the family home in Buena Vista, a small town near the Blue Ridge Mountains. My father commuted as a day student, earning his degree in just three years as the Depression began to wreak havoc. The family business went bankrupt.

My father's mother borrowed tuition money from a friend to help my father get a master's degree from Ohio State. He finished that degree in 1930. That same year, the family home in Buena Vista was auctioned off. My father, only twenty-one, with a graduate degree in hand, took a teaching job at Shenandoah College. They paid him Depression wages. He taught for room and board.

My mother, Gundred Howe, grew up in New England, her father working retail at a haberdashery and her mother working for a social services

Gundred and Royal B. Embree Jr, 1933. *Embree family photo.*

agency. My mother finished high school in Hartford, Connecticut. There, she trained with a voice teacher and performed in repertoire musicals and local opera productions. Hartford newspaper reviews mentioned her beautiful contralto.

My mother learned of a secretarial job in the Shenandoah College president's office. Shenandoah had a well-known music conservatory as well as potential employment. She took a train from Hartford, Connecticut, to Dayton, Virginia, cramming from a shorthand book along the way. She was eager for a job and the adventure of leaving home.

I can't rely upon my parents' memory of meeting, but I imagine that my father was attracted to my mother's spunk, and that she found my father intriguing, tall and gregarious, a young man already credentialed with two degrees. They were an unlikely couple. She was barely five feet tall to his lanky six foot two; her New England reserve clashed with his Virginia charm.

A sepia photo captures my parents young and full of life. They are arm in arm, a corsage pinned to my mother's lapel, her hat stylishly angled on her head. I like to think it was the day they eloped.

There wasn't money to be wasted on a fancy wedding, so my parents didn't have one. A Presbyterian minister in Staunton, Virginia, married them in 1933. There were no bridal showers, attendants, rehearsal dinners, or receptions. Only a wedding certificate and a simple announcement sent out by my maternal grandparents marked the occasion. There is also the photograph that I imagine was taken that day they married.

After my parents died, my sister recorded oral histories with my mother's brother and my father's sister. My uncle and aunt accompanied my parents as they drove to Hartford to break the news of their elopement to my mother's parents. After my parents told my maternal grandparents that they were married, their siblings were let in on the secret.

In 1933 my English-major father compiled his poetry into a book, *Fifty Selected Poems*. He had the collection bound and he dedicated it to his mother. One of the poems, written in 1930, strikes an ironic chord. Over the course of my father's academic life, he supervised more than 40 doctoral dissertations and more than 150 master's theses and reports. But in 1930, he wrote these words about academia:

HYPOCRISY
Royal B. Embree Jr.

We laugh at dogs
That chase their tails
In frenzy wild,
Until strength fails.
But we commend
A college student
Without end
For moving on from class to class,
Pursuing knowledge
While years pass.
We view the whirling dog
With most superior laughter;
Yet it at least has something solid
To chase after!

My parents worked briefly in Meriden, Connecticut, before moving in 1935 to Minneapolis, where my father became a graduate student at the University of Minnesota. He worked as director of guidance at the University High School while he pursued his PhD. My father always referred to his PhD advisor, Wilford Stanton Miller, as "Dr. Miller of Miller Analogies," the latter a standardized test developed by Miller for graduate admissions.

My sister, Mary Ellen, was born in Minneapolis in 1937. My father's only sister, Jean, came to live with my parents while she finished her undergraduate degree at the University of Minnesota. I imagine this early period of my parents' lives to have been happy, filled with the magic of a young toddler, friends, and a mild flirtation with radical politics.

My parents acquired a Paul Robeson record then, a scratchy 78 rpm. As a teenager, I was fascinated by the album, *Songs of Free Men*, with its dramatic cover. A black hand, with a broken wrist shackle, is plunging a dagger into a swastika-emblazoned snake. My father spoke of his fascination with the Abraham Lincoln Brigade that mobilized in the 1930s to fight the fascists in Spain. Sorting through my father's papers after his death, I found a 1930s training manual for union organizers and learned he had been president of a teacher's union local.

In 1941, my parents moved back to Virginia, where my father became director of counseling at the College of William and Mary. Pearl Harbor and World War II interrupted his academic career. My father's three younger brothers signed up to serve. Even my father's sister went to work in Washington, DC, on a plan to transform the automobile industry to wartime production. Because she was a woman, she was banished from the room when the plan was presented to industry chiefs. My father, married with a young child, could have avoided service, but he took military leave to train as an officer in the US Navy.

My mother returned to Hartford to be near her parents. One family story was told so many times that I thought I must have been present, at least in utero. On the afternoon of July 6, 1944, my mother took my sister to the circus accompanied by her sister-in-law, Ethel, and Ethel's two sons. During the middle of the performance, the big top of the Ringling Bros. and Barnum and Bailey caught fire with seven thousand people inside. An enclosed steel runway for circus animals blocked the main exit.

My mother and my sister dropped down through the bleachers and escaped under the flap of the tent.

My mother saw a father carrying his daughter on his shoulders, unaware that fire was singeing her hair. At least 167 people died and 700 were injured. My family members made it outside to safety. My father was stationed at a naval training base. He got his news through the mail, the first letters only saying they were going, not that they were safe.

I came into the picture while the war was on. My mother had suffered a miscarriage before I was born and had been told that another pregnancy was unlikely. I was therefore a surprise baby, born by cesarean, with a caul on my head. By some accounts, a caul is good luck for seafarers. Maybe it was.

My father was the commanding officer on a medium landing ship, *LSM-160*, in the middle of the Pacific Ocean when I was born. He didn't know of my birth until seventeen days later, when a package of letters arrived. One of my mother's letters said, "I hope you aren't disappointed that she is not a boy."

My father returned to his job at William and Mary in Williamsburg, Virginia, after the war, and the family lived in Yorktown. According to my fifth-grade report "The Story of Alice Embree," they lived on the "exact spot where Cornwallis surrendered to Washington during the Revolutionary War."

My father finally finished his doctoral dissertation. In a true act of love, my mother typed all 574 pages, replete with tables. She also produced flawless carbon copies. My mother's spelling and grammar were flawless as well. I have no doubt that she contributed her editing talent as well as her secretarial skill to his opus.

My sister, Mary Ellen Embree LeBien, discovered family lore that my parents never knew. In her book *Embree Remembered*, she traces our family ancestry as direct descendants of Effingham Embree, a New York clockmaker during the Revolutionary era. Three of Effingham's clocks are in the White House. The Colonial Dames of America donated an Effingham Embree tall case clock as a Bicentennial gift in 1976. That clock was placed in the White House Diplomatic Reception Room.

Effingham wasn't only a clockmaker. He was a member of the standing

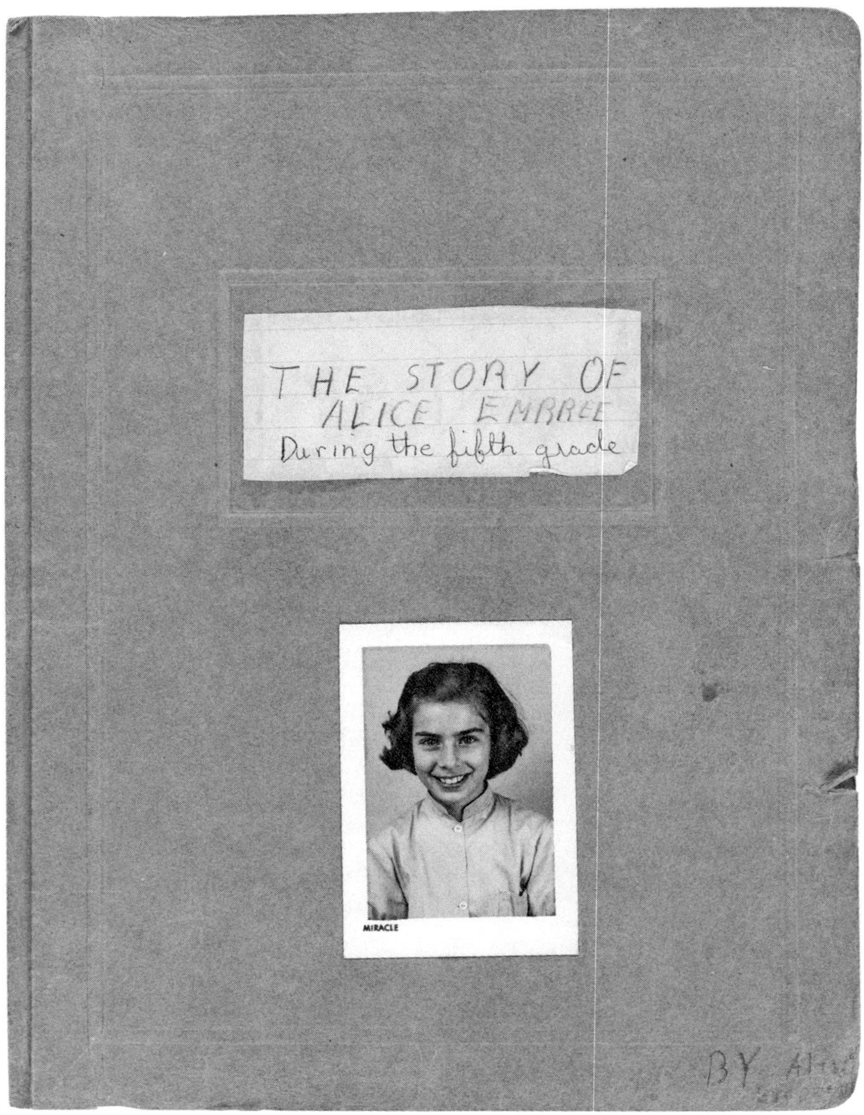

My first autobiography, from fifth grade at St. Andrew's Episcopal School.

committee of the New York Manumission Society, advocating the manumission of slaves.[2] The society started a free school in New York for African American boys in 1786, admitting girls after 1792. Effingham Embree served as one of the school's first trustees.

The particular family chowder that nurtured me had many seasonings. My Virginia-born father and my New England mother made their way to Texas when I was a toddler. The Depression had ended and the war had been won.

My parents brought a liberal vantage point with them, perhaps acquired in Minneapolis, to a state where Jim Crow laws were visibly on display, from separate drinking fountains to poll taxes. The Red Scare was visible as well. The University of Texas required faculty and staff to sign loyalty oaths, a vestige of McCarthyism. You had to answer the question "Are you now or have you ever been a member of . . ." about a long list of left-wing organizations. My father told me he was glad he had never joined the Abraham Lincoln Brigade because he wouldn't have been hired at Texas.

The economic uncertainty that shaped my parents' early years gave way to economic optimism. I grew up in a modest house with a modest mortgage. My parents added to the square footage, upgraded the appliances, and parked a new car in the driveway every few years.

When I read the Students for a Democratic Society's *Port Huron Statement* in 1964, this description resonated: "We are people of this generation bred in at least modest comfort, housed now in universities . . ." I took that modest comfort for granted. My parents never did.

Sleepy College Town

With his PhD pending, my father secured a job in 1947 as assistant director of testing and guidance at the University of Texas. Austin was at that time a fairly sleepy college town.

My father turned thirty-eight that year. It was a pivotal year for him, and he wrote his memory of it in a birthday note to me when I turned thirty-eight: "I came to Texas in February. My mother died in March. Gundred, you and Mary Ellen arrived in May. . . . I got my Ph.D. in August. You were two years old in October."

My sister was ten and I was nearly two when my parents came to Texas.

We lived briefly in the University of Texas Married Student Housing before my parents purchased a modest, cinder-block, stucco-covered home. It was in a new development called Delwood 2, just north of Airport Boulevard and just east of East Avenue, now Interstate 35. The purchase price was $10,000, the monthly mortgage $75, the property tax about $50 a year. The home was on the north edge of Austin, and the backyard nestled up to a relatively quiet airport where a few propeller planes took off and landed each day.

Delwood 2 is a cookie-cutter neighborhood. Most houses were constructed of cinder blocks on a concrete slab. There were several different configurations of two or three bedrooms and just one bath. A few fancier wooden, or stick-built, homes were sprinkled in. The typical house included a one-car attached garage. As families grew, the garage became a family room or additional bedroom. Then the parents of the postwar baby boom added bathrooms.

In my preschool years, my mother would arrange "excursions." We might go to the library or the fire station near the house. I was five when she took me down to the police station. It must have been a boring day on the *Austin American* cop beat, because my visit warranted a story on page 13, "Little Miss Inspects City Jail, Okehs [*sic*] It, Has Few Suggestions." A photo appearing on April 5, 1951, showed me peering down the empty barrel of a policeman's shotgun.

There were no sidewalks in Delwood 2. Kids owned the sparsely traveled streets, roaming by bike and roller skates, playing hide-and-seek at dusk, catching fireflies. Barefoot in the summer, with feet toughened by hot streets, we'd swarm to greet the ice cream trucks that prowled the neighborhoods. A great adventure was to slip through the four strands of barbed wire bordering the airport and take off to the jungle area where runoff formed a pond with tadpoles. Poison ivy was the principal danger, but occasionally copperhead snakes were sighted and killed by the neighborhood men.

Fearless, I would cross Airport Boulevard with other kids to play at the nearby Patterson Park. The city staffed the park and its pool in the summer with lifeguards and an attendant who would check out volleyballs and nets, make sure the tetherball was attached to its pole, and treat the occasional scrape.

From left, me and my sister, Mary Ellen, with our parents in front of our house, c. 1955. *Embree family photo.*

The Delwood Shopping Center was within walking distance, with a typical dime store that had everything from sewing sundries to games to goldfish. A drugstore in the shopping center sold root beer floats, banana splits, and sandwiches. There was a cafeteria, a grocery store, clothing stores, a beauty shop, and an adjacent motel and drive-in theater. Those small stores have succumbed to megastores. A large Fiesta supermarket dominates the site today. A few other small retail outlets are there: a shoe repair shop and an auto parts store. But the drugstore and dime store items at prices within a kid's allowance are long gone. The interstate is a death-defying traffic artery. And the walk across Airport Boulevard that I used to make frequently at a young age is no longer safe for children.

When I was growing up, Tony Gail and her brother, Speedy, were next door. They lived with their divorced mother and their grandmother, who cooked the Southern cuisine my mother didn't cook—scratch biscuits, collard greens, and chicken-fried steak. The grandmother composted her scraps and grew stunning zinnias in her garden. Tony was my best friend then, and I would sometimes sneak a dinner at their house before coming home to dinner with my parents.

I was still in elementary school when I got a Kodak camera with a flashbulb attachment for my birthday. Tony and I staged a photo shoot with us posing as movie stars with scarves and sunglasses. We talked her brother into posing in his cowboy hat and vest. The black-and-white photos capture our innocence against the backdrop of some outrageously flowered curtains in my family's dining room. The curtains covered the largest window in the house, created when the garage was remodeled and the garage door became a window.

In a not-so-innocent move, we also played a prank on my father. He would drink, drooping at the dining room table, eyes glazed, nodding off. Tony and I slipped half a bottle of Tabasco sauce into his shrimp cocktail sauce to see if he'd notice. He didn't. Decades passed before I saw this act of rebellion in a different context.

The Wilsons lived on the other side of our house. Their son, Mark, was my age, and I had a crush on him before I knew what that might be. For me, it was a fantasy of going off to an island on which we would be queen and king. I had picked out some obscure spot on a map and "invented" a language that we would use. It lacked important linguistic features, like conjugation; it was just a series of nouns in English and my invented translations. I am embarrassed now at that blissful acceptance of monarchy and colonial entitlement for my spot on a map.

My parents had a desk in their bedroom with a typewriter. I would retype things. I'm sure all this typing foreshadowed my prefeminist role at underground newspapers. I found a list of movie stars in a comic book that I laboriously retyped. When I left the desk midlist to go to the bathroom, my sister snuck in to see what I was up to. She sat down and typed in her name, condemning my perfect list to the trash bin. Several months later, by complete accident, she received her karmic payback. I had left a compass on the couch, and she sat down on its sharp point.

The occasional propeller flights in the airport behind our house were more entertaining than annoying. Fewer than 160,000 people lived in

My first-grade class at All Saints' Episcopal School. I am in the front row, far right.
Embree family photo.

Austin in 1955, and the thundering roars of jet-propelled commercial flights were far in the distant future. The boys in the neighborhood dug trenches on the airport property behind our house in order to play at warfare. I recall a variation on cowboys and Indians that had a Southern tone—Yankees and Southerners. When it was discovered that I had been born in Hartford, I was told I had to be a Yankee. It sent me crying to my mother.

My October birthday meant I couldn't enroll in a public first grade the year I was to turn six. I went instead to first grade at All Saints' Episcopal School in an older building where ants would invade our lunch bags before we retrieved them. My father dismissed the ant problem by telling me that they were full of nourishing tannic acid.

I was eligible to attend public school the next year and went to second grade at Maplewood Elementary, a school that both of my children later attended. My main memory of Maplewood is not of schoolrooms but of polio vaccines. When the new vaccine was distributed nationally, my entire family went to Maplewood to get it; the children's doses were in sugar cubes.

In 1952, for third grade, my parents sent me to the newly formed Episcopal grade school St. Andrew's. I think they received a scholarship discount. The school was housed in a rambling, two-story house at Twenty-First and Pearl Street. I endured the nickname "Peewee" there because I was the shortest kid in my class. Next to the converted house was a plain building where we went to chapel each day. We played kickball at recess.

Since my father was a professor, we were comfortably middle class, but many of my St. Andrew's classmates were the daughters and sons of West Austin surgeons and judges. They lived in Tarrytown, where the privileged lived before they moved farther west, and they were more likely to go to the Episcopal Church of the Good Shepherd than to the university church, All Saints'. In the third grade, one of these girls said, "You've worn that dress twice this week." I'd had no idea that was a breach of conduct. It was a mild scolding from a position of class privilege. I just knew I was being shamed and put on notice about how to dress.

In the fifth grade, Lynda Bird Johnson, the congressman's daughter, was in the class ahead of mine. My main memory is that she was exempted from recess sports. Once a week, I would walk with Louise Bailey, Reverend Scott Field Bailey's daughter, from the school on Pearl Street, across the university campus, to choir practice at All Saints' Church on Twenty-Seventh Street and Whitis. On our way, we'd stop in the University of Texas Student Union. The university was still small enough that the cashiers would let the two of us charge ice cream to my father's account.

My mother started to work full time when I began third grade. She was registrar and secretary to Dean Gray M. Blandy of the Episcopal Seminary of the Southwest that was then located in a house near All Saints'. I think the television was seen as a substitute for the time my mother wouldn't be at home after school. The black-and-white TV sat in the dining room with rabbit ears on it. We would sometimes watch *I Love Lucy* or *The Loretta Young Show* as we ate.

My Episcopalian parents said grace before every meal. I figured out that we could say grace in the time it took a commercial to air. After dinner, I perfected a technique of filling the bathtub during one commercial and taking a bath during the next so as not to miss a program I wanted to see.

Not Yet Twelve

Everything changed when I was eleven.

My mother was diagnosed with colorectal cancer and underwent major surgery at Seton Hospital. It was the spring of 1957 and I was in the sixth grade at St. Andrew's. After the lengthy surgery, the doctor called my father and older sister into a lab room to show them the tumor he had removed. It was floating in preservative. The surgeon wanted them to know why such drastic measures had been taken. I was not privy to the bizarre viewing, but it is etched into my sister's memory.

I wasn't given much information, but the gravity of the situation churned in my guts. I was dispatched for a brief stay to Louise Bailey's home in West Austin. Her father, rector at All Saints', went on to be a diocesan bishop.

I ate a bland dinner with Louise's family the first night, meat loaf and mashed potatoes. Afterward, I was shown into a study with a couch that opened into a bed where I was to spend the next few nights. I threw up that dinner on the bathroom floor next to the study. I didn't ask for help. Instead, I stealthily cleaned up my vomit and managed not to waken my hosts.

My mother recuperated for some time at the old Seton Hospital on West Twenty-Sixth. The nuns in charge wore the large, white head cornettes typical of the Sisters of Charity in the 1950s. That hospital with its somber statues of bleeding saints evoked mystery. Our shoes would clatter and echo down the long, tiled corridors.

My sister penetrated that somber mood one evening when she took me to visit. She snuck our cat, Ping, hidden in a bag, up the side stairs to my mother's room. It got a welcome laugh from my mother.

The church community and neighbors chipped in. Another classmate's family had their maid pack a bag lunch for me for the remainder of the year at St. Andrew's. Next door, Mark Wilson's mother braided my hair before school.

My mother had a difficult time recovering, with subsequent operations to remove scar tissue. From that time on, she used enemas and colostomy bags to evacuate what was left of her colon. We acclimated to her radically altered life. Predawn enemas that she politely referred to as "ablutions" marked every morning. She'd rise at 5:00 a.m., attend to her ablutions, then carry on—soldier on, as the Brits would say—to wake the rest of us, cook breakfast, and get us on our way and herself to work at the Episcopal seminary.

My sister took off for a church camp in Brazil that summer after my mother's surgery. At Christmas we made one of our hard-driving family trips to Connecticut. My mother was in the bathroom of her parents' home with her ablutions. My grandmother went in to help, coming out with a stricken face.

I went down to my grandparents' basement to explore the oddities— a mangle for ironing sheets, a set of double photos that you could view as 3D through a stereo viewer. My grandfather came downstairs. I remember standing quiet and undetected and watching him weep over what my mother had to endure. It astonished me to see him cry. He never knew that I had.

The surgery inflicted a shame that my mother seemed to internalize. She was a modest woman, and when diarrhea struck while she was working, with its unavoidable smell, when her clothes were stained from a leaking colostomy bag, she suffered with embarrassment. When she traveled, she had to take a makeup case filled with colostomy bags and other necessities. She never wanted that to be opened.

My grandmother could not bring herself to speak the word "cancer," certainly not to describe it precisely or matter-of-factly as "colorectal cancer," as it would be today. Her generation couldn't even say the word "pregnant." She would whisper about my mother's condition the way some families might whisper about syphilis.

IF ONLY YOU COULD HAVE KNOWN ME
June 27, 2003

I was twelve and
small for my age

walking down the
buffed, tiled hallways
of an older Seton Hospital
my older sister steering me
to my mother's room.
The unfamiliar statues
of the Virgin and Jesus
as intimidating as the
dark habits and wide
hats of the Daughters of Charity
who sailed down the corridors
and stood by hospital beds.
In the alcove
Jesus stood solemn
with his heart red and exposed
outside his chest.
It was where life
hung in the balance
as rawly exposed
and vulnerable
as the heart of Jesus.[3]

School Days

After the sixth grade I returned to public school, attending University Junior High in a building that the University of Texas has since reclaimed. In this junior high setting, I had the great good fortune of meeting Terry Clarkson. We collaborated on a joint social studies project, constructing a large board map of Latin America on which we placed flags and miniature figures dressed in traditional garb—gauchos in Argentina, indigenous Peruvians.

Terry's father was a physicist who worked at a small company special- izing in seismic measurement devices. She lived in the Wilshire Woods neighborhood, a short walk across Airport Boulevard. Her house backed up to a creek that was worth exploring if you were willing to risk poison ivy and an occasional leech attaching to your leg. We could cut across the creek and through a neighbor's yard to get to Patterson Park. Terry had an older brother and a younger sister. For me, Terry's home was a window into a world of normalcy. With my sister's departure, I was the only child in the house. Cancer had left its mark on routines. My parents rarely entertained. Dinners with family, after my widowed grandmother and her sister moved to Austin, were formal.

Terry's parents would gather with friends around a card table to drink beer and play bridge. They drank socially with friends. I felt like a Peace Corps volunteer might feel observing an entirely different set of cultural habits.

There was a lot of silence in my home. My sister, nine years older, was in college when I was still in elementary school. Then she left to live her life on the East Coast. My mother would go to bed early so she could rise at the crack of dawn and attend to her colostomy. My father would drink.

I was an overly self-conscious teenager attending a junior high dance at Hancock Recreational Center one weekend. It was my father's turn to pick up our car pool of girls. He didn't show up. I called and knew that I had roused him from a stupor. He arrived smelling of alcohol, with glazed eyes and slurred words. I could hear the girls in the back seat snickering as he drove them home. It was excruciating.

Once, walking home from Terry's after a rainstorm, two young boys raced across Parkwood Road in front of me, crying that their brother was in the creek. They were dashing off for help. I went down to the edge of the creek and saw a young boy in the water. I removed my shoes and jumped in, forgetting to take off my bulky car coat. I couldn't really climb up the slippery bank, but I held the boy up until his parents arrived. Later I heard he coughed up mud but was fine. I came home with dry shoes and a cold, muddy coat. I made sure my kids heard that story when we passed that creek on our way to their elementary school.

My father had rigged up a turntable in the kitchen pantry with a speaker in the living room. I could play my parents' 78 rpm records. Paul Robeson's powerful voice stirred me with emotion as he sang "Joe Hill." Years later, my father would affectionately call me "Josefina Hill." On my sixteenth birthday my dad gave me five paperbacks that he had loved. *For Whom the Bell Tolls* and *Homage to Catalonia* were among them. The Spanish Civil War carved a place in my heart.

I got a portable turntable that could play 45 rpm records and acquired a small collection. Some Elvis, some Chuck Berry, some of it pure schmaltz about love-stricken teenagers and wrecked cars. I went from ponytails to occasional perms that frizzed my hair. I wore loafers and bobby socks with gathered skirts. Terry and I would sometimes take the bus down to Congress Avenue, where there were two movie theaters. Or we'd browse through department stores—the larger ones, like Yaring's and Scarborough's, particularly their bargain basements. Downtown was sprinkled with smaller clothing stores, jewelry shops, a Woolworth's with a lunch counter, and the Piccadilly Cafeteria.

Terry and I gravitated to speech as an elective—a class where we recited poetry, debated, and performed skits for our audience classmates. I was painfully shy, and she was borderline shy. Somehow the organized pursuit of public speaking—debate, and later drama—appealed to the two of us.

A bigger drama was playing out in the Austin Independent School District. University Junior High (UJH) was a local experiment in desegregation. It was part of a gradual step-down plan that began with token integration at the high school level. A fire at Allan Junior High delayed the step-down by a year. But by the fall of 1959, my last year of junior high, integration had reached our school, with five Black kids in the ninth grade and one in the eighth grade.

I became friends with one of those kids, Saundra Kirk, whose brother, Ron, would later become the mayor of Dallas and serve in the Obama administration. Since there had been no Black kids at St. Andrew's, I thought I was in a fully integrated school. At that time, Hispanic origin was not even a designation on the census. While there were many Mexican American kids at UJH, perhaps because of the fire at Allan Junior High, that wasn't referred to as "integration." "Integration" was a term with Black and white connotations.

My friend Saundra Kirk has shared her experience with the final festivities of that year, a ninth-grade picnic at Zilker Park. She and the other Black ninth-graders were called into the principal's office before the picnic. There, they were told how lucky they were to have the day off. Three of their parents met with the principal, the Austin Parks Department, and the mayor about that picnic. At the same time, a Black student and a parent of a Black student were pressuring Austin High School administrators over their end-of-year festivities. Austin's iconic spring-fed Barton Springs Pool was integrated in the spring of 1960 by the Black students attending UJH and the Black students at Austin High.

I knew nothing of those behind-the-scenes battles, nothing of the courage, and nothing of the fierce advocacy by the parents. I am sure that I was wrapped in my own self-conscious cocoon, probably wondering if I looked as awkward as I felt in my swimsuit.

Subtleties of class and race discrimination were not obvious to me then. Mexican American boys were often tracked into shop classes to learn automotive repair and offset printing. The Black kids, having been selected by their parents for this high-stakes experiment, were being tracked toward higher education in universities. At that time in Austin, no community college system existed to provide an affordable associate's degree.

UJH also made small efforts to cross gender barriers. Both boys and girls took a class that alternated from home economics to shop. Boys in the six-week segment of home economics would crack jokes as they learned to prepare macaroni and cheese. I loved shop. I carefully constructed a desktop book holder, cutting the grooves into the wood, then gluing, sanding, staining, and varnishing with great patience. My father kept this in his office, and I got it back after his death. Decades later, my daughter's careful work on a wooden toolbox in an LBJ High School shop class would transcend my effort and remind me of my earlier experience.

Nevertheless, true to gender norms, I did take typing in junior high. I was very good at it. My typing skills proved essential to many jobs, temporary and permanent, throughout my life.

In home economics, I made gathered skirts, sewing wide stitches across the top, carefully pulling them into gathers, and then using a finer machine stitch to get the waistband attached. We wore starched petticoats under the gathered skirts. If you dried the petticoats on a towel on the floor, spread out in a circle, they were even more buoyant. The starch scratched at your waist, and the layers were hard to manage. Thankfully, starched petticoats, like Elvis, have left the building.

I'm not sure what prohibitions my parents were observing, but they didn't explain much of anything about sex. Once, I attended a sixth-grade swimming party while at St. Andrew's. Some girls weren't swimming, a fact that I reported to my parents. My father exchanged a look with my mother that I knew had adult meaning. Later I was called into my parents' room, and my mother asked if I knew about menstruation. I did not, but I said I did and beat a hasty retreat.

My sister might have been a go-to person for information on puberty, but I didn't possess the language skills to ask the right questions. I remember questioning her about undergarments, proxies for a maturing body. "When do you wear a garter belt?" "When do you wear a bra?" "When do you wear a girdle?" Her answers didn't help much.

Health classes didn't happen until high school, so there was no help from official sources. Other sources were dirty jokes. I remember one about three high school football players going out with cheerleaders and reporting on what had happened. The punch line was "Game delayed due to a muddy field." From this, I inferred that sex and periods didn't mix well.

In the back pages of some teen magazine, I found an ad from Kimberly-Clark that offered a free pamphlet on menstruation. I sent off a request for the pamphlet that was to be delivered in a brown paper wrapper. Since both of my parents worked, I could retrieve the mail without detection.

My period finally started in the summer when I was thirteen, fairly old by today's standards. My father's office was located in V Hall then, and I was waiting for him to finish work and give me a ride home. V Hall was an old army barracks building near Sutton Hall.

I found blood on my underwear when I went into the women's bathroom. Thankfully, there were vending machines, and I was able to get one of those cumbersome pads with safety pins. When I got home, I told my mother. She got me a belt and a supply of sanitary napkins.

My friendship with Terry helped me survive junior high—acne, car pools, yellow and royal-blue pom-poms, and a crush on a young male math teacher. We were usually dropped off at the back entrance to the school, and my sister taught me to yell "Y-a-a-a-y E-a-g-l-e-s" as we rode down Red River, making the yell last the entire block.

The University of Texas had not yet made its land grab to the south and east. Quality Seafood was located on Nineteenth Street, now Martin Luther King Jr. Boulevard. A U-shaped driveway off San Jacinto was the front entrance to UJH. A massive live oak sprawled in the U.

At East Avenue and Manor Road, there was a mom-and-pop store, A. H. Ritter Grocery, that my father loved. The butcher would cut filets mignons for special family occasions, and my father could find exotic treats like smoked oysters, anchovies, and pickled pig's feet.

Red Dragons

In the fall of 1960, I began high school at Austin High, now the Rio Grande Campus of Austin Community College. Terry and I found Red Dragons, the drama club. It wasn't hard to find, since Terry's older brother was part of it. It's only a slight exaggeration to say that it saved my life. Self-conscious, more isolated at home without my sister, I lived too much in my head. I found an easy camaraderie in the drama club. I found intelligent life—offbeat, funny, talented—and we spent weekends stretching muslin fabric over wooden frames, priming it with wheat paste, and painting the flats to look like brick or wallpaper for set walls.

I took on many theater assignments. I was an assistant stage manager, an assembler of props, Red Dragons' scribe in charge of the scrapbook, and Helen Keller's mother in our production of *The Miracle Worker*. In 1963, we won a University Interscholastic League contest that advanced our play to the state level, where we got to perform at Hogg Auditorium on the University of Texas campus. We lost first place to a Corpus Christi school. I still remember that scary sensation of beginning the production. I stood in front of the curtain as a spotlight fixed on me, first singing to a doll in a crib, then realizing that "she" couldn't hear me. I let out a bloodcurdling scream. The stage went dark, the crib was moved, and I joined the rest of the cast as the curtains opened.

My mother was hospitalized with shingles and couldn't attend, but my father came to the show.

The drama and speech teacher and director of our play productions was a vivacious woman named Terri Flynn. She was just out of college, full of exuberant energy. A few eyebrows were raised when several years later she married one of my classmates. He had been her student. But it was a

marriage that lasted. I shall always have a soft spot for Terri Flynn because she saw something in me that I couldn't yet see in myself.

Theater is an odd space for the self-conscious, but it is often where introverts can find an outlet. We can test our voices, with someone yelling from midaudience, "PROJECT!"

Turkish Coffee

Margaret Rideout, my high school friend, was also in Red Dragons. She was tiny and intense. With glasses, she looked bookish, and she was an early convert to contact lenses. Her father and mother were also short, wore glasses, and were decidedly bookish. They lived in a two-story house at 910 West Twenty-Sixth Street. It was an older house, full of bookshelves and books, with a side porch. It was just a few blocks from the university in the West Campus area then dominated by fraternities and sororities.

When I would visit Margaret to go over homework or lines for a play, I was treated to a family ritual. Her father would brew strong Turkish coffee and serve it in their kitchen in small cups, sweetened with sugar.

John Rideout, Margaret's father, served that Turkish coffee to me along with politics. I have a precious memory of sitting across the kitchen table, drinking the thick brew down to the remaining sludge at the bottom of the cup and talking about foreign policy and civil rights. It was a delight to be treated as someone whose opinion was valued. Strong coffee and politics became habit-forming intoxicants.

Margaret's father taught at Huston-Tillotson, the historically Black university in East Austin, and her mother worked in the library there. Much later, when I knew more about politics, I was curious about what brought them to a Black college in Austin.

Decades later, I learned more from Margaret. She told me her parents had moved from the Northeast with several families, including one Black family, to South Carolina. The children all attended Black schools and settled in a predominantly Black community. Their intentional disruption of segregation got them red-baited out of South Carolina. When Margaret began high school in Austin, she didn't divulge that history, perhaps eager to start a new chapter in her life. I later told her how much her father's mix of caffeine and conversation had influenced me.

Glodine

Austin High School, like UJH, was "integrated." Again, just as in junior high, there were only a handful of African American students in 1960, when I was a freshman. Anderson High School and Kealing Junior High were the predominantly Black schools. Sometimes I hear my white peers talk about the number of Austin high schools when we were in school. They remember only those that were predominantly white and have to be reminded of Anderson.

My parents didn't tolerate racist epithets, so I was outraged and mortified in high school when a girl in my car pool yelled "coon" at some Black kids as they drove down Rio Grande after school. But I couldn't bring myself to confront the perpetrator. Terry's brother did. He was driving us home one afternoon when the same girl yelled at a Black kid. He pulled the car over to the curb and said he wouldn't take her home if he heard another word.

In 1961, an incident in a Corpus Christi restaurant foreshadowed my future activism. I was in the Austin High drill squad, the Red Jackets. We wore severe maroon blazers and white skirts modeled after the University of Texas Orange Jackets, a service organization that my sister had been part of. Other schools had much trendier outfits, but we had a stern drill sergeant, Miss Corrinne Herndon. Red Jackets marched in formation with the band during half-time performances.

When I was in the eleventh grade, the Red Jackets went by bus to a Corpus Christi football game. Hungry and ready to move around, we all got out of the bus at a Corpus Christi cafeteria. In a short amount of time we were told that we should all get back on the bus, but no one explained why. We went to another restaurant, where we filed in, taking up a number of tables.

I was sitting with Karen Kieke and Glodine Propps, the only Black member of the Red Jackets drill squad. We were waiting to order when the waitress came over, addressing Glodine in the sweetest voice, "I'm sorry, honey, we just can't serve you here."

We rose to leave, and I said to the other Red Jackets nearby, "They won't serve Glodine. We have to leave." I remember Charlotte, a blonde girl who lived nearby, saying, "But, Alice, we've already ordered." Karen, Glodine, and I left in search of a place where Glodine would be served.

I wasn't afraid to speak up, but I expected others to respond, to get up as well. No one else did. The adult sponsors didn't intervene. They didn't follow us outside. I don't recall anyone directing us to a place where we could eat. I don't recall the Red Jackets' faculty sponsor asking us what had happened when we returned to the bus. It was the silence that shocked me.

Age distills these memories—the white of Glodine's socks against her skinny, brown legs, the racism wrapped in Southern manners, the waitress who was sent out by her manager to deliver the message with apology in her voice, "we just can't serve you here," and my classmates who really couldn't upset the restaurant decorum after their orders had been placed. Truly, the orders had been put in place for all of us, laid down as though they were immutable law, and the fact that the three of us didn't act our parts was somewhat amazing.

I still remember details as though they occurred in slow motion, the intonations, the familiar accent concealing ugly racism. And I reflect on our own impotence with no adults offering to intervene. We didn't know then how to make a collective fuss and raise the issue up a chain of command. We could have embarrassed the school administration for putting us in that position. Instead, the three of us left and found a Woolworth's, which we knew had integrated in response to national protests. We ate a solemn meal at the counter before returning to the group, pretending that nothing life changing had happened. It was an early voice lesson, a lesson in needing other voices.

As a child, I remember awkward rides on Austin's buses with signs telling "Colored people" to sit in the back. I remember two sets of drinking fountains in the department stores, the nicer ones for white people and the unrefrigerated water marked "Colored." From first grade through eighth grade, I attended segregated schools, two of them private Episcopal schools, two of them public schools: Maplewood Elementary and the first two years of UJH.

I believed my junior high had been integrated, but in contrast to the Maplewood classrooms that my children attended in the late '80s and early '90s, it wasn't. I was in my twenties when I learned from Saundra Kirk, one of the handful of Black students in my junior high and high school, how difficult it had been for them. They were plucked from their comfort zone. They would have preferred to stay with their junior high classmates. Saundra's parents, the Kirks, along with other African American families, the Andersons and the Means, pushed their kids to break this color barrier.

In 2013, at our fiftieth high school reunion, Saundra Kirk told me more about Glodine. Her Kealing Junior High classmates knew Glodine as gifted. Glodine's family wasn't one of the prominent African American families who pushed so hard at desegregation. Saundra told me that the city bus driver sometimes would not stop for them to take them home from Austin High. The Kirks, the Means, and the Andersons called for meetings with the bus company. Once, Glodine tried to get on the bus with an ice cream cone. The bus driver slapped it out of her hand. The Kirks and the Andersons got the bus driver taken off the route.

The Jim Crow world that my African American friends navigated was a minefield. White people had to exit their comfort zones to experience any of the daily insults and violence that Jim Crow laws inflicted on my Black classmates.

The African American students who went to Austin High had been pushed to break through barriers. A lot of expectations were placed upon them. A similar dynamic occurs with first-generation immigrants who expect their children to succeed at all costs. While I was becoming a college radical, Glodine was hard at work on her studies.

Glodine graduated from the University of Texas with a pharmacy degree. I found out from Saundra that she died at the age of twenty-six in the summer of 1971. Her death certificate says only that she drowned in Town Lake at First and Congress. She was working as a pharmacist at the time of her death.

Learning to Speak Out: 1963–1967

IN THE SUMMER OF 1963, MY FATHER TOOK A TEMPORARY teaching position at the University of Southern California. I applied to Southern Cal and was admitted to attend summer classes there. My parents and I drove two cars from Texas to California, making the long slog across the straight highways of West Texas and through the desert to the land Woody Guthrie called, tongue in cheek, the "garden of Eden."

We lived in Whittier in the home of a professor who was also away for the summer. With the theater bug alive and well, I took a beginning acting class. My father and I would drive the Dodge Dart, with its manual transmission, through the thick traffic, rarely getting the car out of second gear. Still, the vegetation climbing up the sides of freeways seemed magical compared to the concrete that lined Texas freeways. I felt the initial rush of collegiate freedom at Southern Cal, frequenting bookstores and reading novels under a tree until my father was free to make the return trip to Whittier.

In the fall of 1963, I began classes as a freshman at the University of Texas. The theater bug was no longer as virulent. I chose anthropology for a major that fall semester.

My sister had been in a sorority when she was in college. She found a home away from home in her Alpha Phi house, and her sorority sisters found someone who could bring up their grade point averages. She thought I should give it a try. I felt as awkward dressing up, drinking tea, and making small talk at sorority Rush Week as I had felt taking those halting steps down a chapel aisle as a bridesmaid in my sister's wedding. Even so, I pledged a sorority—not Alpha Phi—and after a few weeks found myself disgusted by the racist talk I heard from my "sisters." Alone in the bathroom of the sorority house, I broke the chain—metaphorically and literally—that held my tiny sorority pledge pendant. My only regret was that I had wasted some of my parents' money on an attempt to fit that mold.

Liberal and idealistic, I gravitated to the Young Democrats. Because the voting age was still twenty-one, few of my peers had the opportunity to vote for President John F. Kennedy, but we were inspired by his youthful idealism. I also joined my high school friend Saundra Kirk in a campus civil rights organization, the Campus Interracial Committee. Segregated university dorms and athletics became the initial targets of our actions.

I was an innocent freshman in the fall of 1963, the year the country lost its innocence with the assassination of a young president on the streets of Dallas. I was walking across the West Mall when I heard the news. I made my way to the Student Union, where there was a television.

I had expected to be part of a welcoming group for President Kennedy at the Austin airport along with other Young Democrats. Instead we watched in shock as the story of his death was broadcast. The Thanksgiving weekend that followed the assassination was marked by grief, shared with my family. I was devastated.

Kinsolving Dorm

Austin's population had just passed two hundred thousand in 1963. The baby boom was pushing the envelope of enrollment at the University of Texas (UT). The student population was about twenty-three thousand. Restaurants and movie theaters in the capital city had just integrated—except for a few holdouts.

An earlier wave of student activists, Students for Direct Action, had organized stand-ins at university-area movie theaters in 1960. UT student

Sandra "Casey" Cason helped lead that effort with its innovative strategy. Protesters would line up for tickets at the theaters with Black students. When they were refused admission, they'd return to the back of the line, effectively blocking access to the theaters.

In 1963, there were about 150 Black students at UT. The university was technically integrated, but segregation was still in force. UT dorms, athletics, band, and many student activities were segregated. A lawsuit by African American students had been filed in November 1961 to desegregate campus housing, activities, and facilities. The university delayed its progress through the court system.

Black students had staged sit-ins at UT dorms but had failed to get university action. On November 22, Lyndon Johnson became president, sworn in on the plane returning to Washington, DC, with President Kennedy's body. The new president's daughter, Lynda Bird Johnson, was living in UT's Kinsolving Dorm.

I was part of the Campus Interracial Committee, and I know that the decision to demonstrate outside Kinsolving Dorm was not easy. The action was controversial in the aftermath of a national trauma. It would bring adverse publicity to the new president, but publicity was guaranteed. It was a cold December 20, less than one month after the assassination, when we assembled across from Kinsolving to walk in a slow picket line. The picket signs were carefully worded. They placed the blame on the university for its delays in settling the lawsuit, casting the president as victim of those delays. Signs read, "Delay Causes President's Daughter to Be in Segregated Housing."

The Secret Service was out in force, newly attired in Stetsons to look "discreet." The demonstration made national news, as expected. It wasn't long before we heard that LBJ advised the university to settle its [expletive deleted] lawsuit over university housing.

With Lyndon Johnson scheduled to speak at the 1964 graduation ceremony at the end of the spring semester, the only African American plaintiff who was still a student, Sheryl Griffin Bozeman, was asked by UT chancellor Harry Huntt Ransom to drop the lawsuit. She did so, and the board of regents affirmed a policy of desegregation in May of 1964.

UT integrated its university-owned housing but would not deal a full blow to segregation by outlawing it in privately owned college housing, such as Scottish Rite Dorm. UT began, instead, to relax its housing requirements.

In 1963, the university required that unmarried women students live in approved housing. From Sunday through Thursday, the curfew was 11:30 p.m. On Fridays and Saturdays, the curfew was 1:00 a.m. The approved housing list even restricted a divorced single woman from living in a dorm. Clearly, the taint of divorce conflicted with the virginal ideal that in loco parentis housing rules were intended to uphold. As the university requirements for approved housing relaxed, a Pandora's box of premarital cohabitation opened up, but that is another story.

One of the courageous University Junior High and Austin High students, James Means, integrated UT track. But it wasn't until 1970—almost a decade after the 1961 lawsuit—that a Black student received a UT scholarship to play varsity football.

Students for a Democratic Society

I made my way quickly from Young Democrats to Students for a Democratic Society (SDS), a far more radical student organization. Young Democrats lost its sparkle after the Kennedy assassination as members reeled from the loss of a young, vibrant president. Few Young Democrats harbored illusions about the idealism of Lyndon Johnson. He was known as a masterful congressman and an arm twister who had won his 1948 Senate race by a slim margin rumored to have included a few dead voters in Duval County. He wasn't John F. Kennedy.

In the spring of 1964, we were still using old-fashioned computer cards to register for classes in Gregory Gym. Students went from table to table, picking up class cards. When I finished registering for classes and exited the gym, I saw a ragtag crew sitting on folding chairs around a rickety card table. They were recruiting for SDS. They had hand-lettered signs about voting rights, civil rights, and poverty. They were selling a modest pamphlet, *The Port Huron Statement.*

The SDSers outside Gregory Gym were Robert Pardun, Judy Schiffer, Jeff Shero, and Gary Thiher. They had in common a kind of beatnik, unkempt quality and the most deliriously appealing critiques of everything. They

Gary Thiher at a University
Freedom Movement rally, April 1967.
*Photo by John Avant, John Avant
Photographic Archive, Briscoe
Center for American History.*

were focused on social justice, not on advancing themselves within the socially acceptable corridors—Greek organizations, student government, and, depending on gender, either marriage or career. They were funny and welcoming. I was hooked.

Gary Thiher was an uncommon cross between cow country and philosopher. Tall and lanky, from Fort Worth, Gary trucked cattle as a summer job. His eyes were heavy lidded, with a hint of Elvis. With his philosophy skills, Gary could eviscerate a debate opponent, returning fire with a question aimed at demolition, but he had a sweet side and a charming chuckle among friends.

Judy Schiffer fascinated me. She was tiny, with hands that animated her conversation. She was born in New York City and came to Texas by way of Pittsburgh and Philadelphia. When her family relocated to Port Arthur she was in the eleventh grade. She was perhaps the only red diaper baby of that original crew of Texas SDSers. Her father was a leftist who worked in the petrochemical industry. She wore no makeup and her hair fell into soft waves and curls. Her casual look was the antithesis of the sorority norm, with its bouffant hairstyle and cosmetic enhancement. What fascinated me was the way Judy held her own in SDS debates. I was still emerging from some tight '50s cocoon. What I had to say was locked behind layers of how I might be perceived saying it.

Robert Pardun's blue eyes, tall forehead, and fair complexion probably came from his German immigrant ancestors. He grew up on the edge of prairie country in Pueblo, Colorado. He was funny and the best organizer I ever encountered in SDS. Asking, reframing, asking again, he was genuinely interested in what I thought and how I thought. I always felt I could talk with Robert without being judged.

Jeff Shero was lithe and lean. Well, almost all of us were lean then. Later, people would say Jeff and I looked alike with our dark hair and prominent noses. He was an air force brat who had gone to high school in Bryan, Texas. He referred ironically to his stepfather, from his mother's second marriage, as the "Good Colonel." I learned in the '70s that the Good Colonel was anything but good. Jeff was nearsighted and wore contacts. I found him attractive, clever, and worldly wise. He had traveled in Europe, an aspirational goal I had yet to consider within the realm of possibility. And I was in awe that he wrote a column called "Myopia" featured in the *Daily Texan*.

These SDSers bore a resemblance to my high school drama club cohorts in Red Dragons, a bit bohemian, smart, feisty, and nonconformist. Conversations with them were engaging. They believed that poverty and racism were connected, not operating in separate zones. They talked about the power structure in the United States, referencing the work of C. Wright Mills. They believed that consumerism had a deadening influence on society. I was already active in the campaign against segregation, and they were as well. They were radicals, interested in challenging the root causes of problems.

The Port Huron Statement seemed written for me:

> We are people of this generation, bred in at least modest comfort, housed now in universities, looking uncomfortably to the world we inherit.

When we were kids the United States was the wealthiest and strongest country in the world; the only one with the atom bomb, the least scarred by modern war, an initiator of the United Nations that we thought would distribute Western influence throughout the world. Freedom and equality for each individual, government of, by, and for the people—these American values we found good, principles by which we could live as men. Many of us began maturing in complacency.

As we grew, however, our comfort was penetrated by events too troubling to dismiss. First, the permeating and victimizing fact of human degradation, symbolized by the Southern struggle against racial bigotry, compelled most of us from silence to activism. Second, the enclosing fact of the Cold War, symbolized by the presence of the Bomb, brought awareness that we ourselves, and our friends, and millions of abstract "others" we knew more directly because of our common peril, might die at any time.

I didn't even stumble over the gender exclusion of *Port Huron*'s declaration: "We regard men as infinitely precious and possessed of unfulfilled capacities for reason, freedom, and love." I had been raised on these words, after all: "We hold these truths to be self-evident, that all men are created equal." The "forefathers" had enshrined gender exclusion in the Declaration of Independence. In a few years I would be noticing every instance in which language excluded women, every time "men" should have been rewritten as "men and women." Every time "chick" was used to refer to my sisters.

The Port Huron Statement was drafted in 1962, when SDS was emerging from its previous incarnation as the Student League for Industrial Democracy. Much to the dismay of the oldsters in the League for Industrial Democracy, SDS was challenging some of the ossified dogma of Cold War rhetoric. At UT, we still had to sign a loyalty oath for employment. Like most of SDS, I was ready to move past red-baiting.

I was captivated by the SDS concept of participatory democracy. I was still eighteen. I couldn't vote. But I could participate in democracy as the students had in Greensboro, North Carolina, sitting down at the counters of Woolworth's. Those students made change happen through direct action. It was a breathtaking antidote to the limitations of representative democracy that we had been taught in school: the belief that democracy meant you could vote—after you were twenty-one—for representatives. End of story. Democracy in SDS meant something far greater: that all people could participate in the decisions that affected their lives.

SDS had a simple, small membership card. I remember signing it in 1964 and thinking that I would never again be invisible to the FBI. The card contained the preamble to the SDS Constitution:

> Students for a Democratic Society is an association of young people of the left. It seeks to create a sustained community of educational and political concern; one bringing together liberals and radicals, activists and scholars, students and faculty. It maintains a vision of a democratic society, where at all levels the people have control of the decisions which affect them and the resources on which they are dependent. It seeks a relevance through the continual focus on realities and on the programs necessary to effect change at the most basic levels of economic, political, and social organization. It feels the urgency to put forth a radical, democratic program whose methods embody the democratic vision.

I eagerly adopted the small, understated, white button with its lower-case, brown "sds" letters. I was welcomed into a community of like-minded folks and was transformed.

Piccadilly

I had picketed, but in the spring of 1964, I took part in my first sit-in, a far more intense form of direct action. I was recruited by Hunter Ellinger to an action at the Piccadilly Cafeteria. Hunter was two years older, a former Austin High Red Dragon, and we had gone out on a few dates. My high school friend Terry Clarkson was there as well. David Martinez, whom Terry later married, had mapped out a series of sit-ins as a local organizer for the Congress of Racial Equality. David, having attended a national meeting of the congress, was one of the few card-carrying members in Austin.

Many restaurants in Austin had been integrated. My father had played a role, as a member of the Austin Council of Churches, in urging city leaders and the restaurant association to end segregation. But there were holdouts. The Piccadilly Cafeteria on Congress Avenue was one of them.

We joined about ten students gathered in two cars on the north side of the capitol building, out of sight from the cafeteria, waiting for the Piccadilly to open for its Sunday lunch trade.

I was in Jeff Shero's car, a two-tone, tan-and-white 1956 Pontiac station wagon, also known as "Butterscotch." Jeff was reading the Sunday paper, aloof and seemingly oblivious to the others in the car. He showed no nervousness about the upcoming action.

Because Terry and I were newcomers and wouldn't be recognized, it was decided that we would enter the cafeteria line and sit down with our trays. A Black student from Huston-Tillotson would join us. That's what we did. We ate. The Black student paid for the ticket, dumbfounding the cashier for a moment before she took his money. We had integrated the cafeteria. The walls didn't cave in, the other cafeteria customers didn't rebel, and no arrests were made. It was another chip in the barrier of segregation, although it would be a while before it became official Piccadilly policy.

Despite his indifferent manner, I must have made an impression on Jeff as well. He approached me at an SDS meeting a few weeks later and invited me to go with him and others to the Holiday House, a hamburger joint several blocks south of campus. It wasn't exactly a date.

I went, and after milk shakes and hamburgers, Jeff pulled out a thin paperback with a black-and-white picture of an amusement park on the cover. It was Lawrence Ferlinghetti's *A Coney Island of the Mind*. He read from a poem at the back of the book.

> I am waiting for my case to come up
> and I am waiting for a rebirth of wonder

He had me at the first line. And he knew it.

Three years older, he seemed to have a decade more life experience than I did as a freshman. He was an activist, a writer for the student paper, a reader of Ferlinghetti. What could be more romantic?

Our relationship went from dates and making out to more over the course of a year. By the next fall, Terry and I were sharing a boardinghouse room on Whitis north of where the Dobie complex now stands. We were in a separate converted garage with a bathroom and toaster oven. We'd sign in to obey a still-standing curfew requirement at the main house, then go to our separate dwelling, then sneak out the bathroom window to spend the nights with our boyfriends. This was the beginning of the sexual revolution, when subterfuge was required.

As my relationship with Jeff evolved, his role in the national work of SDS was ramping up. He and Robert Pardun took Jeff's station wagon, Butterscotch, to meet coal miners in Hazard, Kentucky, in the spring of 1964. The Hazard meeting was part of an SDS community-organizing strategy under the umbrella of the Economic Research and Action Project. Jeff and Robert also went that spring to the inaugural meeting of the Southern Student Organizing Committee. In the summer, Jeff was elected to the National Council of SDS, and that same year he became a regional organizer for SDS. Robert was increasingly involved with SDS national leadership as well. Their tether to student status began to fray as they both became full-time movement activists.

I was a sophomore and very much a student. Jeff's role as an SDS organizer frequently took him away from Austin to regional meetings and to the national office in Chicago. As I later told a writing partner, "A lot of the time that Jeff and I were together, he wasn't there."

•　•　•　•　•

SDS was growing like a weed in Austin, thriving within a community of malcontents that ran the gamut from longhaired hippies to political activists. An early addition to the SDSers who had tabled at Gregory Gym was a Houston crew, a cohort that had attended Bellaire High School. They included Thorne Dreyer, Judy Gitlin, and Dennis Fitzgerald. Dennis had published a daily high school newspaper at Bellaire. Thorne and Judy had bonded through high school drama. They were all incoming freshman the same year I was. Thorne and Judy joined forces with another Houstonian, Gary Chason, to put on a UT Curtain Club production of *Winnie the Pooh*. Thorne was a perfect Eeyore, intoning his lament, "Miserable.

Utterly miserable." Judy, with long, chestnut hair, was full of energy. Dennis was skinny and smart. The three of them were highly skilled punsters and pranksters.

Robert Carnal and Paul Pipkin joined Texas SDS as well. Robert was tall and thin. His dark hair grew longer and longer with each passing year. In the summer of 1965, Robert and Paul showed up in cowboy boots and hats at the SDS national conference in Kewadin, Michigan. They made an indelible impression on the brainy bunch of graduate students from East Coast colleges. It was a bit like mixing Perrier and unrefined petroleum.

George Vizard and Mariann Garner joined the ranks in the fall of 1964. George was from San Antonio, Mariann from Fort Worth. It wasn't long before they were together, bringing a raucous audacity into the mix.

Chuck Wagon

SDS was not an exclusive club, but we had a clubhouse. The Chuck Wagon in the UT Student Union building was our home base. You could buy breakfast—eggs, toast, and bacon—for less than a dollar. The coffee was just seven cents. The hamburgers were greasy but cheap. Cooks and cashiers were paid by UT but not paid well. As I remember, some dishwashers were on work release from the State Hospital. This was before the university contracted out food service to fast food chains.

We were a nascent body, gathering together like a developing organism, stretching our limbs and our imaginations, adding tables to accommodate our growing numbers. We built community and drank from the rich cup of camaraderie, welcoming the like-minded and the curious. Occasionally we would subdivide to accommodate class schedules, returning to the Student Union after attending class. We might study or cram for tests at the nearby Academic Center.

I had found my people, like my theater crowd—often disheveled, always passionate with ideas. I learned from reading SDS literature and from a modest antiwar publication, *I. F. Stone's Weekly*. But I mostly learned from the steady diet of conversation that accompanied our cheap caffeine.

Issues of war, of poverty, of racism had always been presented to me in discrete packages as though they had no relationship to one another.

We took pride in connecting issues, discussing root causes, and fleshing out a radical analysis. We paid little attention to the statues that stood like sentinels of racism to the south of the Tower. The reality, the deep crevice of racism, was as close as the segregated dorms and the all-white football team. We paid attention to those markers instead.

A debate could take over the grassy area of the West Mall outside the Union, drawing in people like a magnet. I would listen to arguments made by Robert Pardun, Gary Thiher, and others against the war in Vietnam or, prompted by concerns of Black students, against fraternity slave auctions or minstrel shows with blackface.

We could reserve rooms for SDS meetings in the Student Union, make picket signs in the third-floor crafts center, and watch the news in a lounge area with couches and a large television. At night in SDS meetings we'd debate strategies to challenge segregation and later to end the war.

The men consumed most of the oxygen in those rooms, their voices arguing points and counterpoints. When leaflets were needed, women were usually the ones typing and mimeographing. Judy Schiffer was the exception, bold and articulate. I wanted to learn her skills.

We lived within walking distance of the campus. I spent two semesters in a dorm and then a boardinghouse, "approved housing" for unmarried women. Many SDS friends moved into ramshackle houses that could accommodate four or five housemates. A high rental price was about $150. Outside the boundaries of university housing, we began to experiment first with marijuana, then many of us tried mescaline capsules made from peyote cactus. LSD made its way from California to Austin among people I knew in 1965.

In those early days of SDS, very few of us had cars. Jeff and Gary were exceptions. We lived at the Chuck Wagon, but we could walk to the places where we slept. Sometimes, we'd pile into a car and go to San Jacinto Café. It was a restaurant just south of Scholz Garten and Saengerrunde Hall on San Jacinto. We called it San Jack's. The building has succumbed to a state parking garage. The waiter, Ray, was nice to us and took to our banter. Gary, perusing the menu carefully, asked what the difference was between the $1.99 steak dinner and the $2.99 steak dinner. Without missing a beat, Ray answered, "The knife"; then, pausing for effect, "It's sharper with the

A UT Chuck Wagon sign prohibiting non-students seen through broken glass, 1969.
Prints and Photographs Collection, Briscoe Center for American History.

$2.99 dinner." His wry words were endearing. He was written up as "Rag Man of the Week" in a December 1967 issue of *The Rag*.

I have fond memories of that community we built, the one that sustained us for many years. Our SDS chapter grew from a dozen members to become one of the largest in the country. Later I could see the sexism, but I had no vocabulary for those criticisms in those early years. My insecurities could overwhelm my voice and keep me from speaking up or seeing myself as a writer. It took a sisterhood in the 1970s to give me a feminist perspective on this precious period of discovery. Those bonds of friendship and affection are deep; only a few are brittle with age.

In November 1969, the university administration imposed rules to keep nonstudents out of the Chuck Wagon. I wasn't in Austin then, but I heard

The Chuck Wagon "riot" as police arrest students and non-students, November 1969. *Prints and Photographs Collection, Briscoe Center for American History.*

about the Chuck Wagon "riot" from afar as students and nonstudents were dragged from their beloved home base. Charges were filed against the "Chuck Wagon Twenty-One" for conspiracy. Movement attorneys scrambled to the defense of those arrested.

I'm sure the university intended to kill the clubhouse where radical politics thrived. They went about eliminating the grassy areas where people would congregate, favoring fountains that rarely worked but that broke up the landscape. The shuttle bus system allowed students to live in cheaper apartments farther away. Now the campus empties at night as students commute in and out. The student activities center has moved away from the Student Union building now. Pockets of resistance may be thriving somewhere on that vast campus, but they are no longer sustained by a Chuck Wagon with cheap coffee.

• • • • •

I'll call him "Dr. R." He was the only physician in Austin in 1964 who would prescribe birth control pills to unmarried women. The University Health Center offered no birth control information, and they certainly didn't provide actual contraceptives. There was only our word-of-mouth network. Via scribbled notes, Dr. R. went viral among women who were becoming sexually active in the '60s.

You had to go so far afield from the dictates of "only having sex after marriage," a great distance from "Why buy the cow when you can get the milk for free?" Well, you get the picture. We were willing to go far afield. Willing to go all the way. And after the initial shock was absorbed, we were unabashedly open about sex outside of marriage. Among ourselves. Not necessarily around our parents.

I remember Mariann Garner and George Vizard embracing in the Chuck Wagon. I'm talking unabashedly, in a way I could never quite manage. In a lifetime, I've never quite shaken that New England reserve my mother bestowed upon me. Except when I curse like a marine.

After the initial clumsiness of spermicidal foam and applicators, the pill seemed gloriously undramatic and brilliantly effective in preventing pregnancy. It allowed spontaneity. Of course, we were the unwitting guinea pigs of hormonal overdosing. This information came later. Who knows how many breast cancer diagnoses can be laid upon that era, when we were such eager guinea pigs.

West Twelfth

Jeff rented a basement apartment at 506 West Twelfth Street. The building, just one block from the original Austin High, now houses professional offices.

In the '60s, it housed the Dorf photography studios. Eugene Dorf was a high school classmate and member of the theater group Red Dragons. His photographer father took stunning black-and-white photos of our plays. The Dorf family subdivided the two-story building into a family residence and photographic studio, an upstairs apartment, and a basement apartment.

As someone raised in Austin, I guess it shouldn't have surprised me that only a few degrees separated me from Jeff's landlords.

Jeff's apartment entrance was behind the house. A narrow flight of stairs led down to a tiny, dimly lit space with natural light coming in from short, ground-level windows. A skinny hallway connected a small bedroom on one end and a kitchen on the other. There was also a small closet and a bathroom. Jeff pasted up a colorful collage of photos, prints, and postcards on the stucco walls of the hallway and kitchen.

In 1964, I would sometimes stay the night in that apartment, creeping out of my mandatory approved housing in a boardinghouse. Not too many months passed before we were living together.

Jeff was not there, and I was asleep in the basement apartment, when I woke to the loud noise of the door being kicked in, splintering the wood around the lock. "Who the hell is there?" I yelled, mustering a lot more adrenaline-spiked bravado than I really felt. The intruder left. I crept into the kitchen and grabbed a knife.

By small-town coincidence again, the upstairs apartment was rented to Bobby and Trudy Minkoff. They had come to UT from Buffalo, New York. I did not know them well at the time, but they became good friends in the SDS community.

With my knife, I went outside, crept around the house, and climbed the stairs leading to the Minkoffs' second-story apartment. They let me sleep on their couch, but I overheard their whispers as they questioned how well they really knew the guest with the knife.

I called the police about the break-in the next morning. The detective who showed up asked, "Do you have any enemies?" I paused for a few seconds, thinking it was a trick question. *Only the Austin Police red squad,* I thought. They certainly made their presence known at demonstrations, and they occasionally attended SDS meetings. They had likely known that Jeff was in Chicago at the SDS national office and might have believed that this was an opportunity to search through his belongings in an unoccupied apartment. In any case, no suspects were found.

I picked up the mail one day to find a letter from the draft board that I wasn't sure was for Jeff. He had used every parent and stepparent's name when he registered for the draft. He won IV-A deferral with the help of several professors. One of these was Gideon Sjoberg, a sociology professor.

Gideon found the two of us fascinating. I think he viewed us as a sociological case study in radical politics and alternative lifestyles. We invited him for dinner one night. I cooked beef teriyaki. It was the height of my culinary talent at the time. I purchased ingredients at the grocery store nearby and cut beef into slender strips, using brown sugar and soy sauce to make the dish sweetly tart. I enjoyed that feeling of entertaining someone at that small kitchen table as though Jeff and I were a typical domestic partnership.

I had a recurring dream in that small apartment. It was about a hallway door that stayed closed. Behind the door were spacious rooms that were never accessed or used.

•   •   •   •   •

Charlotte Pittman came to Austin and into my life in 1965. Jeff and Char were fast friends, both air force brats. Char's father and Jeff's stepfather had been stationed at a North Dakota air force base. Char and Jeff had attended the University of North Dakota. The two of them could slip into a spirited rendition of a song they had learned there.

> You oughta go-ta North Dakota
> See the people and the wheat[4]

Jeff played a matchmaker role, arranging for Char, who was on the East Coast, to meet an Austin SDSer from Seminole, Texas, Scott Pittman. Char and Scott met under the clock in Grand Central Station. Char came to Austin and then traveled to Hazard, Kentucky, with Jeff and Robert Pardun in early 1965. I remember meeting her a bit later that year. She made an impression—petite, artistic, and beautiful. Char was one of those envelope-pushing women in my life. She wore European clogs before anyone else did and sported a white bikini at Shipe Pool long before other bikinis were seen in Austin. She put her artistic skill to use creating giant death masks for an antiwar march in the fall of 1965.

Rick Robbins and Charlotte Pittman carrying the SDS poster in a Death March protesting the war in Vietnam, UT West Mall, October 1965. Charlotte's boss at Kmart asked if it was her in the photo and fired her when she said yes. *UT Texas Student Publications photo, Briscoe Center for American History.*

1965

The events at Selma, Alabama, in 1965 hit home when Jeff went there with several other reporters from the *Daily Texan.*

Poll taxes, intricate literacy tests, job intimidation, and violence were all used to keep Black voters away from the polls in Alabama and throughout the South. Selma made headlines as voter suppression was challenged. In February 1965 civil rights leader Jimmie Lee Jackson was beaten and shot by an Alabama state trooper. He died eight days later, his death mobilizing civil rights advocates across the nation to act.

The Southern Christian Leadership Conference called for a march from Selma to Birmingham. The nonviolent protest was brutally attacked by Alabama troopers as marchers tried to cross the Edmund Pettus Bridge. Later, under National Guard protection, the march finally proceeded along the fifty-four-mile route, arriving in Birmingham at the end of March.

In Southeast Asia, the war in Vietnam was escalating, and SDS made plans for the first national march on Washington, DC, against the war. It was to happen Easter weekend, April 17, 1965. In Texas, SDS decided not to travel to DC but to go where the president was going—the LBJ Ranch, on the outskirts of Stonewall, Texas, seventy miles southwest of Austin. We staged a vigil there, with Secret Service and state troopers nearly outnumbering us.

We had an impact beyond our numbers. As Texans, we were bringing the war opposition to the president's home turf. The president couldn't escape antiwar sentiment, and his administration couldn't say it was just an East or West Coast phenomenon. We were there. A photo taken by a United Press International photographer identified several of us, including Jeff and me. The UPI photograph was the 1965 equivalent of going viral.

The national demonstration drew far greater numbers than expected. SDS president Paul Potter delivered a speech to that gathering of twenty-five thousand, and the reprint of that speech became a standard item on SDS literature tables.

In April of 1965, I took on my familiar role of typing the materials for a teaching event on Vietnam. Billed as "The Faculty Colloquy on Viet-Nam," the Austin event did not have the edgy quality of teach-ins happening on other campuses. It was adapted for a more conservative Texas setting

PUBLIC TELEPHONE
MASTER BURGLAR ALARM CO.
BRING THE CIVIL RIGHTS ACT TO AUSTIN
INTEGRATED PUBLIC ACCOMMODATIONS FOR ALL UT STUDENTS
I CAN DIE FOR MY COUNTRY BUT I CAN'T BE SERVED HERE

Demonstrators demanding integration at Roy's Lounge on Guadalupe. *UT Texas Student Publications photo, Briscoe Center for American History.*

with a handout entitled "Viet-Nam: An Inquiry." I typed a large part of that material onto stencils that were mimeographed and assembled. The typing was tedious because mistakes had to be painted over with a noxious correction fluid. Despite its rather tame format, the faculty colloquy forged new alliances between antiwar students and faculty.

I was on another picket line in the spring of 1965. Roy's Lounge, a small dive of a bar at 2610 Guadalupe, refused service to an African American student, Linda Tolbert. SDS activist George Vizard was with her when she tried to use the pay phone and was refused access. George marched into the Student Union Chuck Wagon and got another interracial couple to attempt to enter the bar. They were also refused service. George told the owners he would return with a picket line. And that he did.

We kept that picket line going for weeks, gathering at the university

Roy's Lounge demonstration, with me pictured in the lower right panel. Excerpt from *Students for a Democratic Society: A Graphic History*. Text copyright 2008 by Harvey Pekar and Paul Buhle. Artwork copyright 2008 by Gary Dumm. Reprinted by permission of Hill and Wang, a division of Farrar, Straus and Giroux. All Rights Reserved.

YMCA/YWCA, the "Y," at Twenty-Second Street, where we would stand on the steps, arms linked, and sing civil rights anthems. Those songs still send shivers up my spine.

> We shall overcome
> We shall overcome
> We shall overcome someday

We would march five blocks north to picket the bar at Twenty-Seventh Street. The demonstration often drew a crowd from nearby fraternities that would jeer and taunt us with racist slurs, aiming ugly sexist insults at the women. George was arrested at the first demonstration there.

Roy's Lounge closed at the end of the spring semester. Perhaps the protests played a part in its demise. In a later incarnation, Roy's Lounge became a legendary punk bar, Raul's.

What Is to Be Done?

With my SDS comrades, we launched a student rights campaign in 1965. It was edgy and irreverent. We ridiculed the current student government apparatus as powerless. The campaign was provocative in every way, in its vision and platform and its attention-grabbing skits and songs. It was fun.

SDSer Gary Thiher ran for student government as a presidential candidate. His mimeographed platform was titled "What Is to Be Done?" It was a lighthearted nod to Vladimir Lenin's broadside by the same name. The platform began with an explanation from Gary: "I am entering this campaign to effect change in the University—to return power over academic affairs to the academic community and control over student life to the students. I am not entering in order to play the timeworn game of student politics for personal prestige."

The campaign put forth a bold Bill of Rights: "Free discussion and evaluation being vital to an academic community, the University shall make no regulation abridging the freedom of speech or of publication and distribution; nor abridge the right of persons to peacefully assemble and petition."

The Thiher platform addressed housing, contraceptives, adherence to the federal minimum wage, and the elimination of questions on race and religion from housing questionnaires. It included radical ideas and even revolutionary ones when it came to free tuition and an accredited program of "peace study" with funding similar to that provided for the Reserve Officers' Training Corps. The platform advocated an end to mandatory approved housing, noting that women in particular were restricted, scrutinized, and overly regulated by the system in place. Birth control was addressed as follows:

> Recognizing the fact of pre-marital sexual relationships between students, the University Health Center should provide the same services as other health centers. This plank does not condone or condemn any individual's sexual ethics, but expresses concern about undesired conceptions which lead to hasty marriage, abortion, or illegitimate children.
>
> I THEREFORE ADVOCATE that the University Health Center should make available birth control information and prescriptions to any student seeking them.

The campaign was feisty and nonconformist, complete with a ballad by John Clay, who sang it while playing a banjo:

> You know he cannot win
> Cause he's advocating sin
> And if you vote for Thiher
> They'll wonder what you're in
> But, if you want to show them how you feel
> Vote for Gary Thiher if you don't like this kind of deal.

Well, Gary Thiher didn't win that race. In 1967, he ran again on an SDS slate, which I was on as well. We did not win then. But we paved the way for a successful campaign by SDS member Jeff Jones in 1970. Jeff was elected president of the student government.

Vietnam consumed the attention of SDS as the war escalated. The conflict had barely grazed my consciousness in 1963. In October of that year Madame Nhu, the sister-in-law of Ngo Dinh Diem, president of South Vietnam, spoke at UT's Gregory Gym. A few students in the Young People's Socialist League leafleted on the steps before and after her talk. President Diem, a Catholic in a majority Buddhist nation, had grown increasingly unpopular, criticized for lining his family's pockets and imposing repressive measures against Buddhists. He was assassinated in a CIA-backed coup d'etat just days after Madame Nhu's speech. His assassination came three weeks before President John F. Kennedy's.

As 1963 drew to a close, sixteen thousand US soldiers were in Vietnam. The Gulf of Tonkin incident became the pretext for declaring war in 1964. By the end of Lyndon Johnson's presidency in 1968, there were half a million soldiers in Vietnam, and in that year alone, there were sixteen thousand US casualties and unnumbered Vietnamese dead.

SDS had printed a poster in 1965 intended for the New York subway system. It had a photo of a Vietnamese child, her back horrifically scarred by napalm burns. It said, "Why are we burning, torturing, killing the people of Vietnam? . . . To prevent free elections." In the fall of 1965, Austin SDS held a somber death march on the UT campus. Marchers dressed in black, carrying that poster at the front of the procession.

I was working as a lab clerk for a professor of genetics whom my parents knew. He studied the inherited traits of *Drosophila*, a fruit fly with traits easily tracked by examining its eyes. I typed and filed reports, but I also had lab duties, specifically the care and feeding of the flies. I had to move the flies periodically from their old bottles to new bottles with fresh gruel. This involved putting them to sleep with chloroform. Too much and you would lose a few. Too little and they would wake up during the transfer and escape. It wasn't arduous work, and I spent many hours arguing with administrative assistant Carol Whitcraft about the war in Vietnam. On many days, I received her final dismissal of my views: "You can't understand; you didn't live through World War II."

During the fall semester of 1965, Terry Clarkson, David Martinez, and I rented a house on Tom Green Street in Austin. Terry and David married in January of 1966 in the Methodist Student Center chapel. The Tom Green house has since been demolished and replaced by apartments. It was very close to the Episcopal Seminary of the Southwest, where my mother worked. I didn't have much anonymity at Tom Green. If our parties in that house were too rowdy, they would be reported to my mother by a neighbor.

Campus Traveling

I didn't enroll for the spring semester in 1966. Instead I got my first job totally on my own merits—as a waitress. It was a lesson in stamina and humility. I waited tables at the Rome Inn, an Italian restaurant at Twenty-Ninth and Rio Grande. It had dim lights and candles mounted in fat Chianti bottles with straw baskets. Wax dripped down the bottles. The menu offerings were pizza, lasagna, spaghetti and meatballs, eggplant and veal parmesan, and a modest variety of wines.

On March 18, 1966, I walked up Rio Grande Street for my afternoon shift to find the restaurant charred by fire. The outdoor sign was blackened, and the dining room and kitchen had suffered major damage. Scorched chairs and tables had been pulled out into the parking lot behind the restaurant. Stacks of red plastic water glasses were now surreal towers of melted plastic. The fish in the restaurant's picturesque aquariums had perished as their water heated.

Without a job to go to or classes to attend, it was an easy choice: organizing the old-fashioned way—campus traveling with Jeff. We had no way to email or text. We had a mimeographed list of names from the SDS national office of people who had either filled out membership cards or signed up to receive the SDS newsletter, *New Left Notes*. We took off, bound for the places where there were people but no active chapters.

Gas was cheap and Butterscotch was sturdy. We had boxes of SDS literature—*The Port Huron Statement*, copies of *New Left Notes*, pamphlets with the speech Paul Potter delivered in 1965 at the first national demonstration against the Vietnam War. Some of the material was printed; more was just mimeographed. It was graphically challenged, sometimes barely legible, but thought provoking. This was before underground newspapers began to pop up around the country.

We drove the long, straight stretches of West Texas listening to the radio or singing union and civil rights songs. When we finally reached El Paso— in a different time zone from Austin—we called contacts at Texas Western, now the University of Texas at El Paso. We located two separate places to stay, so as not to offend the parents of our main contact. In the morning, I went with the student in whose home I had stayed to set up a literature table. It wasn't long before our antiwar literature attracted several Vietnam vets. Discussion quickly escalated to a fight and an overturned table. Jeff had slept in and missed the altercation.

En route to Greeley, Colorado, we stopped at the Denver Zoo. Maybe it was the petting zoo, because the animals were young and only a low fence separated the elephants from the visitors. A boy had been taunting a young elephant by feeding him pebbles. Suddenly, the elephant took his frustration out on me, wrapping his trunk around my arm and tugging me toward the fence. Jeff pounded on his trunk, trying to unwrap it from my arm. I was saved. I only lost a button on my jacket.

Jeff and I were a team, traveling to the University of Northern Colorado in Greeley, the University of Utah in Salt Lake City, the University of Wyoming in Laramie, and Northern Arizona University in Flagstaff.

In Greeley, the movement people shared a big house, turning the spacious bedrooms with high ceilings into communal space and placing their mattresses in the large closets. In Salt Lake City, the Mormon influence had resulted in a university-wide prohibition on smoking. Students there wanted to organize around their right to smoke as well as in protest against Vietnam. We went as far north as Laramie on that trip. Wyoming was the only state without an SDS chapter; after our visit, SDS had chapters in every state.

I think it was the tail end of this trip when we ended up in Pasadena, California, where Jeff's mother and sisters lived. Margot, Jeff's mother, was nice to me, but she had five children and was wary that I might get pregnant. By then, I was on the pill and not so worried.

From his mother's home, Jeff and I could cut through backyards to Jeff's grandparents' home. Neen and Gramps welcomed me with gusto, introducing me to cribbage and special breakfast waffles. They had a secret system for betting on the horses. We went with them to the Pasadena racetrack and had a great time. But they wouldn't divulge their betting strategy.

I returned to Austin without Jeff. He had SDS national office responsibilities in Chicago. I got a job as secretary to Dr. Carl Hereford, my father's university colleague, in a Peace Corps training project. Signing up for the

Peace Corps was an alternative to military service in 1966. When the project introduced a "peer assessment" requiring trainees to evaluate each other, all hell broke loose. The trainees worried that a bad assessment might result in a fellow student being dropped from the Peace Corps assignment and losing their draft deferment status. My professor boss walked into the auditorium to administer the test. I trailed behind carrying the copies. No one would put his or her peers at risk. No one would take the exam.

Sniper Fire

I was working at the Peace Corps office on Rio Grande Street on August 1, 1966, when a coworker received a call from her husband in the UT Tower. He told her that shots were being fired from the observation deck. She could hear the gunfire over the telephone, and soon we could hear the sirens. Along with everyone in Austin, we began to listen to the radio coverage. After the ninety-six-minute ordeal ended with the death of Charles Whitman, his name was announced as the apparent shooter. A young woman coworker cried out that he was married to her cousin. She scrambled to leave. Her cousin was found dead at their home in South Austin.

Two of my friends from SDS were shot. Claire Wilson was the victim of Charles Whitman's first shot from the observation deck. Whitman had trained as a marine sharpshooter in Guantanamo. He targeted Claire's very pregnant abdomen, killing the baby boy inside her. Whitman's next shot took her boyfriend's life. Thomas Eckman fell beside her. Claire lay bleeding on the university's main mall for ninety-six minutes. Whitman would fire at anyone who tried to reach Claire.

Another friend, Sandra Wilson (no relation to Claire), was walking on Twenty-Third Street near the intersection with Guadalupe. A shot tore through her upper arm and into her chest, collapsing her lung.

Jeff and I went to Brackenridge Hospital. I said, "We love you, Claire," as she was being wheeled down a corridor. But we did not know how to help Claire or Sandra as they recovered from the trauma. We didn't have the tools we needed to process this type of campus violence. We were young and inexperienced, a generation that had just seen a president gunned down and carnage on the campus. We were about to see the violence of war escalate in unspeakable ways.

The Rag

The fall semester came hard on the heels of the Tower shooting. A student election had ushered in a new editor for the *Daily Texan*, making it unfriendly turf for progressive thought. Under the editorial control of John Economidy, we lost an avenue for antiwar coverage, opinion pieces, and even letters to the editor. It was time for alternative media.

Four SDS stalwarts had spent the summer months of 1966 working on an SDS project in San Francisco's Haight-Ashbury. They were Carol Neiman and the Houstonians Thorne Dreyer and Dennis and Judy Fitzgerald. In San Francisco, they had picked the brain of Michael Kindman, whose East Lansing *Paper* was a pioneer in a new breed of journalism. The new periodicals were organized under the banner of the Underground Press Syndicate.

When those four returned to Austin from San Francisco, the newspaper idea continued to percolate. Jeff Shero, David Mahler, Gary Thiher, Mariann and George Vizard, and I were early converts to the idea. Trudy Minkoff, whom I had surprised with a knife one night on West Twelfth Street, was a tireless contributor of artwork. Another artist, Clelie Moore, contributed the first psychedelic masthead. *The Rag* began its life on October 10, 1966. Dennis Fitzgerald recalled the beginning this way: "I was privileged to be in the delivery room at the birth of *The Rag*. 'Breathe, breathe, breathe!' It was a long, hard labor. But what a beautiful child she was. For just over a year, I changed my share of dirty diapers and delighted in watching her first tentative steps."[5]

The Rag was just comic-book size, not yet grown to tabloid, when it became the sixth member of the Underground Press Syndicate. Abe Peck, founder of the *Chicago Seed* and later a professor of journalism history, said that *The Rag* was the "first undergrounder to represent the participatory democracy, community organizing and synthesis of politics and culture that the New Left of the midsixties was trying to develop."[6]

The Rag was a scruffy newspaper only a parent could love. A new offset technology made it possible, and it was originally printed with sheet-fed newsprint on Larry Freudiger's Multilith press.

What was revolutionary about offset technology was the flexibility it allowed in design and layout. It was not bound by "hot type" constraints.

The Truth »beep« Is On Page..

by Carol Neiman

Yeah, babes, you've finally hit the bigtime rah rah scooby dooroo beat the hell outa SMU these are the best few years of your life so learn to think for your self make your place in society be a phi beta kappa sigma chi omega doo wah. Hello??

I dunno about you but that really turns me off. So what can you do? Of course the logical, sensible thing to do is to try getting turned on to something else that makes sense.

But woe and alas! Most people seem to remain turned off, unplugged, and militantly apathetic members of the soggy green masses. Why, oh, why this dusty fate for so many once-eager scholars?? Why do they retreat behind stacks of textbooks and class notes, venturing CONTINUED on page 10

THE RAG

volume 1
number one

Gen. John Economidy: The First 100 Days

by KAYE NORTHCOTT ~ Past Editor, DAILY TEXAN

Soon after John Economidy was elected editor of the Daily Texan last spring he made a grand entrance into the newspaper office wearing an Air Force ROTC uniform and carrying a makeshift swagger stick.

He marched to the copy desk, banged the stock on the table rim and announced, "General John is HERE!"

The Texan has not been the same since.

The public relations and government major is hard to put into any political pidgeon hole for he often changes perches.

During the campus-wide campaign last spring, Economidy presented himself as a

YEAH, But wait til you see What we got INSIDE:

The Tinseled Seductress - SEX & SOCIETY

THE BENT SPOKESMAN - OUR REGULAR MOTORCYCLE COLUMN

A REVIEW OF WHO'S AFRAID OF VIRGINIA WOOLF

Psychedelic Drawings

and Rag Bag - an esoteric guide to where the ACTION IS.

October 10, 1966   AUSTIN, TEXAS   PAGE 1

The cover of the first *Rag*, October 10, 1966. *Clelie Moore, artist.*

Using a lot of rubber cement, typed copy, rub-on letter headlines, counter-cultural cartoons, and lively graphics, each page could be an individual creative act, with artwork in the margins, type in different sizes, and headlines running vertically. To eyes accustomed to traditional newspapers, it looked like chaos. To the counterculture, it looked like artistic genius. The completed layout sheets were photographed with a copy camera and converted to negatives. The negatives were "stripped" into a flat, burned onto an aluminum plate, and positioned on a press. Later, as an offset printer, I gained an immense respect for Larry Freudiger's ability to feed sheets of newsprint through his small press. Huge rolls of newsprint are typically used to print newspapers, not sheets.

The address on the first masthead was a house in the West Campus area at 2506 Nueces. Thorne and Carol were listed as Funnel and Funnella, a nod to the lack of hierarchy. Artists were identified. Writers had bylines. George was named a Super Salesman by the second issue. Those who typed copy, cut it to column size, slathered rubber cement, and laid out the paper were identified as Shitworkers and later, more elegantly, as Shitteworkers.

I was a Shitteworker. My master-level skills at typing, acquired in junior high, were relied upon for issue after issue. We used a tedious process to justify columns, typing copy first with Xs at the end of each line, then retyping it and manually inserting space within the column. This was long before affordable typesetters and decades before computers made justifying a convenient menu choice. We also performed a literal "cut and paste" before that function also showed up as a word-processing option.

Although it is usually carried out in silence, writing is a voice exercise. I didn't think of myself as a writer, nor was I encouraged to write. I typed and diligently participated in the all-night layout sessions. I even borrowed a Selectric typewriter from an office where I worked as a secretary, stealthily returning it in the wee hours of the morning on several occasions. Layout sessions required all hands on deck and relied heavily on the artists to fill space, make staff boxes sparkle, and create advertisements.

The paper graduated from its comic-book size after twelve issues. In its tabloid format, it began to feature some of the legendary countercultural artwork of Jim Franklin and Gilbert Shelton. Shelton's "Furry Freak

Brothers" first appeared in *The Rag*. Hippies bought the paper to find out who was playing at the Vulcan Gas Company. Radicals bought the paper to read about the last demonstration and find out when the next one was scheduled.

Always a volunteer effort, the paper miraculously survived from October 1966 until May 1977, spanning nearly eleven years of advocacy journalism with unabashed reporting on the political and cultural upheaval of the era. *The Rag* was connective tissue for a community of resistance. During the UT student rebellion of 1967, the University Freedom Movement, I was one of six students, and the only woman, put on disciplinary probation. Five of us were in SDS and were Ragstaffers. In the best tradition of participatory journalism, *The Rag* covered that student rebellion in detail.

Draft Board

On October 27, 1966, I was one of ten women who staged a sit-in at the Texas headquarters of the Selective Service System. We were still processing the violence on campus. We conceived of this action, planned it, drafted a joint statement, and carried it out, arriving in the late morning to sit down in the hallway and risk arrest. We caught the Selective Service administrators and staff by surprise.

The police were called, and the press showed up. We were warned that we were in violation of a city ordinance, and if we interfered with Selective Service business, we would be in violation of federal law. After an initial scramble and huddle out of our view, those in charge chose to leave us there and to step over and around us until we left in the late afternoon. We were never arrested. Still, we all had decided to take that risk.

This was years before I engaged in consciousness-raising and women's study groups, before organizing with women was commonplace. While four years may not seem like a lifetime, it was a movement lifetime. It was before women's liberation.

Even the way we signed our names on that 1966 statement would be different four years later. The four of us who were unmarried signed our names Sandra Wilson, Julie Cadenhead, Carol Neiman, and Alice Embree. The married women signed with "Mrs." Some used their own first names: Mrs. Judy Pardun, Mrs. Judy Fitzgerald, and Mrs. Judy Binder Kendall.

Draft Protested

All-Woman Sit-In at S.S. Office

BY THORNE DREYER

"Oh my goodness, a bunch of young ladies. We usually have boys in here." The woman, middle-aged and hefty, beamed at the ten girls as they entered the office of the state draft board. her smile would soon fade.

Thursday, October 27, ten young women conducted a sit-in at the Texas state headquarters of the Selective Service System. They remained in the office for four and a half hours, from eleven until three thirty in the afternoon. It was the first such demonstration in Texas.

The girls entered the office at eleven A.M. with a statement addressed to Col. Morris S. Schwartz, state Selective Service director. Col. Schwartz was out of town and they were taken to

CONTINUED on 3

photos by
ben mc guire

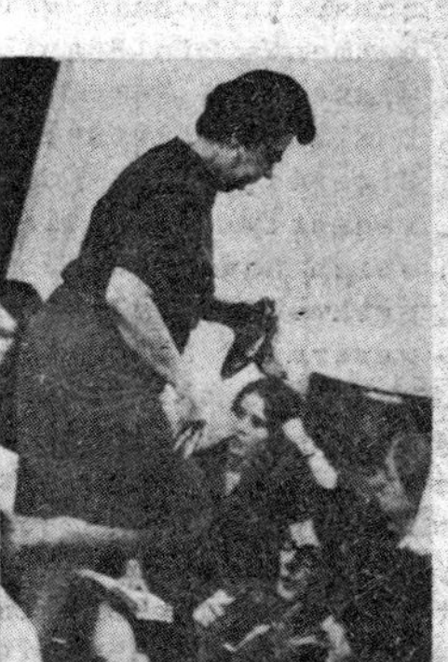

The Rag, October 31, 1966, has Thorne Dreyer's story about the sit-in at the draft office.

Three used their husbands' names: Mrs. Larry Freudiger, Mrs. G. J. Vizard IV, and Mrs. R. Minkoff. The designations were like the clothes we wore to demonstrations at the time, an effort to appeal widely, assuming the mantle of respectability that marriage conveyed.

Sandra Wilson, who had recently survived Whitman's sniper bullet, was with us, and our statement referred to that campus tragedy:

> We protest the brutalizing effects of compulsory military training upon our society. The tower sniper shot one of the signers of our statement. We are concerned with the lack of compassion and indignation in our society concerning acts of violence—whether it is violence on the University of Texas campus or in Vietnam.

The death toll of US soldiers had risen dramatically. Our statement said, "We feel compassion for the families of the over 36,000 American men who have been killed so far in Vietnam, and the unnumbered Vietnamese dead."

We were speaking as sisters, wives, and mothers affected by the war. Nancy Freudiger, who was married to the *Rag* printer, had an infant with her. Judy Binder was already producing powerful antiwar artwork that graced the pages of *The Rag*. She would later establish a creative teaching space in West Virginia to draw upon her many talents—dance, sculpture, painting, and lithography. Carol, Judy Fitzgerald, and Trudy were all working on *The Rag*. Julie was a peace activist. Within a year's time, Mariann would be widowed.

Judy Schiffer Pardun was a trailblazer in several ways. She had been a participant in Mississippi Freedom Summer, taking part in community organizing and voter registration in 1964. I was also impressed when she and Bob Pardun began to live together unabashedly in 1964. Although it may not merit equal stature with voter registration, I recall vividly the first time I rode in a car with Judy. Some items were on the front seat. She said, "Just throw that crap in the back seat." I swear to you, I had never heard a woman say "crap" with such matter-of-fact ease.

I do not recall whose idea it was to stage this sit-in, but I know we met separately and secretly at the *Rag* office. It is remarkable to me that we did this as women, not potential draftees, boldly asserting our opposition to both the draft and the war.

Thorne Dreyer wrote an article for *The Rag* about the action. It begins with the comment of the receptionist: "Oh my goodness, a bunch of young ladies. We usually have boys in here." Sometimes Thorne refers to us as "girls," other times as "women," straddling terminology that was typical at the time.

As for the titles we used, I never imagined in 1966 that I'd keep my name if I married. "Ms." would not be popularized until *Ms.* magazine hit the newsstands in 1972. We were not yet the women of women's liberation. That change was on the horizon and closer than we knew.

• • • • •

I began 1967 as a UT student, taking a full load of classes that spring semester but majoring in SDS. I didn't return for the fall semester. It would be more than a decade before I enrolled again as an undergraduate.

In January of 1967, SDS called for an antiwar protest of Secretary of State Dean Rusk. I was standing next to George Vizard at the state capitol, my knees literally shaking, while George fearlessly informed the Texas Department of Public Safety trooper of our constitutional rights.

In February, I got to know several Chileans who were at UT as part of a Chilean exchange program. The connection was through Philip Russell. Philip, a high school friend of Jeff's from Bryan, Texas, was fluent in Spanish, an invaluable translator, and would become a Latin American scholar. Through Philip we learned that two of the Chileans were interested in the farmworker organizing taking place in the Rio Grande Valley. Philip, Jeff, and I took them on a road trip to South Texas. We spent the night in sleeping bags at the union headquarters. The next day, when we went to see one of the grower's buildings, we were warned off the property by a security guard with a rifle. I'm sure it made a lasting, Texas-style impression on the Chileans.

Soon after the trip to the valley, the Chilean exchange program heated up. Two of the Chilean journalist students left. Before their departure, they were interviewed by Jeff for *The Rag*. It was the first of two articles on the

Chilean students. I became increasingly interested in the exchange, the UT-Chilean Student Leadership Seminar.

Jeff, with Philip's translating assistance, wrote a March 6, 1967, story about the two Chileans who left: "Two Chilean students, angered by their exchange program's tie with the State Department, decided Saturday to cut short their visit and return home. Edmundo Villarroel and Arturo Saez said they learned Thursday the exchange supposedly sponsored by the University of Texas was in fact a State Department contracted program."

A week later, on March 13, 1967, Jeff reported on an agreement signed by UT and the Chilean students. UT Austin student body representative Cliff Drummond and another student, Richard Wright, signed for the Texas students. Augusto Samaniego and Claudio Venegas signed for the Chileans. Samaniego, a member of the Communist Party, had been elected as president of the Federación Estudiantil de la Universidad de Chile. He helped draft a five-point program to guarantee autonomy for the exchange and greater student representation in the decisions about the exchange.

As it turned out, the exchange was terminated before the agreement could be fully implemented. I would be at the center of that storm.

In April 1967, in New York, Martin Luther King Jr. gave his powerful speech at the Riverside Church, declaring for the first time his opposition to the war. Many of his associates wanted him to stay narrowly focused on civil rights. Antiwar activists welcomed his stand, feeling that it was overdue. King spoke to the moral implications of the war: "Now, it should be incandescently clear that no one who has any concern for the integrity and life of America today can ignore the present war. If America's soul becomes totally poisoned, part of the autopsy must read: Vietnam."

One year after his Riverside Church speech, to the day, King was assassinated in Memphis.

University Freedom Movement

SDS, having run a 1965 campaign for Gary Thiher as student body president, launched another campaign in the spring of 1967, this time with a slate of candidates. Gary Thiher was running for president. I was running for vice president. The slate included four other candidates, Dick Reavis,

Jeff Ludlow, Harvey Stone, and Virginia Leonard. The platform began as follows:

QUESTION:

- Why the hell are students second-class citizens—denied even basic Constitutional rights?
- Why are so many dissatisfied students without the power to change their circumstances?
- Why is education such a dull, static drag?
- Why is the Student Assembly an ineffectual machine which merely perpetuates the present stagnation at the cost of a truly creative education?

ANSWER:

- Because you the students are individuals without organization or direction.
- Because you the student are subject to the manipulation of a non-educationally oriented administration.
- Because you the student have never before been faced with the reality of your situation.

The platform called for student-faculty governance, proposed a Black history curriculum, and addressed university employee issues. It demanded that graduate student teaching assistants be included in the retirement system and that all employees, including cafeteria personnel, groundskeepers, and library staff, receive at least the federal minimum wage of $1.40 per hour. Military recruiters, we said, should be handled through the employment office, like any corporate recruiter. We advocated abolition of the Reserve Officers' Training Corps and restrictions on defense research. The 1965 campaign demand for birth control information at the University Health Center was no longer necessary, because the Health Center had changed its policies.

Events that spring in 1967 moved forward on a fast current of activism, with classes playing only a small role. We would gather and talk in the Chuck Wagon over seven-cent coffee. We'd sit on the couches near

The Rag cover from Flipped Out Week, April 10, 1966. *Trudy Minkoff, artist.*

the Student Union television to see Walter Cronkite deliver the nightly news on Vietnam. We would have meetings at night. We were busy with a biweekly *Rag* schedule, writing, typing copy, laying out the paper, taking it to the printers, picking it up, and selling it.

As part of a seamless stream of activity, SDS sponsored Flipped-Out Week from April 10 through 16, coinciding with a national mobilization against the war in Vietnam. The week's events ran the gamut in quick succession: a Gentle Thursday "celebration of our belief that there is nothing wrong with fun"; advocacy of Black Power by the militant Student Non-violent Coordinating Committee (SNCC) leader Stokely Carmichael on Friday; a Saturday Gathering for Peace at Wooldridge Park complete with rock bands, speakers, and poetry; an Angry Arts event at the Methodist Student Center; a campus visit by Beat poet Allen Ginsberg; and a Sunday picnic at Pease Park.

The first salvo from the university administration was to ban Gentle Thursday. Their objection: "Program too vague and certain activities could not be sanctioned by the University. For example—kissing, mellow yellow, en masse, and 'all over campus.'"

"Mellow yellow" had been popularized in Donovan's 1966 song by that title, which was rumored to be about the hallucinogenic properties of smoking banana peels. It was simply a joke, but the UT administration took it seriously. The ban only increased the publicity for and the success of the guitars, balloons, poetry, picnics, and other gentleness that took over the West Mall on Thursday.

We had invited Stokely Carmichael to speak at UT the Friday following Gentle Thursday. As a SNCC activist, he had popularized the call for Black Power. Dick Reavis and I made a trip to Houston to finalize his travel. Stokely had come to Houston to support Texas Southern University's Friends of SNCC. The group was seeking reinstatement of a faculty member who had been fired for being the group's faculty advisor. On April 3, two Black activists, Reverend F. D. Kirkpatrick and Franklin Alexander, had been arrested on the Texas Southern University campus. When we met Stokely and delivered a plane ticket, he looked at it dismissively and said he needed an upgrade to first class.

On Friday, April 14, a large crowd gathered in Austin to hear Stokely speak at an outdoor theater near the UT Art Building. The outdoor movie venue is now the location of Bass Concert Hall. I remember the stressful wait before he arrived about forty-five minutes late. He captivated the audience the moment he stepped onstage, taking the microphone and reciting from memory the first words of the Declaration of Independence: "When, in the course of human events, it becomes necessary for one people to dissolve the political bonds which have connected them with another . . ."

We collected money to give to Stokely and his entourage. An economics professor, Clifford Grubbs, had a spread ready for a post-speech reception. Stokely stood up that offer. We were entering an era in which Black activists saw white college students as suspect allies in the struggle, privileged and protected from the reprisals that were escalating against the Black Power movement. The arrests at Texas Southern University, a historically Black college, were evidence of the disparity in police response.

Only a few days after the intensity of Flipped-Out Week, we learned that Vice President Hubert Humphrey was coming to Austin. On Sunday, April 23, SDS called a meeting to plan an antiwar demonstration at the capitol, where Humphrey would speak. With no time to spare, we met on the West Mall.

The Texas Union building has a prominent arched doorway that leads into the foyer of a large ballroom. On the Sunday afternoon that would reverberate for weeks, I walked up the Union steps to the landing. A limestone wall served as a lectern of sorts. There were other SDS speakers, but I think I was the only woman. I looked down at the crowd that had gathered to plan a demonstration. I'm sure my voice had a nervous tremor. I spoke about the urgency to act in the face of a major escalation of the war—the bombings of North Vietnam. I spoke briefly, for only a few minutes. I was motivated by one thought: a war that escalated every month in destruction and deadliness. I urged the crowd to oppose the war and the war makers.

The chairman of the UT Board of Regents, Frank Erwin, was on the terrace below instructing his aide to take down names. We were violating an order of the chancellor in assembling for that meeting. We had not reserved a room. The news of the vice president's trip to Austin had broken over the weekend, and the office handling room reservations was closed. My maiden journey into public speaking cast a long shadow. I was one

I spoke at a University Freedom Movement rally in April 1967 after being put on disciplinary probation for an antiwar speech. *Photo by John Avant, John Avant Photographic Archive, Briscoe Center for American History.*

of the six charged with violating an administrative order. The campus erupted into a free speech fight.

Frank Erwin was incensed by our plan to protest the vice president, embarrassing the president in his home state. Erwin was not only the powerful chairman of the board of regents, he served as a Democratic committeeman for Texas. He was a loyal friend of Lyndon Johnson's, protective of the image of the president and the Democratic Party. And Frank ruled with a heavy hand.

On Monday, April 24, six of us received a notice that the university administration

> has filed charges against you alleging that you did knowingly and willfully violate an order of the Chancellor of the University of

Texas System in that you did participate in a meeting and rally on the West Mall of the Campus of the University of Texas at Austin on . . . Sunday evening, April 23, 1967, after such meeting and rally were expressly prohibited by the said Chancellor.

With one exception, John Lefeber of the Young Democrats, those of us facing charges were all in SDS and were Ragstaffers, or "on *The Rag*," as I sometimes say with irony. We had all spoken on April 23.

We were summoned to appear at a 10:00 a.m. hearing on Tuesday, April 25. Technically, the university went after us for not using proper channels to reserve a room for a meeting. Fortunately for us, a constitutional law professor at the UT Law School, Fred Cohen, saw the situation as clearly as we did. The university had abridged our right to free speech. He volunteered to defend us before the disciplinary committee.

Fred Cohen, sometimes called "Fred the Red," was a former college basketball star. We gathered at the Student Union with him before the scheduled disciplinary hearing. He towered over us, striding ahead as we walked into the hearing room.

Based on alphabetical order, I was singled out to go first. Embree preceded Lefeber, Mahler, Reavis, Smith, and Thiher. It was an administrative strategy to divide us in this way, so that we did not have a collective presence in the room. I walked into the hearing room and was startled to see my parents sitting in chairs reserved for observers.

It was the first time I had seen them since the disciplinary actions began. I was only able to nod at them before being seated at the table. I know my parents were there to support me. In retrospect, I am grateful. But I didn't feel comforted. It felt like a collision between my activist world and their world, something the other "disciplinary defendants" never had to navigate, because they weren't hometown radicals.

I don't remember the questions that were asked. Attorney Fred Cohen was quite skillful in reframing the issue as one of constitutionally protected speech and assembly. I left the building after the hearing and was surrounded by a swirl of supporters and reporters. There was no opportunity to speak with my parents. I made my way across campus to report on the events near the statue of George Washington on the South Mall. I spoke about the need for a real student union to replace the sham of a student assembly that had no power.

Throughout the events that were known as the University Freedom Movement, I felt that we were propelled forward on a churning current. We had responded to a disastrous escalation of the war in Vietnam. We were motivated by events unfolding on a grand stage, a national stage, a world stage. It was hard to maintain my footing in that treacherous current. That is what it felt like to be at the center of the storm.

To add to the week's intensity, Jeff told me he was involved with another woman. I didn't react with tears or anger. I guess I had good training in silent acquiescence. In retrospect, I thought that it was his prerogative to alter the relationship, that he didn't owe me an explanation. Women were part of a highly hyped '60s sexual revolution that was, by and large, defined by men. On a personal level, I felt that he left at a time I needed support. I was in the center of a storm as the free speech fight simmered and roiled on campus.

I remember almost flipping out in the aftermath of Flipped-Out Week—near meltdown from the constant diet of coffee, adrenaline, meetings, and microphones. When I closed my eyes, staccato, strobe-lit images of days without margins kept flashing. Events moved at warp speed that entire April. Jeff was unavailable for emotional support.

Conversations with Robert Pardun kept me from collapse. By coincidence, Robert and Judy had split up. Judy left Austin and was living with SDS activist Mike Davis in California. I had appreciated Robert's organizing ability, but it was his friendship that was invaluable that spring. I needed a shoulder to lean on, and I suspect he did as well.

I moved out of the apartment Jeff had rented on West Thirteenth Street, just a block north of the apartment on Twelfth that had been broken into. I moved into a screened-in porch at the *Rag* office on West Twenty-Sixth. Governed by the laws of synchronicity, it was the same house where my high school friend Margaret Rideout had lived, the same place I had been treated to Turkish coffee and political conversation by Margaret's father. I had more ghosts to trip over than most of my SDS peers.

A fellow student cited for disciplinary probation snuck through the window into that back porch for a late-night seduction. Jeff wasn't quite

Jeff Shero chairing a University Freedom Movement meeting at the Campus Guild housing cooperative, April 1967. *Photo by John Avant, John Avant Photographic Archive, Briscoe Center for American History.*

prepared for me to get involved with someone else. Later, I would hear Molly Ivins use the phrase "gander sauce." "What's good for the goose is good for the gander." I hadn't really thought of it that way. Still, it was comforting when I saw the way Jeff looked at this guy who was also caught up in disciplinary hearings.

The university escalated the conflict into one of free speech, and the University Freedom Movement took shape. A UT veterans' group defended us with signs that read, "UT Vets Fought for Free Speech." They went so far as to replicate the actions taken by SDS to demonstrate that the university was singling SDS out for special treatment. Hundreds of students signed a declaration of equal responsibility and came to the first disciplinary hearing to demand they also be "tried."

Planning meetings at the Campus Guild housing co-op drew hundreds each evening. Thousands filled the university's main mall in demonstrations as disciplinary hearings continued. The semester ended with SDS stripped of its status as a campus-approved organization. Rather than immediate dismissal, the six of us facing disciplinary action were placed on one-year probationary status. Demonstrations, petitions, and resolutions in our support had drawn thousands on campus into activism.

• • • • •

I had become familiar with the Chilean exchange program through the *Rag* interviews and our trip to the Rio Grande Valley. I decided to apply for the exchange. When I was accepted, I took conversational Spanish classes at the International Office taught by Cecilia Ubilla Garcia, known locally as "Che Che." The exchange was to be three weeks long, taking place during the North American summer break and the Chilean winter. I began to look for warm clothes.

In July, only weeks before we were to depart for Chile, my friend George Vizard was shot to death. When George was murdered on July 23, 1967, I lost a friend and comrade.

Grief mingled with disbelief.

Mariann, George's widow, learned so early to embrace grief and to grow strong with loss, her pale skin like marble, her eyes reflecting wisdom acquired too early in life, at such a heavy cost.[7]

George J. Vizard IV

George, two years my senior, was born in 1943. He grew up in San Antonio and attended San Antonio College before transferring as a junior to UT in the fall of 1964. In the three and a half years he lived in Austin, he played a major role in the battles for racial justice, free speech, and an end to the war in Vietnam.

As a dorm resident my freshman year, I'd occasionally meet my parents at All Saints' Episcopal Church and return home with them for Sunday dinner. To my surprise, George was at a church service in vestments. He was serving as an acolyte, technically a crucifer, carrying the cross down the aisle. After his death, I learned he had considered becoming a priest. Since I knew him from civil rights meetings, I invited him to dinner at my parents' home. George was the kind of person your parents wanted you to bring home. He didn't sit behind a newspaper, speaking only when spoken to. He engaged easily with my family. Mariann told me he had won over her mother when, at the sound of her car in the driveway, he had jumped up to help bring in the groceries.

George was serious about politics—so serious that he later joined the Communist Party—but he wasn't a dour, droning politico. He had a playful side. He read poetry at Ichthus Coffeehouse. When *Mary Poppins* opened at the Varsity Theatre in the fall of 1964, George and I stole away from the Chuck Wagon to see the Disney film. We loved the silliness, the tea party rising up into the air. We came back to the Chuck Wagon serenading our fellow comrades with "A spoonful of sugar makes the medicine go down." Mariann memorialized our duet in a poem she wrote after George's death.

George had an easy presence, a comfort in his own skin. It was a good fit for his job running the customer counter at Home Steam Laundry, where he worked off and on. The owner liked him so much that he loaned him a suit when George married Mariann in December of 1965. Reverend Bob Breihan performed the services in the chapel of the Methodist Student Center.

An iconic photo of George shows him in front of the University Co-op in the fall of 1966. He stands on one leg on a folding chair, his arms extended, newspapers in hand, hawking *The Rag*. He's wearing his "whites," so the photo was taken either before or after his shift at the Austin State Hospital. His wife, Mariann, is seated beside him. George peddled the paper on the UT campus as well. The second issue of *The Rag* carries George's account of his confrontations with the UT Police over whether *The Rag* could be sold on campus. This argument went all the way to the US Supreme Court and was settled in *The Rag*'s favor years after George's death.

George's political beliefs made him bolder than most. In 1965, he initiated the picket line at Roy's Lounge. At a January 1967 protest of

Mariann and George Vizard selling *The Rag* on the Drag, 1966.

Secretary of State Dean Rusk, Mariann and Mary Mantle were pushed by Department of Public Safety troopers. Mariann recalls George coming to her rescue as a trooper held a baton against her throat. That got George arrested.

Just months later, in April, at the SDS protest of Vice President Humphrey, George saw a counterprotester strike Sandra Wilson in the face with a picket sign. He confronted the police, which led to his arrest several days later. In fact, the UT Board of Regents obtained an injunction to prohibit the presence of George and two other nonstudents on campus, declaring that "openly opposing the actions of the United States of America in its foreign policy" was "against the best interests of the University of Texas."

George was eating breakfast at the Chuck Wagon when police presented him with a warrant for his arrest. Going limp, as was nonviolent practice, he was dragged across the cement and pavement, his back bloodied so badly that he had to be taken to Brackenridge Hospital before being booked.

On July 23, 1967, George Vizard was shot to death in the cold locker of the convenience store where he worked. It was a Sunday. We knew Austin Police lieutenant Burt Gerding from his nonstop surveillance and would sometimes alert him to demonstrations. I called Gerding to tell him George had been murdered. Referring to our activism, his response was, "Well, Alice, I always told you this sort of thing could be dangerous." Whether this was the provocative bravado typical of Gerding, or had a darker meaning, I will never know.

On the Sunday we learned of George's death, there was a community gathering at the "Y." Mariann did not think a demonstration at the Austin Police Department was appropriate. As news spread to other cities through our activist network, letters demanding action poured into the offices of the Austin Police and local officials. There was no action. Instead, Mariann was subjected to a polygraph, and friends of George were questioned. Law enforcement officers filled the rear seats of the funeral service at Weed-Corley.

Reverend Bob Breihan, who had married George and Mariann, presided over the funeral at Weed-Corley. My mother came with me out of respect for the young man whom she had met. Reverend Breihan, as he had done at the wedding, read from Ecclesiastes 3:

To everything there is a season,

and a time to every purpose under the heaven:

A time to be born, and a time to die . . .

As was discovered much later, the lead homicide investigator concealed evidence that would have led immediately to Robert Zani, a former UT student with right-wing leanings who had recently been fired from the convenience store. Zani's fingerprints were on a loaf of bread and wrappers on the counter, witnesses saw him there that Sunday, and a tip had come in identifying him as a possible suspect who had asked for help robbing the store.

It would be fourteen years before Zani was arrested, after he and his wife, Erma, had committed several other murders, including, it is believed, of Zani's mother in Tulsa, Oklahoma, and of a San Antonio realtor in 1979. When Zani was arrested with credit cards of the murdered realtor, his wife reportedly said he had killed that "smart-ass communist." Sentenced to ninety-nine years in 1981 for George's death, Zani died in the prison infirmary in 2011.

While Zani was imprisoned, papers belonging to the former UT Police chief came to the attention of former Ragstaffers. They had been kept at Chief Allen Hamilton's house and sent to Half Price Books after his death. They revealed that Zani had volunteered to be a "narc" as early as 1964 and that Hamilton had introduced him to contacts at the Texas Department of Public Safety for assessment. Because Department of Public Safety records from the era have been destroyed, the question of whether Zani was a police "asset" at the time that he murdered George Vizard remains unanswered.

I boarded a plane to Santiago, Chile, on August 9, just two and a half weeks after George's death, and I didn't return to Austin until December 1969. But Mariann and I will always be connected by the shared bond of knowing and loving George.

Santiago to New York: 1967—1969

CHILE, THAT SLENDER EXPANSE OF A NATION BETWEEN THE
Andes and the Pacific Ocean, is on average 110 miles wide—about the
distance from Austin to Waco. But it stretches more than 2,600 miles
from north to south. The northern expanse is desert—the driest desert in
the world—and the southern part of Chile gives way to lakes and islands
and then to Antarctica. Chile made its entrance into my life through the
intercambio, the exchange.

The UT-Chilean Student Leadership Seminar was in its ninth year of
existence. It was to be its last. According to an oral history with Joe Neal
of the UT International Office, it began with riots. Vice President Richard
Nixon had visited Latin America in 1958; his entourage was rocked by
violent demonstrations in Venezuela and Colombia. When he returned,
he instructed State Department personnel to engage with Latin American students. Ten exchange programs were established, relying on State
Department funding and influence but administered by universities.

These were not academic exchanges but cultural ones, lasting a few
weeks, with South American students traveling to the United States during

The UT Chile Exchange participants meeting with Senator Ralph Yarborough before leaving for Chile, August 1967. I am fourth from left and future congressman Lloyd Doggett is on the far right.

their summer months of January and February, and US students traveling to a wintry Chile in August.

By 1967, the contradictions had heightened. The Chilean delegation included many student leftists, and there was increasing suspicion about the autonomy of the exchange. The Chilean president of the student organization signing the accord for the exchange in 1967 was in the Communist Party. The Chilean journalism students interviewed by *The Rag* prior to their departure from Austin were members of the Socialist Party.

My disciplinary charges had been reduced to probation by the end of the 1967 spring semester, and I was accepted as a participant in the Chile exchange.

There was pushback from the State Department when they realized that our delegation included several students critical of the Vietnam War and active in civil rights struggles. But we survived that pushback when UT chancellor Harry Huntt Ransom argued that many points of view should be included.

We took off for Washington, DC, on August 22. There, we learned that the University of Chile's Pedagógico in Santiago had voted to break the exchange agreement. After a scramble on the part of the UT International Office, we were diverted to a university in the port city of Valparaíso.

There were two African American students in our group—Norm Bonner and Grace Cleaver. When we toured poor neighborhoods in Santiago, children unaccustomed to Black skin would shout "Pelé" at Norm. To them, he resembled the Brazilian soccer sensation who played in the World Cup in Chile in 1962.

We were feted with pisco sours and empanadas. We heard Nicanor Parra read poetry. With a small group, I was able to go to the famous Peña de los Parra, where I heard the music of the Nueva Canción movement. In my journal, I recorded that I gave Isabel Parra an antiwar button. I even attended a production in Spanish of *MacBird!*, the play written by Barbara Garson that satirized Lyndon Johnson with an adaptation of *Macbeth*.

On the political side, I met with some of the leftist students of the Pedagógico even though they refused to meet with others in the delegation. These Chilean students were affiliated with the major left parties, Socialist and Communist. In the United States, Cold War politics had demonized leftist parties. They had been blacklisted and split asunder over views on Stalin. SDS had originated as the student organization of the League for Industrial Democracy, a labor left organization that was anticommunist. Renamed SDS, we called ourselves the "New Left." We were neither fish nor fowl among traditional left parties. Embracing the counterculture as we did, we were a formation unknown in much of the world.

I brought SDS buttons and posters to Chile. I gave students there copies of an SDS poster of Malcolm X that read, "He was ready, are you?" Our Chilean peers were very interested in the emerging Black Power movement. We were asked by a socialist student group in Valparaíso to speak about the war in Vietnam. A right-wing student in our US delegation told the group that we had a duty to support our president. I said that we

Jim Pape, one of the exchange participants, took this photo of me in Chile, 1967.

had no right to be in Vietnam and should unilaterally withdraw. That, of course, was applauded. Lloyd Doggett said he agreed with both positions.

Lloyd Doggett, who had just been elected UT student body president for the 1967–1968 academic year, already had the DNA of a politician. He went on to be a crusading Texas legislator, serving on the Texas Supreme Court and in the US House of Representatives. Even though gerrymandering now prevents me from voting for him, I'm grateful he made it to Congress.

I was on a different path, not destined to hold office. It was a path that would take me to Cuba in six months on an SDS delegation, a path that would include demonstrations, disruptions, and a few misdemeanor charges. I was on the streets at the 1968 Democratic National Convention in Chicago, not part of any delegation. Lloyd Doggett went in a more orderly direction. Congressman Doggett does remember something I had forgotten. I took the Beatles' *Sgt. Pepper's Lonely Heart Club Band* down to Santiago to share with our Chilean counterparts. I had remembered taking the SDS posters but not the record.

An informal gathering took place as the exchange was drawing to a close. Several of us from Texas were with several Chilean hosts, gathered around a table after a meal, having consumed a few pisco sours. The Chileans stood up and sang the Chilean national anthem a cappella. To follow suit, most of the US students stood up, responding with an a cappella "Star-Spangled Banner," slightly slurred by alcohol. I stayed seated, and so did another Texan who had been active in civil rights battles.

Participating felt like condoning a naked nationalism that fueled the Vietnam War and cloaked an ugly and systemic racism. That is why we did not stand up. It was the equivalent of "taking a knee" on the football field, as NFL quarterback Colin Kaepernick did in 2016 when he protested police violence against African Americans by going down on one knee during the national anthem. His gesture spread across the nation into many sports arenas after the white supremacist violence in Charlottesville, Virginia, in August 2017.

In 1967, we did not know that Salvador Allende, a doctor and a member of the Socialist Party, would win a presidential bid three years later. As part of the Unidad Popular, the Popular Unity coalition, Allende succeeded on his third run for the presidency in 1970. Nor did we know that the United

States would conspire to overthrow his government in 1973, unleashing a level of brutality that ignited solidarity throughout the world.

New York

There are several New Yorks in my life. There is the one I remember from my sister's wedding. When I was still in high school, I made trips to visit my older sister and her husband in their Upper East Side apartment, once with my cousin from Maryland. On another occasion, Hunter Ellinger, whom I knew from Austin High, came up from Washington, DC, visiting me while my sister was away. While utterly chaste, the visit alarmed my sister.

Then, there is the New York of 1967. My sister and her family were no longer in Manhattan, having moved to Larchmont, New York. As my fellow student leaders on the exchange returned to the States for the fall semester, I took the road less traveled. Actually, it was tarmac less traveled, with stops in Uruguay, Argentina, Brazil, and then Peru. I made my way as a tourist through Montevideo and Buenos Aires, stayed with a contact in Rio de Janeiro, and met a friend of Philip Russell's in Peru. While I was still in Chile, I got a letter from Jeff Shero telling me of his plans to launch an underground newspaper in New York. He urged me to come there. In October, I flew from Peru to New York and became another Texas transplant in New York for the next two years.

Jeff picked me up at JFK Airport in New York and drove me to the Upper West Side apartment of Marge Piercy and her then husband, Robert Shapiro. They had a guest room that they were willing to share. We took my bags in, but when Jeff returned to his car he saw that his bag had been stolen. He had not locked the car, thinking he would only be gone for a few minutes. In a "New York minute," someone spotted an opportunity.

Jeff had just returned from Russia, where, as an SDS delegate, he had attended a celebration of the fiftieth anniversary of the Bolshevik Revolution. In that stolen bag was a ring from the Vietnamese delegation that he had intended to give me.

Marge Piercy, our gracious hostess, was not yet a famous author. She had a book of poetry, *Breaking Camp*, accepted for publication by Wesleyan University Press. She would go on to publish many books of poetry, many novels, and a memoir, *Sleeping with Cats*. That memoir allows me to rely on Marge's memory of her six-room apartment on the fourteenth floor at Ninety-Eighth and Broadway. She writes, "Off the left of the big foyer was a narrow hall leading to our bedroom and my office, with an elderly black daybed in it for guests."[8]

Marge was born in 1936 and was slightly older than my sister. She had jet-black hair, long bangs, and dark, penetrating eyes. Her husband Robert's computer skills were well compensated, and the two of them opened their house and cupboards to movement activists, dinner guests, and partygoers. She remembers in her memoir, "We had one couple with us for several months, Jeff and Alice who came to New York from Texas to start an alternative newspaper (which I named *The Rat*)."[9]

I don't remember that our stay lasted for several months; maybe it just seemed that long to Marge. But I do remember the meals—stews and pasta dishes—made to stretch for many dinner guests. Dinners were served with good wine, followed by gourmet coffee, dripped through a Melitta filter into a carafe that had to sit upon a metal ring above low heat. It wasn't the Turkish coffee that had impressed me in high school, but it was also quality caffeine. Dinners were followed by long conversations around the table, what Chilenos call *sobremesa*.

I learned that the Chile exchange program had been canceled by the UT Board of Regents and that the chair, Frank Erwin, blamed the "Embree girl." Both the blame and label made me angry. I wasn't referred to by my full name, as a male student might have been. Frank Erwin used the diminutive "girl." The moniker seemed to carry a subtle threat to my professor father. It lit a spark like a match to dry kindling. Out of that anger, I wrote my first article for *The Rag*.

No longer the silent typist for others, I put my fingers to a typewriter in New York and wrote out my response. My article, "Dead for the Wrong Reasons," appeared in the November 6, 1967, issue of the paper. It was another voice lesson for me. I became a writer through the alchemy of anger.

North American Congress on Latin America

The North American Congress on Latin America (NACLA), now over fifty years old, was in its infancy when I arrived in New York. Marge Piercy, who had offered us a temporary home, was a member of the first collective.

Through her I met Peter Henig, Procter Lippincott, Mike Locker, Edie Black, and Fred Goff. NACLA had published its first mimeographed newsletter in February 1967. The organization had some church funding and an official address at 475 Riverside Drive, the Interchurch Center.

I was familiar with NACLA's work, had seen their pamphlets at SDS meetings and had pored over several before I left on the Chile exchange. NACLA was gaining a reputation for its power structure analysis. The organization's focus on Latin America interested me. NACLA also offered me an opportunity for an independent movement identity, with several degrees of separation from Jeff as he launched the *Rat* newspaper. I contacted Fred Goff about joining the group. Over the phone, he quizzed me skeptically. I must have passed Fred's inquisition because I was invited to a meeting in the Upper West Side apartment near Columbia University that NACLA used as an unofficial office in 1967.

I didn't know all the details of NACLA's backstory but was impressed with all the early members. They were a bit older and more experienced with civil rights struggles and opposition to the war. They were all skilled researchers.

Fred had been to Mississippi in 1963 to plan Stanford's participation in Mississippi Freedom Summer. Edie had been part of SNCC's Mississippi Freedom Summer in 1964, teaching children in a Freedom School and returning the following summer to register voters. She met Fred in New York when he was recruiting election observers for the upcoming elections in the Dominican Republic.

In July 1966, both Fred and Procter served as election observers in the Dominican Republic. It was the first election to take place after the 1965 invasion and occupation of the country by US forces. In a lengthy history of NACLA, Fred Rosen describes Fred and Procter's concerns upon returning from the Dominican Republic: "Dismayed by this experience and frustrated by the lack of any independent sources of information on the Dominican Republic, they discussed the formation of an independent research center that might play a critical role in the transformation of U.S. foreign policy, particularly in Latin America."[10]

In the fall of 1966, two meetings took place, the first at Princeton with a University Christian Movement committee on Latin America and the second in Chicago. "To the best of everyone's memory," Fred Rosen wrote, "it was at the Chicago meeting that the name 'North American Congress on Latin America' first emerged."[11]

Alarmed by the US invasion of the Dominican Republic, many activists began to turn their attention to Latin America. In Ann Arbor, SDS's Radical Education Project provided Jon Frappier with funds to travel to Guatemala for research on the 1954 coup that overthrew the democratically elected Jacobo Árbenz government. Jon had joined the NACLA collective by the time I did.

John Gerassi's *The Great Fear in Latin America,* published in 1965, was a primer on US interventions. It was widely read by movement activists, and I read it before my trip to Chile. NACLA research aimed at documenting connections between corporate agricultural interests (sugar, bananas), mining interests (copper, nitrates, gold, silver) and US foreign policy. I discovered another author's work much later in life, Stephen Kinzer's 2013 book *The Brothers: John Foster Dulles, Allen Dulles, and Their Secret World War*. It impressed me as the prequel to Gerassi's primer, describing decades of imperialist debacles originating with the policies of the Dulles brothers.

NACLA housed files and held meetings in the apartment near Columbia. Fred, Jon, Mike, Procter, Edie, Marge, and Linda Kerley were at the first meetings I attended. We all crowded into the small living room. The group discussed ideas and research assignments for the monthly newsletters. Daunting, four-foot-high stacks of *Wall Street Journals* filled the bathroom tub. We clipped and filed articles, focusing heavily on financial publications, *Forbes*, the *Wall Street Journal*, corporate stockholder reports, and *Moody's Industrials*.

Marge Piercy introduced a primitive information retrieval system to NACLA, developed with the help of her computer-savvy husband. Decades before Google's search engine, we used edge-notched computer cards. Information was typed on the card: for example, "Rockefeller," "Exxon," "Chase Bank." Subject categories were linked to the numbered holes along the edge, and relevant holes were punched. You could sort data with knitting needles. Two or more needles through a stack of cards could refine a search, making chosen subjects fall from the stack. It's cumbersome to describe and was cumbersome to use. Ever the typist, I zealously entered information onto those cards. I still have a small stack of them, but I've given Marge's instruction manual and many of the cards to the Briscoe Center's archival collection.

At perhaps the third or fourth meeting I attended, Marge Piercy and Linda Kerley announced they would no longer be at meetings. As a relative newcomer, this announcement shocked me. Maybe it wasn't a surprise to others, because the meeting facilitator quickly went on to the next item. As I have learned since, Marge left to work in the SDS regional office. She kept working on related research and continued to maintain the database.

Jeff and I talked Linda into making an Austin stop on her way to the West Coast. Our friends Arnie and Judy Kendall embraced her with Austin hospitality when she arrived, and in Austin she met my SDS friend Bob Pardun, whom she later married.

Marge Piercy provided a feminist teaching moment for me when I innocently introduced her in the elevator as Marge Shapiro, using her husband's last name. She directed a withering gaze my way and corrected me. I never forgot the vehemence with which she protected her name, and I would come to understand her response quite well a short time later.

Edie Black provided another teaching moment when she stormed into the NACLA office one day. Posters about Che Guevara's life were mounted in a series on the wall. Without warning or explanation, she removed one and replaced it with a poster of the Marxist theorist Rosa Luxemburg. It didn't make for gender parity, but it made a distinct mark on my memory, and no one dared remove Rosa's intrusion into Che's life.

I clipped articles and participated in research projects, spending hours in the Columbia University business library with *Moody's Industrials* and *Who's Who in America*. Mike Klare, a graduate student at Columbia, joined the NACLA staff in 1968. He parlayed his prodigious research skills into monitoring defense contracts. His research was published as *The University-Military-Police Complex*.

My work with major projects came late in the tumultuous year of 1968, prompted by three events—the May strike at Columbia University, the August Democratic National Convention in Chicago, and the September Tlatelolco massacre in Mexico. I often served as the liaison to the *Rat* newspaper on joint projects. I helped compile research on Columbia University for both NACLA and *Rat*. NACLA staff worked on the special edition of *Rat* prior to the August 1968 Democratic Convention. We worked late into the night as events forced us to respond in the way we knew how, with power structure research and analysis. We scrambled to publish a special NACLA pamphlet on Mexico immediately following the student massacre. The bonds forged during those late-night work sessions remain fond memories.

We were a movement intelligence-gathering operation. We honed skills that some of my compatriots have later used in corporate campaigns mounted by community coalitions and unions. We learned to follow the board connections and the money.

1968

I went home for the Christmas holidays in 1967 and returned to New York for what was to be one of the most explosive years in US history. Nineteen sixty-eight moved with breakneck speed, beginning with the Tet Offensive in Vietnam. North Vietnamese and National Liberation Front forces coordinated surprise attacks on cities and outposts throughout South Vietnam. The massive show of strength contradicted presidential assurances that the US war was going well. Nineteen sixty-eight was a pivotal year also marked by assassinations, a siege at the Ivy League Columbia University, an international uprising in France, a massacre of students in Mexico, and the Democratic National Convention, where the world watched Chicago police run roughshod over demonstrators.

Rat newspaper rolled off the press with its first issue on March 4. Just a month later, Jeff and I were at a New Jersey printshop, watching the newsprint feed through the giant offset press, when the printer, an African American man we knew as "Red," told us that Martin Luther King Jr. had been shot and killed in Memphis.

I remember the look of anguish and despair that passed between us. It seemed that the country was poisoned by violence—the prediction King had made in New York a year earlier at the Riverside Church. There were uprisings in one hundred cities. In New York, it felt as though we were in the center of the storm.

SoHo

Jeff and I relocated from a West Side apartment near the Port Authority Bus Terminal into a basement apartment south of East Houston at the corner of Norfolk and Delancey Street. SoHo, "south of Houston," is a trendy New York destination now, filled with boutiques and galleries. It wasn't in 1968. And Houston was not then, and is not now, pronounced the way Texans pronounce it.

We had almost nothing to move, but Jeff and I unloaded what we had from Butterscotch. Within a week or two, we returned to find a handwritten note taped on the apartment door: "We have the perp." It was signed by a New York Police Department robbery detective and included a precinct phone number. When we opened the door, we saw that our apartment had been robbed.

I was still an urban novice and didn't know what a "perp" was. The police explained to Jeff and me that the perpetrator who had broken in to our apartment had taken, among other things, a hunting rifle that Jeff had brought from Texas. The rifle was not returned. In fact, I'm not sure anything was returned. The thief had broken into the apartment through a window that opened onto a courtyard. I remember napping one Saturday afternoon on a mattress near that window a few weeks later. I woke to a hand reaching through the broken glass. I yelled and scrambled out the door. It wasn't a great place, but the rent was about seventy dollars. Even better, it was just a few blocks' walk north to the first *Rat* office at 201 East Fourth Street. We made it a habit to eat at a cheap Polish restaurant on the way to and from the *Rat* office, and I acquired a taste for borscht.

Cuba

SDS planned to send a delegation to Cuba. I was eager to see revolutionary Latin America, and I applied to go. The selection committee chose twenty of us to make this trip, intentionally breaking the travel ban. Our delegation preceded the Venceremos Brigades that sent many delegates down to help with sugar harvests. We did not work. We toured.

Several of us from New York carpooled to Chicago, where we talked with folks in the national office. Philip Russell, Dick Reavis, and I were from Texas. Mark Rudd, Mark Hardesty, Nina Clamage, Sheila Ryan, and others were part of the delegation. The FBI has the complete list. And a congressman made sure it was read into the *Congressional Record*.

On the plane to Mexico City, I sat next to Mark Rudd, who would become a leader of the Columbia strike a few months later. When the flight attendant came by to take drink orders, I was shocked to see that I had gone to high school with her. Her name was Claudia. A small world indeed. We did not disclose our ultimate destination, telling her only that we were going to Mexico City.

We were delayed several days in Mexico City while arrangements were finalized. When we boarded the Cuban plane, Mexican authorities—no doubt assisting US intelligence—took our photos and stamped a giant CUBA in our passports.

We arrived in Havana on February 9, toasting with Cuba libres when we landed. We stayed at the Hotel Habana Libre, a luxury hotel, for our first nights in Havana. I'll never forget the waiter serving us steaming coffee and milk from silver pots poured simultaneously into our breakfast cups. It was another memorable mix of caffeine and revolution.

We visited with student representatives and went to Playa Girón—the Bay of Pigs—to see where Cuba had repelled CIA-sponsored invaders. We visited the Casa de las Américas, Cuba's famous international cultural center, ate ice cream at Coppelia, toured a sugar factory, and saw Cuban movies: *Manuela, Death of a Bureaucrat*, and a bio on Camilo Cienfuegos, a Cuban revolutionary. Toward the end of our stay we went to the North Vietnamese embassy and then to the embassy of the Vietnamese National Liberation Front. For all of us who had labored to end the war in Vietnam, these encounters were the most meaningful.

On March 1, we boarded a vegetable boat for our return trip. The boat made its way up the East Coast to unload cargo—including us—at a port in Canada. In Canada, we took buses to the US border and went through customs before returning to New York on the bus. I remember the assault on my senses when we passed into the US advertising culture, feeling blasted by commercialism. In Cuba, soap didn't come in a wrapper. People recycled bottles and even medicine containers. The billboards advertised the revolution with images of Che Guevara and Camilo Cienfuegos and the slogan "Hasta la victoria siempre."

I was stunned by the reentry into racist culture. There is, of course, racism in Cuba, but it had not been palpable in the way it was in the United States. We had seen a struggling and poor but proud and dignified country that believed absolutely in international solidarity, had eradicated illiteracy, had increased maternal health, and provided free health care and education. It was also a country graced with stunning Caribbean beaches.

Our trip happened more than a year before the Stonewall rebellion galvanized the gay liberation movement in the United States. Soon, criticism began to be voiced within the US movement about Cuba's antigay policies.

The FBI made several attempts to contact me after I returned. They wanted to see whether I had altered the page in my passport that said I could not travel to Cuba and a number of other countries. With the advice of a movement attorney, I finally agreed to meet them at the *Rat* office and show them the passport. Two clean-cut FBI agents showed up at the *Rat* office door. I took them through the chaos of stacked newspapers and layout supplies back to a worktable and handed them my passport. They examined it. Nothing had been altered. The names of five countries to which US citizens were banned from traveling, including Cuba, were printed in my passport. Another eight Middle Eastern countries had been added, stamped in red ink. We knew there was a travel ban. They knew we knew. Within about ten minutes, they departed. In the '70s when I requested my FBI file under the Freedom of Information Act, I saw that the Cuba trip was prominently recorded.

Columbia

NACLA's apartment office was blocks from Columbia University. The Columbia business library had been one of the first places in New York that NACLA staff had taken me. We did research there to map out the connections in the power structure. Looking for overlapping boards and corporate connections was NACLA's thing. We researched the empire in that library, delving into the corporate self-interest that shaped US foreign policy, prolonged the war in Vietnam, and supported coups d'etat in Latin America.

By April of 1968, a volatile mix was brewing at the Columbia campus. The university was displacing about 7,500 low-income Puerto Rican and

Black residents from affordable housing as it pushed forward its expansion between 110th and 123rd Streets in the adjacent Morningside Heights neighborhood. Students were mobilizing to sever the relationship the university had with the Vietnam War effort. University president Grayson Kirk was imposing restrictions on students' rights to petition, mobilize, and demonstrate.

Beginning on Tuesday, April 23, demonstrators tore down the fence at the Morningside Heights construction site. The Student Afro-American Society and SDS then occupied Hamilton Hall. In the early morning hours, the Student Afro-American Society asked white student allies to leave and take over another building. Wednesday morning, students entered Low Library, the iconic domed building housing the offices of university administrators, including President Grayson Kirk. Protesters seized a third building the next day.

The occupation of the president's office was briefly interrupted by security guards who removed a Rembrandt, but occupiers had several days to peruse correspondence and copy documents that were particularly revealing about Columbia's real estate shenanigans and its ties to the Institute for Defense Analyses, a consortium of twelve universities aiding the war effort with their research expertise. The president's correspondence also included correspondence with foundations known to be conduits for CIA funding.

This is where I came in. Jeff called me, asking me to come by Low Library. He yelled out to me, and I could see him in the open second-floor window. He tossed a package of documents out the window. It glanced off my eye, but I made the catch and took off. These documents were leaks before computers—no hacks, no thumb drives, just old-fashioned intelligence gathering.

In the courtyard in front of the business library one evening during the occupation, I saw police remove a piece of the iron fence on the west side of the campus. They entered that way rather than through the gates. I ran. I was wearing flimsy shoes with low heels, the kind I would never wear again to a demonstration. I tripped and fell hard, slamming my chin against the sidewalk. The cut was gushing blood. I got bandaged at a Barnard first aid center and spent the night nearby on my NACLA friend

Mike Locker's couch. The next morning, I went down to the Lower East Side, my trench coat stained with blood, my chin bandaged. I looked at the headlines on the papers commuters were holding. They were about bloodshed at Columbia. Fellow passengers' eyes kept shifting from the newspaper headlines to me.

In the early hours a week after the occupations began, police entered the campus and arrested over six hundred protesters. Jeff was one of them. He was taken down to the Tombs, New York's House of Detention. Bernardine Dohrn served as an attorney for the defendants. She would later become a leader of an SDS faction, the Weather Underground.

The Columbia strike occupied the next two issues of the *Rat* newspaper, and NACLA produced a pamphlet on the university power structure that became a model for many other campuses. I was involved with both efforts.

The cover of the May 3 through May 16 issue of *Rat* said "Heil Columbia" and featured a drawing of a swastika-emblazoned helmet perched on top of Low Library. A cover headline announced that the issue contained "liberated documents." Correspondence documented the "five month runaround" of the Morningside tenants' council. Michael Klare of NACLA wrote an article in that issue on Columbia's deep connections and funding dependency on the military-industrial complex. The next issue of *Rat* included an article I wrote, "The Urban Removal Masquerade," on Columbia's role in bulldozing affordable housing and the sweetheart relationship they had with corporate media.

NACLA turned its attention to the Columbia University Board of Trustees, documenting the shocking level of interlocking interests among these very powerful men.

The board of trustees looked like Exhibit A for a C. Wright Mills presentation in *The Power Elite*. The trustees sat on the most important corporate boards in media, finance, real estate, and the military-industrial complex. The trustees and the corporations they represented benefitted financially from defense research and real estate land grabs. NACLA scrambled to research those connections and to publish the pamphlet *Who Rules Columbia?* NACLA's power structure research was soon copied by student activists at several other universities.

My favorite feature was a seventeen-by-twenty-two-inch pullout chart,

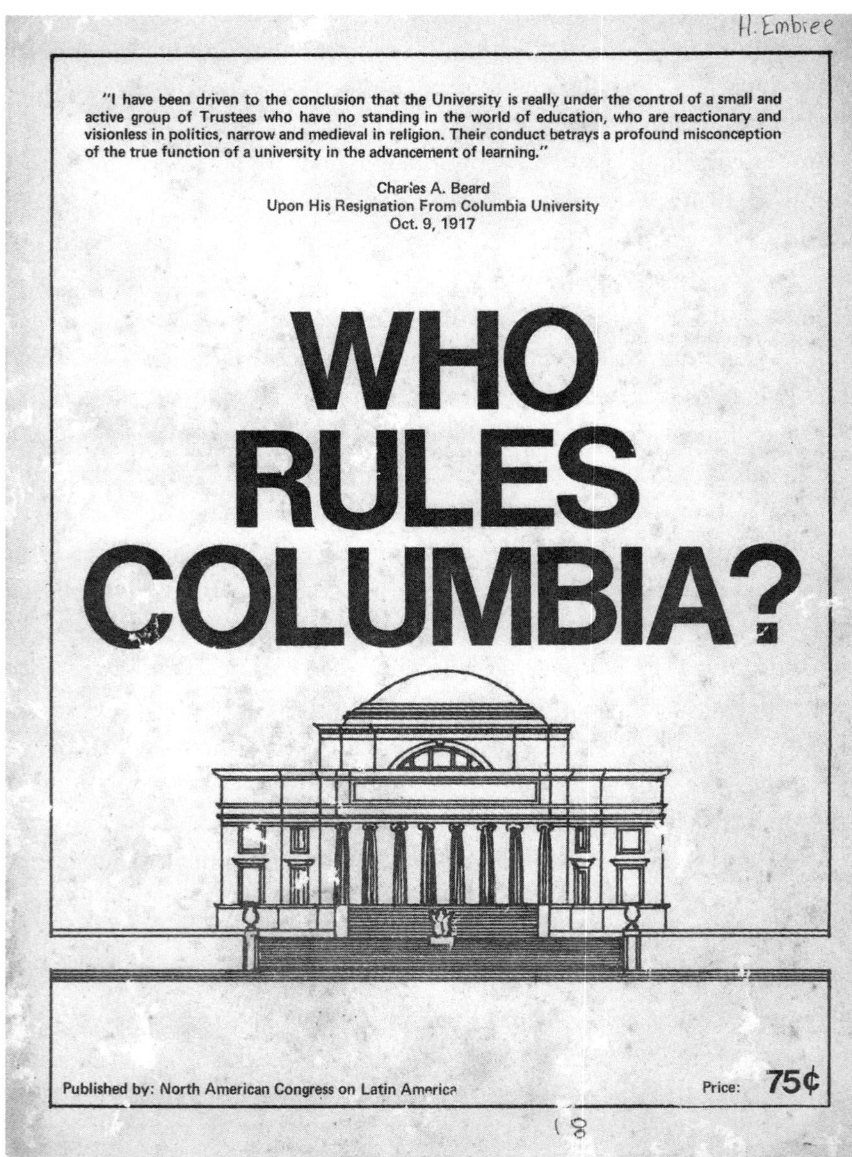

NACLA's June 1968 research guide *Who Rules Columbia?* published at the time of the strike at Columbia, designed by Mike Klare.

"The Top 22: Columbia's Ruling Elite." Mike Klare did the layout. Eleven names ran across the top, and eleven ran across the bottom. They were connected by lines to five different nodes of power: mass media, defense research, real estate and finance, administering the empire, and administering the home country.

Luminaries in corporate media, William Paley of CBS and Arthur Hays Sulzberger of the *New York Times*, were among the trustees. Real estate tycoon Percy Uris was a trustee. The trustees included board members of Lockheed, the district attorney of New York, and the secretary-general of the United Nations. Grayson Kirk, the president of Columbia, served on the boards of Socony-Mobil, the Institute for Defense Analyses, Morningside Heights, Consolidated Edison, and the two nonprofit entities that had been exposed as conduits for CIA funds.

Perhaps my research-heavy articles from the '60s are a bit ham-fisted and short on nuance, but what I wrote in "The Urban Removal Masquerade" in the May 17–30, 1968, issue of *Rat* still resonates for me. As veils of innocence were removed in those early years, so much was revealed:

> It is a great and mysterious maze of interlocking interests which the Columbia upheaval has brought to light. Columbia moves community people into tighter ghettos in Harlem, Uris makes money off the expansion projects, and the *New York Times* covers up the information. As one student at Columbia put it, "They keep saying we've disrupted education, but we've learned more from this than we have in the last three years in college."

Chicago

Working with both NACLA and *Rat* staff, I helped prepare a special issue of the newspaper for the Chicago Democratic Convention in August. On the cover was a cartoon of Lyndon Johnson's birthday party; a specter of Bobby Kennedy floated above the celebrants. Jeff rented a van, and we loaded papers hot off the press into the back and set off for Chicago. The *Rat* had a map of Chicago with alternate demonstration sites—corporate offices and the CIA office at the federal building. Mayor Richard Daley called it the "Terrorist Guide to Chicago."

The stage had been set for another perfect storm in Chicago. Lyndon Johnson had surprised the nation with his announcement on March 31, 1968, that he would not run again. Eugene McCarthy had stepped in to the nomination race, followed shortly thereafter by Bobby Kennedy. Kennedy had just defeated McCarthy in the California primary, demonstrating his ability to bring together young people, Latinxs, and Black people. He was gunned down on June 6 in Los Angeles—just two months after Martin Luther King's assassination.

Despite the friendly turf in a town run by an old-style Democratic boss, Mayor Richard Daley, trouble was brewing in every quarter. The Democratic Party was facing a challenge from the Mississippi Freedom Democratic Party, a challenge that exposed the racism within the Mississippi delegation and within the party. Antiwar forces were mobilizing for a major demonstration. The National Guard was called out.

Meanwhile, back in Texas at Fort Hood, another drama was playing out as five thousand troops were ordered to go to the Great Lakes Naval Training Center in Chicago to be used as backup for local police. Tom Cleaver, a navy veteran I had met while student traveling in Colorado, was working at the antiwar GI coffeehouse near Fort Hood. He would write this account forty years later:

> As the soldiers were preparing to board the airplanes, the bravest act of antiwar protest I ever knew of happened. 43 Black soldiers, all combat veterans, refused to board the airplanes. Due to the self-separation of the races on the base, we had no idea this was going to happen. The Black troops had organized themselves. They knew what they were going to get for this. The minimum qualification to be one of those who would refuse was the Bronze Star and the Purple Heart, so the Army wouldn't be able to call them cowards.[12]

Ten thousand protesters gathered at Grant Park. Some were enticed by the Yippie Festival of Life and entertained by the nomination of Pigasus the pig for president. Others, mobilized by SDS and other groups, were protesting the war. A line of National Guard soldiers stood along the

Protesters at Grant Park in Chicago during the Democratic National Convention, August 1968. *Photo by Stephen Shames, Stephen Shames Photographic Archive, Briscoe Center for American History.*

perimeter of the park. Before all hell broke loose I went down the line of soldiers, offering *Rat* newspapers, surprised at how many, after checking around for officers, would fold the paper and conceal it under their shirts.

The Illinois National Guard and Chicago police were there in overwhelming force. On August 28, police pushed into the crowd, beating protesters with billy clubs. Tear gas filled the streets. I remember running down the street with hundreds of protesters, this time in sturdier shoes than the ones I had worn at Columbia.

It was surreal. Diners in restaurants were watching the chaos outside their windows. A friend told me that he broke through a restaurant's plate glass window in order to escape the stampeding police. What had seemed to be a spectacle on the streets suddenly crashed through the glass barrier to the shock of everyone eating dinner.

On a side street near the rented van, someone asked us to help a demonstrator who had been badly clubbed. He was loaded onto bundles of newspapers. With Jeff driving, we tore off toward a hospital with the injured man and medical students who had been mobilized to provide first aid. I remember one of the medical students checking for a pulse and telling Jeff to drive faster. I never knew the name of the demonstrator, but we learned that he had suffered a ruptured spleen. He survived.

Demonstrators were chanting, "The whole world is watching." It was true that television was beaming the images around the world in a way that hadn't been possible before. The media itself, reporting from inside the convention center, were confronted with the question of how to report on what was going on outside it. The Chicago convention came on the heels of the Soviet invasion of Czechoslovakia, and some demonstrators held signs that said, "Welcome to Czechago." The slogan of Gene McCarthy, "A breath of fresh air," was ironic in a city filled with tear gas. The bedlam outside was more compelling than the orchestrated nomination of Hubert Humphrey.

Mexico

Hardly any time passed before I was part of another NACLA project in response to events south of the border. Mexico was hosting the 1968 Olympics, and President Gustavo Díaz Ordaz was determined to clamp down on all protest. As millions of government funds were diverted to Olympics projects, tensions soared. A massive student strike began at the National Autonomous University of Mexico and spread to other universities and schools. Labor unions mobilized with their own grievances and in support of the students.

On October 2, 1968, approximately ten thousand students marched into the Plaza de las Tres Culturas, the Plaza of the Three Cultures, in the Tlatelolco part of the capital to hear speeches. They were met by sniper fire. Hundreds of students were killed. Many more were detained.

I was part of a NACLA team scrambling to chronicle the Tlatelolco events. On November 1, just a month after the massacre, NACLA published a fifty-page pamphlet, *Mexico 1968: A Study of Domination and Repression*. Fellow Austinite Philip Russell helped research and write the pamphlet. In December, I returned to Texas to visit family. Philip and I traveled from Austin to Mexico City with copies of the NACLA pamphlet. The student leadership had been decimated and pushed underground.

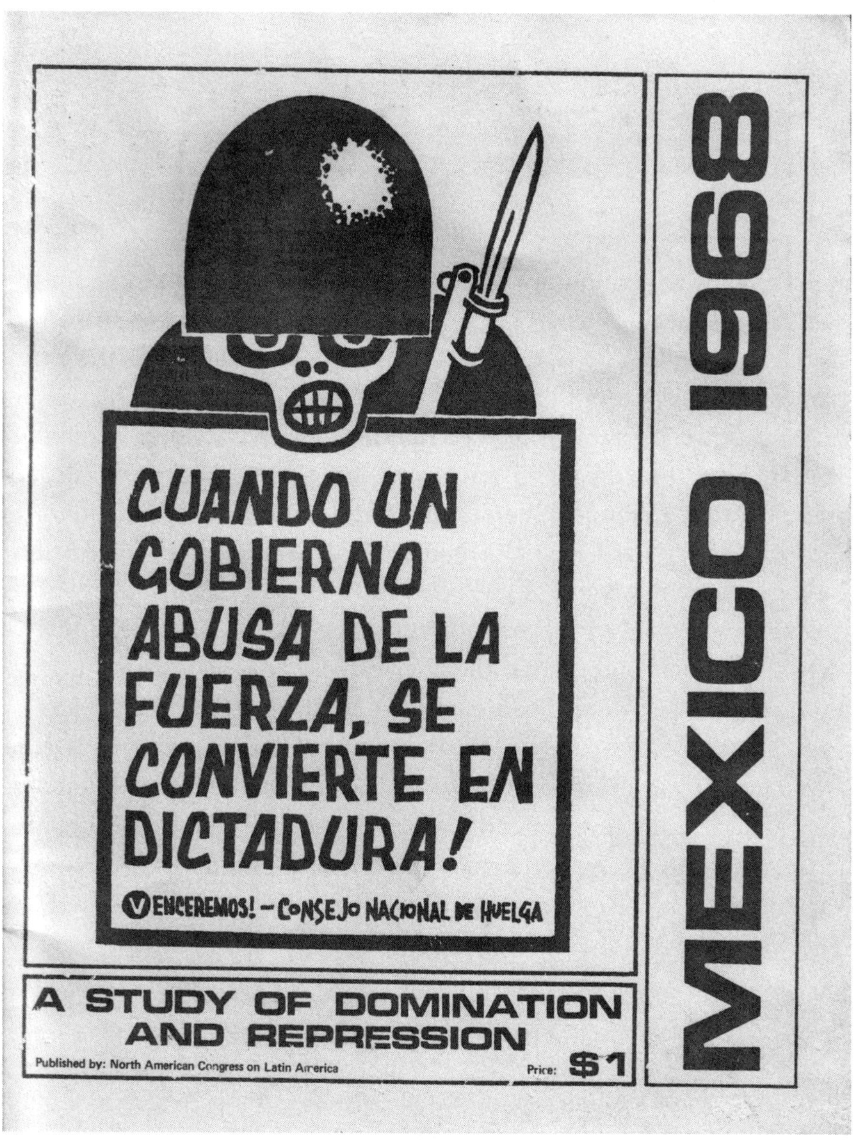

NACLA's 1968 research guide *Mexico 1968: A Study of Domination and Repression*, published after the repression of a student strike in Mexico, graphic by Consejo Nacional de Huelga.

Through Philip's contacts, we were able to meet a few of the participants and to pass on many of the pamphlets.

Tlatelolco cast a long shadow in Mexico. I was mesmerized by an account written by Paco Taibo II. His memoir of the student strike is simply entitled *'68*. Taibo, known now as a prolific and acclaimed writer of fiction, was a student participant in 1968. He writes beautifully of the sense of power the students experienced during the sixty-seven days that they occupied the National Autonomous University of Mexico, the unity that was forged with community and labor leaders. He celebrates the student uprising and he mourns the losses, writing, "And so we go on bearing with us the ghosts of our dead, the ghosts of our occasional traitors, the ghosts of our suicides."[13]

Poet and translator Margaret Randall's recent memoir recalls the student uprising and the brutal repression of 1968.[14] At the time, she was coediting a bilingual literary quarterly, *El Corno Emplumado / The Plumed Horn*. From 1962 until 1969, *El Corno Emplumado* made history publishing the new work of poets in Spanish and English and creating a lively cross-border literary community. Because the journal had supported the 1968 student movement, the quarterly was forced to close in 1969. Margaret and her family fled to Cuba, where she lived for many years.

In 1993, on the twenty-fifth anniversary of the Tlatelolco massacre, a monument was dedicated to the victims, and on the thirtieth anniversary, the Mexican government authorized a congressional investigation of the massacre. Even now, so many people recall 1968 as the year of the Columbia strike, the French student uprising, and the Chicago convention. They leave out Mexico. I always add Tlatelolco. The crushing repression and the decades that crept by without accountability must not be forgotten.

· · · · ·

The 1968 election seemed to many of us to be Exhibit A for a two-party system that didn't reflect what was happening in the streets and on the campuses. If you were under twenty-one you couldn't vote, but males over eighteen could be drafted and sent to Vietnam. The Democratic Party had impaled itself on an imperialist venture. Change was in the air, but not through the ballot box. And in this context, Richard Nixon was elected.

I began 1969 with a trip to Washington, DC, with NACLA friends to what was called the "counter-inaugural." The official inaugural pomp was taking place in one part of the nation's capital. I was with the protesters, and we were met with tear gas and DC cops on horseback practicing crowd control. I did not witness Marilyn Webb's feminist speech to an antiwar crowd. Marilyn, a longtime SDS member, was heckled off the stage as movement men hurled vile comments at her. She described that event as the pivotal one in making her understand that a women's movement had to separate from the male-dominated left in order to survive.

On March 20, 1969, a grand jury issued an indictment sweeping up eight Chicago convention organizers into the Chicago Eight court battle. SDS leaders, Youth International Party "Yippies," Black Panther Bobby Seale, and elder peace activist Dave Dellinger were all charged with conspiracy. The trial would begin in the fall of 1969.

Auden's

At the beginning of April, Jeff and I moved uptown. We left our theft-prone basement apartment in SoHo for 77 St. Mark's Place, between First and Second Avenue. It was the apartment of the distinguished poet W. H. Auden.

This turn of events came about when Jeff and SDS photographer D. Gorton pitched a book idea about Mississippi to Random House. They received a modest advance. Through the publisher, Jeff learned that Auden wanted to sublet his St. Mark's Place apartment while he was in Austria. He typically spent half the year, the sweltering months, in Europe. That was how we moved uptown.

The place was a considerable step up from our apartment at Norfolk and Delancey. A flight of stairs took you up to the front door. The apartment had a narrow kitchen and three large rooms—a living room lined with bookcases, a small dining room with drawings of nude males on the walls, and a sitting area with a television. Three very small bedrooms, each accommodating not much more than a bed, adjoined the common rooms. Auden had moved with his companion, Chester Kallman, into the apartment in 1952. Auden stayed there until 1972, a year before his death at sixty-six.

I had only a brief encounter with the poet. In the great narcissism of youth, I was indifferent to Auden's literary stature. He was just a few years older than my parents, formal and reserved. His apartment was dark, with tall ceilings. He had set aside $1.75 and asked that we pick up his laundry. He had written a note with the necessary contact information and told us how to switch the Con Edison electric bill, ending with this salutation: "Hope you enjoy the apartment."

Decades later, I read *February House* by Sherill Tippins, about Auden's remarkable home in Brooklyn in the 1940s. My youthful and narcissistic take on life had dissipated with age. The house Tippins described was a creative enclave for writers, artists, performers, and composers. As the world careened toward World War II, Wystan Hugh Auden had lived communally with a crazy mix of talent—Gypsy Rose Lee, Benjamin Britten, Carson McCullers, Jane and Paul Bowles. At the time, I'd had no inkling of Auden's audacity or his experience with communal living.

• • • • •

My weekday routine was to take the subway to the Upper West Side NACLA office. In April of 1969, we learned that Governor Nelson Rockefeller had been tapped by President Nixon to embark on a fact-finding mission to multiple locations in Latin America. We launched a major NACLA research project to document Rockefeller corporate holdings and investments in each of the countries he would visit. He went on four separate trips to twenty countries.

The Rockefeller trip prompted anti-imperialist demonstrations at every turn. NACLA's work was translated and carried in publications across the hemisphere, exposing the Rockefeller corporate footprint from banks to petrol, Chase Manhattan to Standard Oil. The Rockefeller tour would later be referred to as the "Rocky Horror Road Show." It ignited anti-American sentiment from Mexico to the Southern Cone of the Americas.

In May, three of us from NACLA, Mike Locker, Jon Frappier, and I, traveled to Washington, DC, to propose a major research project on the media to the Institute for Policy Studies. Our proposal was called the "Study of Function and Structure of Mass Media in the U.S." We said we would delve into the corporate ownership of the media and, similar to our work with the Columbia Board of Trustees, we would examine the interlocking interests of corporate media with domestic repression and imperial policy. By exploring the power relationships, we felt we could expose the motivations for mass media messaging on the antiwar movement and the Black Panthers.

That media research had long legs. I relied on it to write an essay on media images of women for *Sisterhood Is Powerful*. Based on this research expertise and interest, I was asked the next year to organize a media conference in Texas.

We lived at Auden's apartment from April through September. A series of staccato memories, fueled by a life in overdrive, may give a feel to those tumultuous New York days. They tumble into my recall: grits on the stove, a comatose teenager on the couch, Motherfuckers in the bathtub, poets at the door, the moon landing on TV, a night spent posted at the window while sheltering Black Panthers, the folk singer Phil Ochs asking for a joint.

I would occasionally cook breakfast at Auden's for the *Rat* staff after all-night layout sessions at the newspaper's office on West Fourteenth Street. Eggs, bacon, and grits. Grits were unknown on the East Coast, and serving them earned me "Grits" as a middle name in some of the newspaper's staff boxes.

A teenager, Jon, who worked on *Rat* was taken to Bellevue Hospital tripping on acid. Jeff and I went to the hospital, where Jeff vouched for Jon as an employee of the paper. He was released, and we brought him back to Auden's. He lay zonked out on Thorazine on the couch, breathing so shallowly that I went up to him several times during the night to make sure he was still alive.

The radical street gang Motherfuckers came once or twice to avail themselves of Auden's bathtub. They would leave clean, darting disdainful looks at us for our bourgeois setting.

One day when I was at the apartment by myself, three poets stopped by and asked for Auden. Allen Ginsberg was the only one I recognized. I called down from the landing that Auden was not there.

There was a black-and-white TV in Auden's living room. On July 20, 1969, I was able to watch the moon landing. When I later worked on an essay about media images of women, I watched daytime programming for several days. But the ads aimed at women were more compelling to me than the programming. I studied the advertisers, who talked among themselves about women, reading *Advertising Age* as the essay percolated in my mind.

I don't remember the month, but a call went out to shelter members of the Black Panther Party because of imminent police raids. Several Black Panthers came one night to Auden's. I stood with another woman at the window, watching for police as the rain fell on St. Mark's. We had a small revolver that would have been a mere nuisance had a police raid occurred.

In the lead-up to Woodstock, Jeff and I got to know Jerry Rubin and Nancy Kurshan, Abbie and Anita Hoffman, and Judy Gumbo and Stew Albert, the Youth International Party "Yippies." Two of the Yippies once brought folk singer Phil Ochs by Auden's. He was not impressed that Jeff, an underground press editor, could not produce a decent joint to smoke.

· · · · ·

A contingent of Texans, most of them friends from *The Rag* in Austin, were in New York working with Liberation News Service, a self-styled wire service for the movement. Many of the Texas crew had grown up in Houston. At the beginning of the summer, they returned to their hometown to launch *Space City News*. The first issue came out in June of 1969. As the Liberation News Service Texans left, an SDS compatriot from Texas, Gary Thiher, arrived. Jeff had asked Gary to fill in as *Rat* editor while he was in Mississippi.

In the summer of 1969, Richard Avedon requested that several of us from *Rat* come to his studio for a photo session. I have several proof copies in my possession. I guess it is ironic that these proofs were chewed on by rats while in storage in my shed. They include one of Jeff holding the first issue; one of Jeff, Gary, and me; one of Gary; and one of Jeff and me. In the photo of Jeff and me, I am facing him, standing to his side. The photo shows Jeff smiling and the back of my head, with very long hair. I think it was Avedon's favorite. But the one I have seen in print is iconic: Avedon captured Gary's sardonic gaze in a collection of photographs called *The Sixties*. Gary stares into Avedon's camera. He's wearing jeans, with his thumbs tucked behind a Texas belt buckle, decidedly not New York.

The summer was heating up. Berkeley activists took over land owned by the University of California and christened it People's Park. There was a fight to hold the park when the authorities sought to reclaim it. One person was killed by police fire. The Stonewall riots took place in June at a gay bar just blocks from Auden's apartment. It is considered the beginning of a radical gay liberation movement. In late July, a series of bombings began in New York City, initially targeting corporations like United Fruit and Marine Midland Bank.

That summer, Jane Alpert, who had joined the *Rat* staff, paid a call while I was at Auden's apartment by myself. I offered her a soft drink. She spilled it on Auden's couch. Later, when I learned the dates of the bombings, I suspected that I was serving as an alibi.

Woodstock

I had not known any of the Yippies until the lead-up to Woodstock. They were inspired pranksters. They had introduced Pigasus as a presidential candidate in Chicago. I was more inclined toward power structure research. SDS was beginning to break apart for many reasons, and the media-savvy Yippies were getting more attention.

The Yippies had picked up early on the zeitgeist of Woodstock. Jeff had a rather cool relationship with them. When Abbie Hoffman published *Woodstock Nation*, he described his initial relationship with Jeff as distant, in part over an article Abbie had written about SDS. In *Woodstock Nation*, Abbie gives me credit for breaking down barriers between the two of them. He quotes Jeff as saying, "Alice says I have a tendency to snub you."[15] Whether my role was crucial or not, the Lower East Side alliance between *Rat* and the Yippies became a formidable one before Woodstock.

The Aquarian Exposition, now known simply as Woodstock, was billed as three days of peace and music. The promoters leased a six-hundred-acre dairy farm in Upstate New York. As advance ticket sales pushed toward two hundred thousand, it was clear that the concert planned for August 15 to 17 was going to be huge. Nearly half a million people arrived, clogging roads and tearing down fences, converting the event into a free concert.

The Yippies and Jeff, representing *Rat*, made their way into the offices of the promoters, Woodstock Ventures, forcing them to divert thousands of dollars to a tent city where the Hog Farm commune provided food and medics provided first aid. I'm sure the food and first aid probably saved some lives. I wasn't part of any of the meetings, but it was when I got to know many of the Yippies.

Rat published a special issue that was transported to the tent city. Incongruously, the cover art was three images of a gun—not peace or music. It reflected the edgy, not groovy, spirit of the newspaper. After all, Jeff had launched the paper as a counterbalance to the less political *East Village Other*. And the events in New York, from bombings to Black Panther repression, certainly weren't in the vein of peace and love.

At Woodstock half a million young people peacefully coexisted, sharing what they had, without the need for police and security, and that is the stuff of counterculture legend. That it all took place on a sloping pasture turned to mud by rainfall is remarkable. Young people were entertained by most of the best musicians of their generation; they were peacefully inhaling and sharing marijuana and hash; they were imbibing psychedelics. Abbie Hoffman's book *Woodstock Nation* celebrated the promise of youth that was at the core of the Youth International Party.

I occasionally moved from the tent city area to the sloping embankment to hear the music from massive speakers. The pulsating sound and the feeling of camaraderie made a deep impression, but I spent more time in the tent city area. I imbibed the hash and skinny-dipped in the creek. The crowd was the experience as much as the music, a throng of young people who had brought down the fences, literally and metaphorically, in a peaceful challenge to every last shred of 1950s conformity.

•   •   •   •   •

After Woodstock, the Chicago Conspiracy trial took the Yippies from New York to Chicago, providing us with an apartment from October to December after W. H. Auden's return. At the end of September, Jeff and I boxed up our meager belongings and went a few blocks west on St. Mark's Place to the three-story walk-up apartment of Jerry Rubin and Nancy Kurshan. The apartment was just east of Third Street where East Eighth ended and St. Mark's began. I finished my essay for Robin Morgan there, typing at the table of a conspiracy defendant. I can't imagine how many listening devices might have been in those walls. I learned to not talk inside during those final months in New York.

Network television owners were not allowing antiwar sentiment to be aired as part of regular programming. When the *Smothers Brothers Comedy Hour* went on the air with Pete Seeger singing a reference to Vietnam, "Waist Deep in the Big Muddy," CBS fired the Smothers Brothers. I wrote a story for *Rat* about the cancellation of the comedy show. I was able to interview Tom Smothers in a hotel suite. My article laced together his impressions with my own media research. It was published on September 24, the same day that the Chicago Conspiracy trial began.

Jeff had taken off for Chicago to be there during the lead-up to the trial. I joined him for several days after the trial began. There was a rally in front of the federal courthouse. I went to the trial as an observer with Sharon Krebs, who was part of the Yippie circle and would later that fall disrupt a Democratic Party event by walking down the aisle nude with a pig's head on a tray. Both of us refused to stand for Judge Julius Hoffman when he entered the courtroom. We were ushered out. I remember her remark about the number of undercover cops in the courtroom: "You could hear their guns clunking against the back of the benches."

Jerry Rubin and Abbie Hoffman got out of Cook County Jail on bail, and Jeff was among the people picking them up. Their first stop was a meeting in a small Chicago apartment with their attorneys and a few supporters. I was there. While the meeting was going on, Abbie and Anita slipped into the bathroom for privacy. That has always impressed me. Seizing the time, so to speak, during a strategy session on a conspiracy defense. Those are my conspiracy trial memories.

For a contingent of SDS and their allies, the "Days of Rage" loomed large in October. This was the Chicago action that defined whether you were with the Weather contingent or not. The Weather contingent took their name from a Bob Dylan verse, "You don't need a weatherman to know which way the wind blows." I wasn't part of the Weather contingent. But I knew their sense of desperation. There were conspiracy charges against the Black Panthers, trials everywhere. And the war in Vietnam had no end in sight, nothing but bloody escalation.

A series of bombings took place in New York City in 1969, first targeting

United Fruit on July 27. Just days after Woodstock, a bomb went off at the Marine Midland Building. The locations of the eight bombings included the Whitehall Street Army Induction Center and the courthouse where the Black Panther Twenty-One were on trial.

On November 12, the day of the federal courthouse bombing, Sam Melville, Jane Alpert, and David Hughey were arrested on the evidence of an informer. Sam Melville was never released from custody. In September 1971, he was killed in the Attica prison uprising along with twenty-eight other inmates and ten hostages. Jane got out on bail and then lived underground until she turned herself in. In 1974, she was sentenced to nearly three years in prison.

I knew Jane Alpert as a staffer at *Rat*. Jane wrote a tell-all book about this period, *Growing Up Underground*, published in 1981. She describes her relationship with Sam Melville in detail. Jane, Sam, and another couple learned bomb-making skills from several Quebec separatists. The symbolic bombings they carried out were accompanied by warnings that prevented deaths, but the Marine Midland bombing injured a number of people.

That November, Seymour Hersh broke the story of the My Lai massacre in Vietnam. The US Army massacre of hundreds of unarmed civilians had occurred the year before, and it further turned the tide of public opinion against the war. But the tide of public opinion didn't appear to budge the war machine. We felt we were in the belly of the beast. And the Weather contingent argued that the role of white allies should be this: bring the war home. Use your white privilege, if you have it, to open up a domestic front within the belly of the beast. The charismatic Black Panther leader Fred Hampton was murdered in his bed in Chicago on December 4, 1969. His death reinforced the sense of despair and urgency.

Repression, as well as revolution, was in the air as President Nixon ramped up his administration's Counter Intelligence Program (COINTEL-PRO). FBI agents were ordered to "expose, disrupt, misdirect, discredit, neutralize, or otherwise eliminate" the activities of radical movements and their leadership. Grand juries were convened across the country to authorize charges, and conspiracy trials proliferated. The trials diverted the energy of the Black Panthers, the American Indian Movement, the newly visible Chicano movement, and white radicals.

At the beginning of December, I went to a meeting at the Underground Press Syndicate loft near Union Square. A Liberation News Service article that appeared in the *Los Angeles Free Press* describes about thirty people in attendance. Both Jerry Rubin and Abbie Hoffman, who were out on bail, were there. The discussion was about the role that the Youth International Party should play in the vacuum created by a badly factionalized SDS. It is the concluding paragraph that seems prescient:

> Women's liberation may emerge as one of the problems of the Youth International Party. None of the old Yippie leaders are women. While Magdalene Sinclair is brilliant and forceful in her own right, many think of her merely in terms of her husband [John Sinclair]. Nancy Kurshan, one of the hardest workers in the movement and never short on ideas or opinions, is seen by many merely as "Jerry's wife" or "Jerry's chick."[16]

The Liberation News Service article does not carry a byline, but it was likely written by a woman. Soon women's liberation would send shock waves through the movement.

Finding My Voice: 1969–1973

I LEFT NEW YORK IN DECEMBER OF 1969, RETURNING TO TEXAS to spend the Christmas holidays with my parents. I had plans to resettle on the West Coast with the new NACLA office. Jeff was in Greenville, Mississippi, working on his book with D. Gorton, and I took a bus to Greenville to see him. While I was there, he got a phone call that changed my life.

I overheard him talking with Gary Thiher, who had been left in charge at *Rat*. Gary called Jeff with news that the women were taking over the paper.

I remember overhearing the anger and the derogatory words for women. Jeff began to talk about how to put down the insurrection, urging Gary to argue class over feminism. My reaction was volcanic, molten anger. For me, women's liberation got very personal.

I began to simmer as I listened to Jeff's dismissal of women I knew, of women generally. An unfamiliar rage, rooted in a thousand dismissals, came to a rolling boil. By the time he was off the phone, I was planning my exit strategy. I do not remember words, just emotion and fury. I was as astonished by my rage as Jeff was. My voice took on a different register, and my words came out in a menacing growl.

"She exploded like I'd only seen Black people go hysterical in the South." That's what Jeff told fellow underground newspaper editor Abe Peck, who wrote the account in *Uncovering the Sixties: The Life and Times of the Underground Press*.[17]

Even the word "hysterical" felt like loaded language, deriving as it did from a medical diagnosis of symptoms that could land women in an insane asylum, behind lock and key.

Jeff told Abe Peck that I asked for directions to the bus station, ready to bolt from the apartment, from his presence. I don't remember that. I don't remember the return trip to Austin, but I knew everything had changed.

I spoke with several of the women at *Rat*. They called me at my parents' house full of excitement. I listened but let them know I wouldn't be coming back to New York.

Back in Austin, within the safe spaces of women's groups, in conversations with women friends, I began to see myself differently, with new eyes. I felt bolstered and strengthened by sisterhood. I could see how my upbringing had shaped me to accept, not to assert; to acquiesce, not to demand to be heard; to type, not to write. It was baked into our 1950s upbringing, modeled for us in our families, demonstrated to us by teachers, and advised by school counselors. And it was baked into our relationships with movement men. That self-scrutiny, taking place with other women, emboldened us. It was exhilarating. It was also hard.

I wondered what had taken me so long. Women's liberation had been bubbling up all around me in New York, but I had kept my distance from meetings there. I wrote about media images of women, interweaving my power structure perspective, researching the money spent on advertising, the commercial messages, not just the programming. But that writing was a solitary act. I needed to be on familiar turf in Austin to find sisterhood. I needed distance from my identity within a couple.

There were ragged attempts with Jeff to revive our relationship. There were letters. He came to Austin. I went to Houston. We went together to Big Bend National Park in West Texas, but that was a disastrous trip. Jeff wrote that I cared too much what my women friends thought. Though, to be honest, I had realized I hadn't had many women friends before. He had never noticed that I had cared too much what men in my life thought.

SLEEPER CELL

Inspired by women's liberation

We were the sleeper cell.
Sleeping beside you
Our breathing so shallow
That you hardly knew
We were there.
We
Were
There
Typing the leaflets
Working the mimeograph
Listening.
Our voices sometimes trembled
When we spoke.
We went unheard.
We were easily overlooked.
You were taller
You were accustomed to taking up more space.
We woke to sisterhood
To mountain moving time
We woke.
Hot molten lava
Poured through us
You were covered in ash.
Stunned by our raised fists
Our raised voices.
Our rage.
We were there all along.

The male-dominated movement placed a hierarchy on struggles. End-ing the war and confronting racism were considered paramount concerns. Women's liberation was labeled a distraction. That distraction emerged as a major force in 1969 and altered the movement landscape.

Abe Peck, the former *Chicago Seed* editor, interviewed Jeff and me separately for his 1985 book on the underground press. He asked each of us about the women's takeover of *Rat*. To his surprise, he noted, our accounts of the long-distance phone call were similar.

Abe Peck described us as the "quintessential movement couple." In many ways, that phone call began the quintessential movement breakup. Many movement couples split apart as women's liberation dawned.

Robin Morgan's "Goodbye to All That" appeared in the February 9–23, 1970, issue of *Rat*, the first issue after the takeover by women. She described the anger of women as "an amulet of madness":

> There is something every woman wears around her neck on a thin chain of fear—an amulet of madness. For each of us, there exists somewhere a moment of insult so intense that she will reach up and rip the amulet off, even if the chain tears the flesh of her neck. And the last protection from seeing the truth will be gone. [18]

With "Goodbye to All That," Robin Morgan penned a broadside against a male-dominated movement. It was reprinted across the country in newly minted women's liberation newspapers as well as many other underground papers.

At the end of her essay, she listed the names of several movement women, partners of prominent movement men. Robin's words, a gauntlet thrown down, included many women I knew: "Free Anita Hoffman," "Free Nancy Kurshan," "Free Alice Embree," "Free Gumbo," and, yes, "Free Robin Morgan." She included her own name.

After "Goodbye to All That" was published, Jeff asked me if I felt patronized by Robin, by her assumption that I wasn't free. Without hesitation, I said, "No!" Another woman on that list, Judy Gumbo, recalled the same question from her Yippie partner, Stew Albert. "No!" she had said as well.

Movement men who had been leaders suddenly found themselves questioned by current and former partners. Many lost a sense of identity, a core sense of what their role in the world should be. For many women, we had nothing to lose as we gained a sense of ourselves as actors on the stage of history.

From left, Alyce Guynn, me, Cris Cunningham, Sharon Shelton, Vernell Pratt, Vicky Gabriner (in hat), and Charlotte Pittman (with broom), perform a women's liberation skit, August 1970.

When I watched the 1954 movie *Salt of the Earth* in the 1970s, it resonated deeply. This classic film deals simultaneously with class struggle, racism, and male chauvinism. A court order prevents the men from picketing at the mine where they work. The women step forward, and the men are suddenly at home cooking and washing diapers. The film captures the dislocation men experienced as they were plunged into support roles. It also captures that transformative spark of solidarity among the women as they take on the mine owners and the sheriffs.

Jeff was in Greenville, Atlanta, New York, and Washington, DC, before he returned to Texas in October of 1970 and began working at KPFT radio in Houston. Our relationship did a slow, long-distance unravel, evident in journals and letters. Perhaps it is fortunate that so many miles separated us then. I think the collateral damage from splinters and shards could have affected a wide circle of friends. Bob Dylan's words said it best for me: "We're both just one too many mornings and a thousand miles behind."

The first issue of the women's *Rat* hit the New York newsstands in February 1970. The paper would last as long as a women's liberation paper as it had lasted in its previous incarnation with Jeff as editor.

Random House published the book edited by Robin Morgan, *Sisterhood Is Powerful: An Anthology of Writings from the Women's Liberation Movement*, at the beginning of 1970 as well. The New York Public Library called the anthology "one of the most influential books of the Twentieth Century."

In Austin, the women's movement was breaking like a tsunami—women's consciousness-raising groups, a women's center, employment barriers toppled by threatened lawsuits, birth control counseling, and abortion referrals. No longer a student, no longer part of a couple, I embraced women's liberation, and soon I was transformed by it.

Feminism at *The Rag*

Feminism was percolating at the *Rag* newspaper, transforming working and personal relationships. In a filmed interview, Ragstaffer Judy Walther recalled the impact of a feminist pamphlet, *The Myth of the Vaginal Orgasm*, and thinking, "We're going to do it differently." The changes, she said, were "down to that level."[19]

Between 1968 and 1973, Judy Smith and her sister, Linda Smith, were part of a *Rag* collective that embraced feminism, disdained hierarchy, and operated by consensus, not titles. Mastheads and bylines often reflected first names only.

Judy Smith was hard to overlook. She was tall, athletic, smart, and comfortable with leadership. She was also skilled at mentoring and committed to sharing leadership. Judy had followed her sister, Linda, to Austin. She had graduated from Brandeis and served in the Peace Corps in Nigeria before coming to Austin to pursue a doctoral degree in molecular biology at UT. Judy's writing covered a vast array of topics, including Fort Hood, urban renewal, fair housing, apartheid, birth control, fear of vasectomy, the energy crisis, and the coup in Chile.

Judy and other *Rag* women helped launch the Austin Women's Center and a women's birth control hotline. In a filmed People's History in Texas interview, Judy recalls the decision to create a space for birth control counseling in the *Rag* office. Women on the staff literally claimed the space by hammering up plywood walls in the corner of the office. The hotline was an experience that made Judy acutely aware of two issues women faced: access to birth control and access to safe, legal abortions.

Judy Smith answering the birth control hotline phone outside *The Rag* office, 1970. *Photo by Alan Pogue.*

There wasn't easy access to birth control and contraception information, and few Austin physicians would prescribe birth control pills to unmarried women. Abortions were illegal, dangerous, and often required a secretive trip across the Mexico border. Judy Smith, Victoria Foe, and Bea Durden had begun gathering information on birth control. When questions about abortion came up, they began to build a list of places where they could refer women for safe abortion services and places to avoid. Giving abortion advice was then illegal in Texas.

I went twice with women to Nuevo Laredo, where abortions were available after office hours in a doctor's office. And I heard harrowing tales from other women, the worst being from a close friend. When she found herself pregnant, an acquaintance referred her to a Waco veterinarian for an abortion. It took place in a desolate motel, hardly a sterile environment. When she returned to Austin, an infection set in that made her delirious with fever. She nearly died. Her horror story reminds me what it was like before vacuum aspiration, in a medical setting, made abortion much safer and before oral medication was available that could end an early pregnancy.

Sarah Weddington, in her book *A Question of Choice*, credits Judy Smith as being instrumental in the decision to take *Roe v. Wade* to court. Judy's partner, Jim Wheelis, had begun law school at UT. Sarah Weddington was working at the law school. Sarah recalls joining Judy; her partner, Jim; and another law student, Ron Weddington, at a coffee shop:

> Judy talked me into volunteering to file a lawsuit against the Texas anti-abortion law; Jim and Ron enthusiastically agreed to help with research and encouragement. Barbara Hines, a UT law student, was most helpful in preparing the documents in the case. That coffee meeting was the beginning of *Roe v. Wade*, the case decided by the U.S. Supreme Court on January 22, 1973, which overturned the anti-abortion statute in Texas and, by extension, throughout the U.S.[20]

Judy Hart Smith passed away in 2013 in Missoula, Montana, where she moved in 1973. Her passion for feminism and social justice blossomed

Ad appearing in *The Rag*, November 3, 1969.

there. She helped establish a Missoula clinic to provide women with reproductive health choices, advocated for affordable housing, and organized a coalition to encourage low-income women to vote.

Judy's life provides a lens for the struggle for reproductive rights. In the beginning, it was about birth control. The need for legal, safe, accessible abortions grew out of that foundational feminist understanding that women should have the right to control their bodies. Challenging the laws against abortion was a clear next step.

The history behind *Roe v. Wade*, its relationship to the birth control counseling center in the *Rag* office, and the role of Judy Smith have surfaced because of *Rag* reunions, the *Rag* movie, and the book *Celebrating The Rag*. In August 2019, a *Ms.* magazine blog story featured a photo of Judy Smith on the hallway phone at the "Y," answering a call from a woman desperate for information on options for an unplanned pregnancy.[21]

Leonard Street

Char and Scott Pittman had gotten married in Europe. In 1969, after they returned to Austin, Char gave birth to a daughter. When I came back to Texas from New York in 1970, I lived with Char and her daughter in a big house on Leonard Street near Eastwoods Park. Another couple, Mary and John Erler, lived at the house with their young son. I was introduced to the world of toddlers. Scott was sometimes there. Scott's brother, Wayne, had a home in Elgin but occasionally stayed at the house as well. It became my home base, a couch to sleep on and then an upstairs bedroom.

In February 1970, I made my way to California to check out the emerging West Coast NACLA as I had promised. Not much of that trip survives in my memory, but I did end up seeing *They Shoot Horses, Don't They?* Notably, I went to the movie with Tom Hayden and the woman he was living with in a Berkeley collective. I bought a Slo Poke bar and lost a filling to the sticky caramel. Tom reflected on the Depression themes in the movie and the emptiness of capitalism. Perhaps he was also reflecting on Jane Fonda.

Jane Fonda was nominated for an Academy Award for her performance in *They Shoot Horses* and has spoken about the movie as a transition to topics with social relevance. She won an Oscar the following year for *Klute.*

She was famously recruited by Tom Hayden to be part of a 1972 peace delegation to North Vietnam not long after her Oscar win.

I was in California when I heard news that reverberated through the movement. On March 6, 1970, a bomb prematurely detonated in Greenwich Village. The townhouse bombing took the lives of three SDS Weathermen: Diana Oughton, Terry Robbins, and Ted Gold. Two women, Kathy Boudin and Cathy Wilkerson, escaped from the smoldering wreckage on West Eleventh. The Weather faction of SDS became the Weather Underground, assuming new identities and living the lives of fugitives. I knew some of the Weather faction. I had traveled to Cuba with Mark Rudd. Kathy Boudin had driven with us back to New York from the Chicago convention in our van.

Texas Media Conference

I felt an even stronger tug to be on familiar home turf. I returned to Texas with a temporary organizing job. I was asked to put together a three-city Texas Media Conference. It took place at the end of April 1970 in Houston, Dallas, and Austin.

The United Ministries in Higher Education reimbursed my travel costs, and my contact there was Leon Howell. The connection came through the University "Y" director Cris Cunningham, who had attended Union Theological Seminary with Leon.

My research and writing on the media qualified me, as did my experience with the underground press. Again, I benefitted from the long legs of my NACLA work on ownership of mass media.

The United Ministries in Higher Education had sponsored a similar media conference outside of New York City. They were able to provide a modest budget for the Texas project that let us reimburse some out-of-state travel. Many working in commercial media were deeply affected by events in Chicago and the continuing repression of Black Panthers. They were grappling with their role as reporters in changing times. My report to United Ministries set out the 1970 context:

> The upheaval that touched every major institution in the United
> States in the last decade swept into the mass media shortly after
> the Democratic Convention in Chicago in 1968. The power of the

mass media to influence events had never been more obvious. And members of the mass media had been stripped of the protection of "objective observer" status by the "overkill" of the Chicago police. Out of the Chicago experience, the *Chicago Journalism Review* was born. Employees in mass media in Chicago put their journalistic skills to use in analyzing their own work and the institutions that they worked for.

It was just a beginning. In the summer of 1969, initial attempts were made at organizing similar groups in New York, the media capital of the nation. A variety of organizational forms emerged— the New York Media Project, New York Media Women (an early offshoot of the NY Media Project), and Media Mobilization. . . . The New York Media Project sponsored the equivalent of a teach-in for people in mass media during the October Moratorium; they produced a detailed critique of *Newsweek* coverage of the Black Panthers, and they continue to publish a paper, *Pac-O-Lies*. . . . The women's caucus of the group sponsored a dinner and discussion to which all the women employees of *Newsweek* were invited. On the west coast, the Berkeley New People Media Project was formed—several of the founders having come out of the New York Media Project. They maintain a media research center and produce a paper called *Overload*. These emerging groups are beginning the process of criticism from within the institutions of mass media.

I began organizing events in the three Texas cities. Each event had a different character. The three-day event in Houston was the least successful in attracting members of the established media. Houston's repressive climate probably contributed to this lack of success. The office of the underground newspaper *Space City!* had been bombed and broken into by members of the Klan. The Pacifica radio transmitter was destroyed by right-wing sabotage on May 12 after the media conference and bombed again in October. The Southwest Center for Urban Research refused to let their building be used for fear of reprisals. Rumors spread at the *Houston Chronicle* that the meeting might be an attempt at guild organizing.

Those who turned out for the meetings in Houston were almost exclusively from alternative media, *Space City!*, and KPFT.

In Austin, events were more successful. Meetings were held on April 28 in the Methodist Student Center. A women's caucus met at 6:00 p.m., and a meeting with women and men followed. About fifteen women from the *Austin American-Statesman*, the *Texas Observer*, and the capitol press corps attended the first meeting. The mixed meeting drew an additional fifteen attendees.

In Dallas, the following day, nearly forty people met in the journalism building of Southern Methodist University. Reporters from the *Wall Street Journal*, the *Dallas Morning News*, and commercial radio attended, as well as several underground press staff from *Dallas Notes* and journalism professors and students from the university.

The media conference was like organizing a cross-state tour and cultural exchange, moving in rapid succession from city to city. Participants came from all parts of the country. Michael Nolan, Paul Binder, and Paul Greene came from the Berkeley Project. Polly Howells, Honor Moore, and Sharon Shelton represented the New York Media Project. Janis Beaver came from the *Liberated Guardian* and Bob Heilbroner from Liberation News Service in New York. Ron Dorfman represented the *Chicago Journalism Review*, and Marie Moorefield was there from *Motive* magazine in Nashville. Leon Howell represented the United Ministries in Higher Education. Over a few days in Texas, we covered a lot of ground.

A lasting outcome of the Austin conference was that I met two women reporters from the *Austin American-Statesman*, Alyce Guynn and Barbara Worley. Barbara had recently left the newspaper, and Alyce was about to leave. We became lifelong friends. Both of these women were Texan to the core, one from a small town near Waco, smack dab in the Texas Bible Belt, the other from deep East Texas, raised in Marshall. They were not the least bit East Coast intellectual. Their working-class upbringings, their accents, their clever wordplay, their experience as journalists, were authentic, fresh, and new to me. They became sisters to me, part of my chosen family in the 1970s. With them, I learned every word to "I'm Coming Back to You, My Texas." I had come home.

• • • • •

While the Texas Media Conference was drawing to a close, UT student government elections were taking place. The radical community in Austin didn't require student credentials, and it wasn't long before I knew the new people who were involved with *The Rag*, community organizing, and radical student politics. The SDS campaigns for student government didn't prevail in 1965 and 1967. In April of 1970, however, SDS candidates were finally elected.

Jeff Jones, a graduate student who wrote for *The Rag* and had been active in SDS, became president of UT student government. He ran with a slate of candidates called the Yin-Yang Conspiracy. In a 1988 thesis, Beverly Burr, a UT Plan II student, documented the goals of the radical campaign:

> Jeff Jones, the presidential candidate, ran with about 10 others on a four-issue platform. The Yin-Yang Conspiracy called for the following: 1) that UT withdraw all support for the war effort (i.e. ROTC, war-related research, and military recruitment), 2) that there be both an end to racism and efforts to make the racial balance of the student population represent that of the state's taxpayers, 3) that birth control and abortion be provided at the Student Health Center, and 4) that the academic system be reformed.[22]

Jeff Jones, Pat Cuney, Steve Russell, and others whom I came to know better became adept at using the student government platform to connect the campus community with the outside world. From student government offices in the Student Union, they linked students to strike support for a Chicanx-led strike at Economy Furniture; they mobilized volunteers and contributions for the Community United Front, a local Black Panther–affiliate breakfast program; and they provided assistance to Vietnam veteran Terry Dubose for a draft-counseling project. They built lasting ties among students and community leaders, particularly in the Black and Chicanx communities. In 1972, when the voting age was lowered to eighteen, these connections helped transform local elections. Suddenly, a student vote became important. This younger crew of radicals had political skills and community ties honed through student government, and they put them to use in the local electoral arena. It was a shift I couldn't have imagined three years earlier.

Kent State and Jackson State

I felt an ongoing connection to the campus despite my nonstudent status. I knew many of the activists and was known to them as an early organizer and participant in the antiwar movement. The campus was still home base to a vibrant antiwar community.

On April 30, 1970, President Nixon announced the expansion of the Vietnam War into Cambodia, sparking calls for a nationwide student strike. The National Guard was brought in to contain protests on the Kent State University campus in Ohio. On Monday, May 4, soldiers fired on student demonstrators. Over a period of thirteen seconds, soldiers fired sixty-seven rounds. Four students were killed, and nine more were wounded; one of the injured was paralyzed for life.

Student strikes spread across the country, affecting hundreds of universities, colleges, and high schools. Austin was no exception. On the Tuesday after Kent State, UT students and antiwar activists took to the streets without a parade permit, marching toward the capitol. Encountering police lines, they used mobile street tactics, moving to side streets. On the capitol grounds, police fired tear gas at demonstrators. My throat and eyes burned as the gas dispersed. Demonstrators lobbed the canisters back; tear gas fumes filled the capitol rotunda.

That week striking students went into classrooms asking for strike votes, and protesters conducted teach-ins. I remember walking across the UT main mall. Students were camped out with sleeping bags on the grass near the flagpoles. The faculty convened an emergency meeting, and a majority voted to shut down the school and ask the city council to grant a parade permit. On Friday, May 8, the largest demonstration in Austin's history at the time took to the streets. It stretched along thirteen blocks, with over twenty-five thousand people.

Only eleven days after the Kent State killings, police opened fire on students at Jackson State in Jackson, Mississippi, firing shots into a dorm. Two students were killed and twelve were injured.

With the Rev. Frank Doremus of the Episcopal Theological Seminary of the Southwest at the massive demonstration following Kent State, May 1970. *Photo by Alan Pogue.*

In 2016, Tom M. Grace, one of the students wounded at Kent State, came to Austin to publicize his book, *Kent State: Death and Dissent in the Long Sixties.* He recalled in a *Rag Radio* interview that the Austin response was the largest in the country and inspired the Kent State activists.

I was part of the spontaneous demonstration that was met with tear gas. I marched again when a parade permit was secured, amazed by the huge public outpouring, the largest march that had taken place in Austin until that time. The march brought out professors, clergy, veterans, and thousands of people who would never have joined our small numbers in 1965. A student who had gone on the Chile exchange came up to me at the demonstration and said, "You must feel like a mother to all this." The comment stuck with me. I did feel that I had spoken out years before others would.

Alan Pogue, the *Rag* photographer, took a photo of me, long hair streaming, anguish aging my face by at least a decade. We had tried so hard, in so many ways, to end this war. From innocent teach-ins and petitions to draft resistance and GI resistance, to massive mobilizations. And the war was coming home with shootings in Ohio.

The governmental assault on the Black Panthers, the murder of Fred Hampton in his bed, the conspiracy trials, the COINTELPRO programs that were in full swing but still covert had aged us all. We were a generation that had gone from hope to despair to rage. Those of us who were not part of the Weather Underground could understand their motives. When the FBI came to our doors with their pictures, we said what movement attorneys advised: "I'll only speak to you in the presence of an attorney." The FBI left. Later, I saw photographer Alan Pogue's doormat; it put our attitude into words another way: "Come back with a warrant."

GI Resistance

Although the UT campus was still at the heart of antiwar activity, there was another important center of activity seventy miles northwest in Killeen, Texas. It was the Oleo Strut, one of many antiwar coffeehouses that sprang up. The Oleo Strut served coffee and hosted music but also distributed literature, housed organizers, and published a newspaper, the *Fatigue Press*. I was told that they couldn't keep enough Black Power literature on the shelves. It was very popular among African American soldiers. The Oleo Strut was named for the stabilizer on a Huey helicopter. It became an outlet for many returning GIs who were disillusioned with the war, a place away from the brass, a place to decompress.

The most powerful voices against the war were the voices of veterans who had been there. In Austin, Terry Dubose and Alan Pogue stand out. Alan, the documentary photographer who lived at the *Rag* office, was ubiquitous at protests with a camera hanging from a strap around his neck and plastic barrettes keeping his long hair from falling in his face.

Terry was a quiet and thoughtful veteran who had grown up in the cotton country of Brownfield, Texas, and graduated from Hardin-Simmons in Abilene. Despite his good grades, he couldn't get a job without a draft deferment. He enlisted in the army, serving from 1966 to 1969, and was deployed to Vietnam as a first lieutenant.

When Terry returned, GI Bill in hand, he came to study in Austin at UT. He was questioning the war, and he found a community of support.

BOYS CLUBS OF KILLEEN

GI antiwar rally near the Oleo Strut, Killeen, Texas, Memorial Day, 1971. *Photo by Alan Pogue.*

When he saw the spontaneous Kent State demonstration from the window of the state office building where he worked, he got up from his desk and joined the march. He helped set up a draft-counseling center at the Methodist Student Center and then became the statewide coordinator of Vietnam Veterans Against the War. He spoke with veterans across the state, spending a lot of time at the Oleo Strut. In the spring of 1971, he traveled with other veterans to Washington, DC, before the massive May Day demonstration, returning to the demonstration at the LBJ Library dedication and then making the trip to Killeen when Pete Seeger showed up to entertain GIs.

Terry and Alan were the veterans I knew the best. Alan became a celebrated photographer; his documentary photos were published in the 2007 collection *Witness for Justice*. Terry went on to help organize the UT shuttle bus drivers into Amalgamated Transit Union 1549; then he began studies in health science. He said he was recouping his karma. Terry must have recouped it in spades before his death in October 2018. He was a pioneer in the field of diagnostic sonography, training at Harvard, Yale, Baylor, and the University of California; teaching at Austin's Seton Hospital; and then joining the faculty at the University of Arkansas. When he retired he resettled in Austin. Terry made it up to Killeen again, joining soldiers in a 2012 Veterans Day march. Iraq Veterans Against the War were advocating for a soldier's right to heal, and Terry was marching by their side.

• • • • •

Black activists were targeted everywhere, including Texas. On July 26, 1970, a Black activist, Carl Hampton, was assassinated in Houston. Carl, no relation to Fred Hampton, was the leader of the Black Panther offshoot in Houston, People's Party II. Undercover police snipers gunned him down. It was just seven months after Fred Hampton's murder.

The snipers wounded eight others, including Bartee Haile of the John Brown Revolutionary League. In 1971, Bartee Haile would be tried in Houston for assault of a police officer. Austin movement attorneys Cam Cunningham and Brady Coleman successfully defended Haile before a jury. With so many friends and former Ragstaffers now at Houston's *Space City!* newspaper, this repression felt close to home.

Janis and Threadgill

In 1970, friends and fans organized a birthday party for Kenneth Threadgill. He was turning sixty-one in September, but that technicality did not prevent a blowout sixtieth birthday party in July. The party was the brainstorm of attorney turned radical rabble-rouser Martin Wiginton.

Martin knew how to organize an event and draw a crowd. In 1968, Martin had teamed up with the longhaired son of a preacher man Jay McGee to put together the Mother's Grits Anarcho-Terrorist New Left Beatnik Evangelical Traveling Troupe. They took a show on the road to small Texas towns with circus music, booths, rock bands, guerrilla theater skits, and political speeches. It represented the best of Austin's mash-up of counterculture and radical politics. Martin used the same skills again to put together a party for Threadgill.

Kenneth Threadgill was a local Austin legend at the time. In 1933 he bought a small service station on North Lamar Boulevard and turned it into Threadgill's Tavern, where he sold gas, food, and beer with one of Austin's first post-Prohibition beer licenses. The place could only seat a few dozen people and got packed for the house band, the Hootenanny Hoots with Julie and Chuck Joyce. Threadgill would sell beer at the counter but join the band for "Coming Back to Texas." He sang and yodeled like Jimmie Rodgers and danced a crowd-pleasing shuffle. The place became an early cross-pollinator of country and folk music. Julie and Chuck recruited Janis Joplin, who accompanied herself on an autoharp.

By July of 1970, Janis Joplin was a mega rock star. With Big Brother and the Holding Company's *Cheap Thrills*, she had become incandescent. Janis canceled a gig to return to Austin for Threadgill's birthday celebration. The party drew a crowd to a location just south of Austin for barbecue, beer, and music. Janis, without a band, performed two Kris Kristofferson songs, "Me and Bobby McGee" and "Sunday Mornin' Comin' Down."

Only three months later, Janis died. I was working at the Southwest Educational Development Lab as a part-time technical writer. Alyce Guynn had helped me get the job. She was already a practicing poet and a committed journal writer. Her influence rubbed off on me. On the lab's typewriter, I wrote my first poem. It ran in *The Rag* and then in *Space City!* Then the *Texas Observer* ran it.

AND JANIS IS DEAD

oh, janis
Damn!!
damn
from Port Arthur
out of Austin
and finally to a Hollywood hotel,
poison rush
ebbing into death
alone
cold and alone
we let them make you
into an object of our fantasies
when we were saying no more objects
men, never-to-be-lovers, dreamed of fucking you
women, never-to-be-sisters, dreamed of being you
we used you to get closer together
but you never got to get closer
only farther away from home
dylan retreated to Woodstock
and then we followed half a million strong
we watched while the performers were flown in,
separated from us,
eating hors d'oeuvres and drinking cold champagne
while half a million tried to make it together
in the mud
wasn't it clear enough that we didn't need stars
we were doing okay
remember
even bob dylan sometimes must have to stand naked
and when janis joplin looked in the mirror
it didn't make her feel good
remember marilyn monroe
i saw you twice

in nightmare new york, you were incredible
but it was some grandly-opened spot
and I overheard the vice president of Columbia records
and he was bragging about his investment
and then home, in Austin
hair blowing, joking about the guitar
giving threadgill what he always needed
goddam, I wanted to know what was in your head about women
it must have been far out
but I was scared by the feathers and the bluff
now, threadgill who is sixty, still wears an apron to serve beer
and janis is dead
we have to find a way to make music[23]

Pearl Street

In August of 1970, Char moved to a house on Pearl Street in the West Campus area of Austin, and I moved with her as a housemate. It was a three-bedroom, one-bathroom home with a giant oak by the front porch and a garage that became Char's candle-making studio.

Char said she felt like a sorority housemother. She loved making a beautiful home, and a lot of women felt welcomed into her Pearl Street house. She prepared omelets and a wheat berry salad with dried cranberries. Jeff's younger sister showed up. Char's younger brother came to stay.

We listened to Joni Mitchell, Buffy Sainte-Marie, Edith Piaf, Joan Baez, Sweet Honey in the Rock, Linda Ronstadt, and Janis Joplin. And we listened to Bob Dylan and Johnny Cash on *Nashville Skyline*, anything by Kris Kristofferson, and the Band. Barbara Worley began to write songs that we practiced in the living room. Another movement house was across the street, and still another was down the street, where an early neighborhood food co-op flourished one weekend a month.

Our Pearl Street house was a crazy, happening place on a street with a couple of other activists' homes. Pearl Street even got a mention in a 1971 book by John Stickney, *Streets, Actions, Alternatives, Raps*. With typical Pearl Street hospitality, for example, we welcomed a young woman,

Janet, who had just arrived in Austin. She acquired a wicked sunburn while skinny-dipping. She stayed on the couch, wrapped in a sheet, for several days.

I lived with Char for nearly two years. I brought the chaos of an organizer into our shared living space. But Char was trying to provide a nurturing home for a toddler, not an entire movement. After the May Day demonstration in 1971, activity reached a crescendo. At Char's urging, with my drafted language, we posted a note on the door: "This house is not a movement center, movement crash pad, or information center. It is trying to be a home for a few people who are losing their sanity to the traffic and crowds."

Char and I continued to live at a somewhat quieter Pearl Street for another year after the note. Then we left for another communal experiment

Charlotte Pittman, c. 1968. *Photo by Scott Pittman.*

in Arkansas. As with most of the great rentals, the Pearl Street house was passed on, not vacated. Connie Lanham and Cam and Sue Duncan moved in after we left. When Jane Fonda and Tom Hayden came to Austin with the Indochinese Peace Campaign, they stayed there with their infant son.

Uncoupled and happily single, I was free to explore relationships and wary of entanglements. It was exhilarating. The women's community was in its ascendancy. We were becoming actors, taking on agency in meetings and bedrooms. I had a palpable aversion to couple identity. I was militantly nonmonogamous. I fell for, fell into, and enjoyed the freedom of initiating relationships. My journals and letters reveal the occasional havoc that casual intimacy can cause. For me, the '70s were full of experiments in communal living, collective work, and relationships.

I wanted friendships; I wanted brothers and sisters in my relationships. But intimacy collapses boundaries and creates needs, and this was hard terrain to navigate. We were like butterflies, with the gunk of the chrysalis still stuck to our wings, the legacy of '50s expectations shrouding our vision.

My friendships with women flourished. Barbara Worley adopted the name Vernell Pratt, taken from a Charles Portis novel, *Norwood*. She began to play guitar and write music. She has been credited, although I cannot confirm that the headline made it past the editors, with writing a headline to accompany an *Austin American-Statesman* article on Noam Chomsky's visit: "Cunning Linguist Speaks at U.T."

Alyce Guynn and I became lifelong writing partners—in and out of different creative circles and triangles, and sometimes just the two of us.

My NACLA associate Linda had married Robert Pardun. When they left Austin for New Mexico, she gave me her acoustic guitar. I asked my former SDS compatriot Dave Mahler for a few lessons. The first songs I learned were by Bob Dylan: "It Ain't Me, Babe" and "Don't Think Twice, It's All Right." These were the songs of separation that I picked and crooned that spring, summer, and fall of 1970. When I dust off my guitar case and open it up to play a few tunes, I invariably start with these same songs.

I still haven't learned much more than how to strum a few chords on Linda's beat-up acoustic guitar, but I inherited something from my mother, who had a trained voice. It wasn't the voice training, but it was the love of lyrics. Vernell and I would sing Kristofferson's "Just the Other Side of Nowhere," and I would think of the distance I had come, from New York City to picking a guitar on Char's velvet couch with Vernell at 2830 Pearl Street.

Cranky

In December 1970, West Coast visitors brought a street theater script to Pearl Street. Susan Adelman, Terry Cannon, and Terry's sister Carol Cannon shared a women's "Cranky" with our insurgent feminist community. We adopted this street theater as our own. I loved the simplicity of this handheld, no-electricity-required, musically enhanced way of introducing people to women's liberation.

The Cranky was a product of the Bay Area Women's Street Theater, with instructions and graphics published by People's Press in San Francisco. It was a paper movie, a cartoon sequence that you cranked from one reel to a take-up reel. As described by the Women's Street Theater: "THIS cranky is a brief history of women's oppression and struggles. About how the myth of women's inferiority began and has been perpetuated to oppress us, and about how women are refusing to submit to that HIS-STORY any longer." Here is how the Cranky starts:

> In the beginning
> [Cymbal clash, followed by tambourine shake about 5 seconds]
> Women were ALWAYS pregnant.

The cranky was such loveable low-tech media. Char Pittman used her artistic talent to reproduce the Cranky drawings on a roll of butcher paper, a process that might have taken longer than making and posting a video today. It was a great device for introducing women's liberation to a crowd. It had a revolutionary perspective, linking the struggle for women's liberation to other liberation struggles and ending with "Free Angela!" referring, of course, to Angela Davis, who had been arrested in October. We performed it in the UT Student Union, in classrooms, on the UT main mall, and at the Oleo Strut coffeehouse in Killeen. With its compelling graphics and easy script, it made for lively street theater and interaction.

It only took a handful of women—two to crank the story along, one to read, and the others to produce sound effects with tambourines, pots, pans, and kazoos. It should be remembered for its no-software, no-electricity means of production. It never failed to draw a crowd and get them laughing along with a radical message about women's liberation.

Sattva

It was possible to live on very little in the Austin of the '70s. Rents were unbelievably low, houses were shared, utility bills were cheap and divided among housemates. We didn't even have a landline at 2830 Pearl Street. We didn't own a television. Cable, cell phones, laptops weren't invented. We could live on intermittent income.

This was clearly of interest to the FBI. When I received my FBI file, pursuant to a request many years later, it had a notation justifying my continued status as subversive with these words dated September 12, 1971: "Based upon subject's past activities as well as her instability in residence and employment, it is felt that the subject meets the revised ADEX criteria as set forth in Bureau Memorandum 21-72, Items D and E."

Although my residence was fairly stable, I wasn't listed on the lease or the utilities. Both Alyce and Barbara helped me get odd part-time jobs, including editing at the Southwest Educational Development Lab. Along with a little income from vegetarian cooking, that was all I needed.

Sattva was a collectively run vegetarian restaurant first established in October 1970 at the Hillel Student Center on San Antonio Street in West Campus. The restaurant's opening was heralded in a notice in *The Rag*:

> A new restaurant in Austin, SATTVA, at San Antonio and 21st, just around the corner from the Drag in the Hillel building, nonprofit, run completely by members of the Austin community. Good food, macrobiotic and vegetarian cheap, vegetables and rice 35¢, raw milk 10¢ a glass, good whole wheat bread, healthy, filling food, and good people. Open Monday thru Thursday from 11:00 AM to 8:30 PM closed on Friday. On Saturday, free lunch from 12:00 to 1:00, dinner, not free, from 8:00 PM to 10:00 PM, open Sunday from 3:00 to 8:30. Come by.[24]

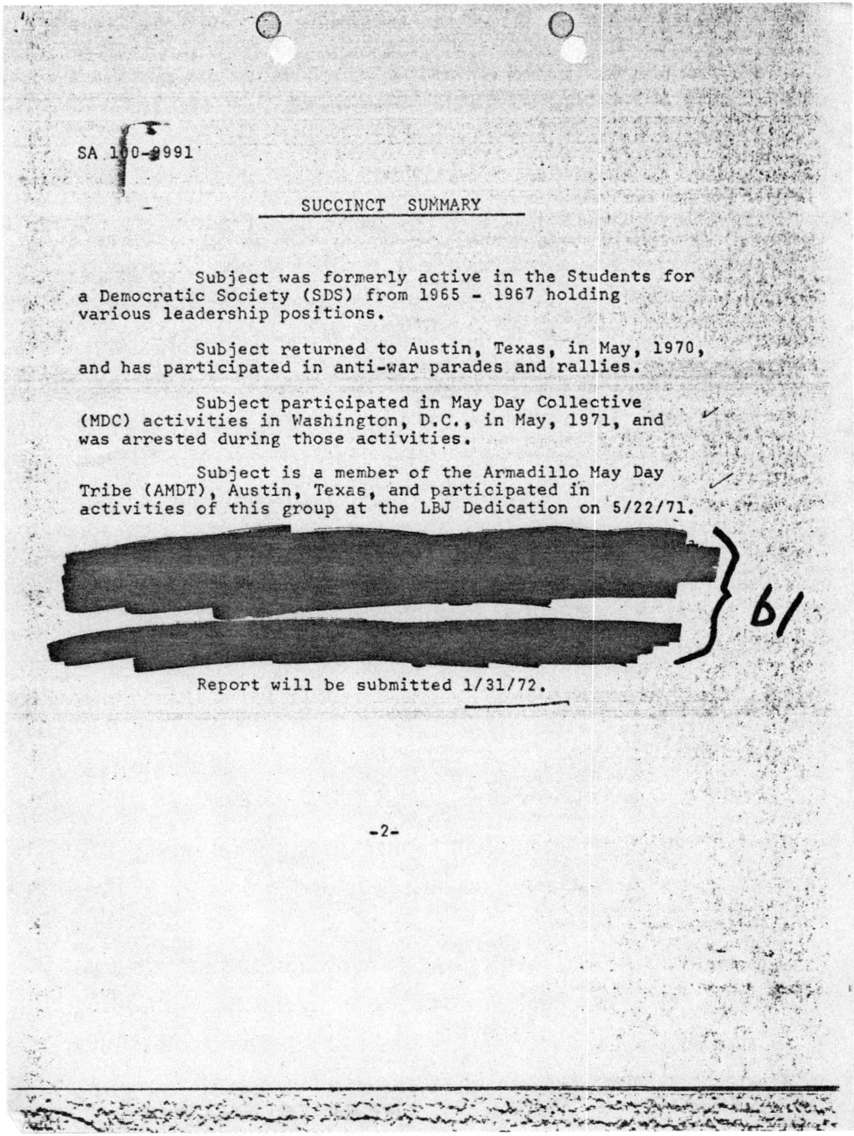

SA 100-9991

<u>SUCCINCT SUMMARY</u>

Subject was formerly active in the Students for a Democratic Society (SDS) from 1965 - 1967 holding various leadership positions.

Subject returned to Austin, Texas, in May, 1970, and has participated in anti-war parades and rallies.

Subject participated in May Day Collective (MDC) activities in Washington, D.C., in May, 1971, and was arrested during those activities.

Subject is a member of the Armadillo May Day Tribe (AMDT), Austin, Texas, and participated in activities of this group at the LBJ Dedication on 5/22/71.

Report will be submitted 1/31/72.

-2-

My antiwar activity as chronicled by the FBI, copy received after a Freedom of Information Act request, September 11, 1978.

The arrangement with Hillel was coming to an end when I helped find a new location for Sattva in 1971. I approached Bob Breihan, who ran the Methodist Student Center, about housing the lunchtime restaurant. Bob was blunt. "The only time I ate there," he said, "I got terrible diarrhea."

Despite his own digestive reluctance, he agreed. We moved Sattva about three blocks north from Hillel into the Methodist Student Center at 2434 Guadalupe in September 1971. My workmates included Jay McGee, Beverly Baker, Curtis Carnes, Jane Anthenien, and Doatsie Shrake. A man named Kimrod had a side business making sesame balls that we offered as a dessert item.

My strongest memory is of garlic. We had to get there in the early morning to feed the lunch crowd. The first thing we did was mince garlic. We peeled the skin off cloves and chopped until we had a mound, aromatic and translucent. After that we chopped a lot of onions. The garlic and onions went in the beans, the soups, and the casseroles. Beans were essential, and rice. A combo bowl was a real bargain—only fifty cents. (It had gone up in price.) We usually had a soup, a tub of salad you could dish out with tongs, and a main entree like squash casserole, eggplant Parmesan, or vegetarian enchiladas.

One morning, the health inspector paid a visit. He looked in on this somewhat bedraggled group of longhairs and asked, "Who's the top banana here?"

Jay, who wore a ponytail down his back and had a mustache like Yosemite Sam, delivered the perfect response in his gravelly, low voice: "We ate him for lunch."

The inspector did his job, checking to see if we stored our onions and potatoes off the floor, looking for signs of rodent or roach droppings, seeing what we used as a cleaner. We passed inspection and he went on his way.

I only worked there for a year, but I have great memories. As staffers, we took turns establishing the day's menu. It was a nonprofit, collectively run, healthy, and inexpensive way to connect with the community. It remained open until December 1976.

May Day

In the early months of 1971, I traveled to Nashville, Houston, and San Francisco. In Nashville I attended my first board meeting with *Motive* magazine. I had been asked to join the board after the Texas Media Conference. I returned through Houston, spending about a week there before traveling to California. I got back to Austin at the end of February. I didn't expect that I would be arrested twice that spring.

Across the nation, antiwar activists began to mobilize for a May Day protest of the war. I was drawn into the local preparations of the Armadillo May Day Tribe. We made plans to caravan to Washington, DC. We went through emergency medical training. I can still remember the warning that a symptom of concussions is projectile vomiting.

Local movement attorneys Jim Simons, Cam Cunningham, and Brady Coleman literally emptied their law office bank account before they left for DC so they could bail us out if we were arrested. The protest had a militant tone: "No more business as usual." The Armadillo May Day Tribe from Austin was assigned to shut Scott Circle down. We even had a song. About thirty people made the trip from Austin. Beverly from Sattva had DC friends who let us sleep on their floor.

The May Day protests in Washington, DC, drew thousands of people from across the country who were committed to bringing the nation's capital to a grinding halt as long as the war raged on. Many churches opened space for the influx of antiwar activists with sleeping bags. Mobile tactics, with contingents deployed to various locations, were effective. Protesters might not have entirely shut the city down, but we were able to interrupt the normal activities of the nation's capital.

Police made a record-breaking number of arrests. More than seven thousand people were rounded up into buses, some taken to a stadium. Sometimes a detainee aboard a bus would open the back door and people would spill out to freedom. One of the Austinites arrested was asked for his first name. "Karl," he said. They typed in "Carl." He gave his last name as "Marx." They typed in "Marks." Sheer volume meant that most of the arrests had to be dismissed for lack of proper procedures.

I was arrested and held overnight. Jeff's younger sister Sal was also arrested, and I was more worried for her than I was for me. I was told I would be charged with a felony. I remember spending the evening wondering whether I was facing prison time and feeling guilty that I hadn't protected Sal from arrest. I was so happy to see Austin movement attorney

Jim Simons in the courtroom the next day when I was arraigned. He arranged for my release on a personal recognizance bond. Sal was also released. I learned later that Jim had asked David Edwards, a UT government professor living in DC, to bring $1,000 in cash in case it was needed for bail. He did, but it wasn't needed. It was years later that I saw him at UT and thanked him for bringing the money.

Hexing the LBJ Library

Back from antiwar protests in DC, Austin radicals were organizing a protest to take place during the dedication of the Lyndon Baines Johnson Presidential Library. President Nixon, Henry Kissinger, Dean Rusk, General William Westmoreland, and other architects of the Vietnam War were to be present. The university went to extraordinary lengths in filing an injunction against thirty-six individuals, identified as organizers, to keep them away from the festivities.

In May 1971, the day before the dedication, I went with a number of women decked out as witches to the library grounds. We circled the newly built fountain and placed a hex upon the library with the words, "The blood of the Vietnamese people will haunt you forever." The granite facing on part of the library complex fell several months later. It had to be replaced. Do not dismiss the power of a witch's hex. Seven of us were arrested the next day when we continued our hexes in downtown Austin.

We were booked at the city jail. While we were waiting for our overworked movement attorneys, the word must have spread among the local detectives. Lieutenant Burt Gerding, who had been assigned to watch Austin "Reds" for years, had left the police department by then. But his accomplice Lieutenant George Phifer was on duty. Phifer made his way to our cell and called out my name. I had my hair ratted out and makeup smeared around my eyes, but I made my way to the cell door, thinking he might have something to tell me.

"Where's Jeff?" he asked. I went stony silent and turned away. Even in jail, I thought, even in my witch garb with my sisters, it's Jeff he wants to know about. I'm sure he never understood why I didn't answer.

When the case came to trial in municipal court in November, the courtroom was packed with witches. Attorney Cam Cunningham was there to defend us. Presiding judge Ronald Earle dismissed the charges, explaining to the crowd that the witches could not be identified since they had been in costume and paint the day of the arrests.

We spilled out of the courtroom onto the sidewalk. One woman read the manifesto of the Women's International Terrorist Conspiracy from Hell, as plainclothes policemen frantically took notes: "WITCH is an all-woman everything. It's an awareness that witches and gypsies were the original guerrillas and resistance fighters against oppression. . . . You are a witch by being female, untamed, angry, joyous and immortal."

Vernell, who had been among those arrested, wrote a song to commemorate our incarceration. It began this way:

> Sittin' in the Austin jail
> Waitin' for someone to go my bail,
> Singing in the street
> Was the name of our crime.

Vernell came up with the name Soeur Queens for a band. The name is a pure Vernell play on words. "Soeur," French for sister, was pronounced "sewer" by Vernell. The Soeur Queens played around town, notably at the One Knite on Red River and at a 1972 Ritz Theatre benefit for the Bach Mai Hospital in Vietnam. In Houston, they played at the 1971 founding conference of the National Women's Political Caucus at the Rice Hotel and for the gay students' association at the University of Houston. A final performance at Liberty Lunch in 1976 was a fundraiser to help Vernell go to China on a cultural exchange. It was billed as "Put Vernell on a Slow Boat to China," but I think she flew there.

Vernell wrote a lot of songs and learned a lot more; one of her first was inspired by our stint in the city jail. She was perhaps best known for "The Only Sin Is Frettin.'" In a 1975 songbook printed by Fly-By-Night Printing Collective, she described the band as an "all girls honkytonk band." The band often expanded to include percussionists and invited guests, but the core group shown on the cover of the songbook consisted of Vernell and Lori Hansel on guitars, Frances Barton at the piano, Nancy Crothers on stand-up bass, and Gail Caldwell on the flute.

Pipestem

Woodstock had taken place in August of 1969, and Janis Joplin died the next year. In the poem I wrote about Janis, I described the Woodstock stars arriving by helicopter and sipping champagne backstage while half a million people sat in the mud. I believed that commercial pressure led to Janis's death. In the end, addiction probably played a larger role, but it was easy for me to focus on the corporate greed fed by her fame.

In August of 1971, I was welcomed into a communal home in Nashville after a *Motive* magazine board meeting. I contributed housework for a couple of weeks in return for a place to stay. Many of these housemates were music lovers; one was an Appalachian clog dancer. They took me to a Nashville bar one night to hear country music. I remember the hush that fell over the room when Kris Kristofferson walked in. He was golden, with an uncommon pedigree, an air force veteran, an Oxford-educated songwriter, the person who had written the song Janis sang at Kenneth Threadgill's birthday, "Me and Bobby McGee." I met Hank Ballard that night. We had a conversation and I gave him my mailing address. He wrote me a letter that I still have.

At Willie Nelson's Dripping Springs Reunion, March 1972. *Photo by Stanley Farrar.*

When some of these Nashville housemates said they were going to a concert in Pipestem, West Virginia, I tagged along. I wrote about my impressions of Pipestem for *The Rag*. Historian Doug Rossinow, author of *The Politics of Authenticity*, called the piece, entitled "People's Music," a "jeremiad."[25]

I was so over reverence for stars, whether they were musical or movement men. I was intrigued by the multigenerational draw of Pipestem, by the beauty of music that resonated with Appalachian culture, and by the way the messages against strip-mining were seamlessly interwoven with the music.

I was critical of youth culture, which I wrote had been "orphaned from the strength that comes from roots and experience. Held together mostly by symbols—long hair and marijuana." I was critical of Yippies and their focus on rip-off culture. I ended that Pipestem piece in a way that still rings true to me:

> I mean for us to stop glorifying superstars and putting energy into national media events. And to start paying attention to real, steady, serious work. Breakfast programs, working food cooperatives, community gardens, tenants' unions, abortion referral services, daycare centers, free clinic[s], communications networks. The kind of things that can cross over lines of privilege, lines of age, and that can make a real difference.[26]

$$\bullet \quad \bullet \quad \bullet \quad \bullet \quad \bullet$$

I returned to Austin from Nashville and the Pipestem concert, stopping first in Atlanta and then in Arkansas. A number of friends had made their way from New Mexico to Arkansas to establish a commune there.

A family tragedy preceded my travel to Nashville. My uncle and cousin drowned while hiking in Washington State. They were trying to cross a flooded river. My uncle was my father's youngest brother—at six-foot-six, the tallest among the siblings. Another brother had died in the '60s, leaving behind a young widow and two sons.

My father was shaken to the core by the deaths of his brother and nephew. He traveled to Seattle for the funeral in late July. When he got back he spoke about how long the coffins had been. Only a few weeks later he suffered a major heart attack. I was in Arkansas. Char Pittman, who was also visiting, was on a county road when a sheriff told her to alert me. She returned to the commune with the news that my father was hospitalized in intensive care. I caught an overnight ride back to Austin. I didn't really know the driver, and I must have been lousy company, lost in my own thoughts until he left me at my parents' home. My mother and I talked and then went to the hospital for visiting hours.

My father recovered from that heart attack. He gave up smoking because of it. He spent a fair amount of time in bed in the back room, where he had installed a record player, an upgrade to the one in another closet that played 78 rpm records. Somehow, housebound, he got poison ivy. The ivy grew along the airport fence, and the Doberman brought it inside on her fur.

It was not long after the family deaths in Washington and my father's heart attack that we got devastating news about my mother. It was Thanksgiving weekend and she was in St. David's Hospital. Her oncologist informed her that she had inoperable liver cancer. Without knowing the news, I walked in to visit on Thanksgiving. My father spoke to my mother about how to tell me. Then, with a blunt statement I will never forget, he said, "I guess we should hit her right between the eyes."

There wasn't much progress at the time in treating cancer that had metastasized to the liver. It was considered inoperable—simply not removable, as the colon cancer had been. That Thanksgiving, my father and I went to the Nighthawk restaurant on Guadalupe. It was a faculty favorite owned by former mayor Harry Akin, who had worked at integrating restaurants. We ate a solemn meal of turkey and dressing, talking a little, trying to swallow both the food and the news.

Nineteen seventy-one drew to a close on the heels of that bad news and sorry prognosis. My parents were spending Christmas with my sister. I went to California, where my friend Alyce Guynn had settled into a communal house on Virginia Avenue in San Francisco. I reconnected with several friends from NACLA and from *Rat* and then made my way back to Austin.

Delta Diner

Sattva provided lunch. In 1972, several of us started the Delta Diner, where we served dinner. It was a short-lived Sattva spin-off specializing in vegetarian cuisine. The diner was located in the Campus Guild housing co-op at 2804 Whitis, a building that had been constructed in 1941 by co-op residents. Char Pittman, Lori Hansel, Vernell Pratt, Michael Lutes, and I were the core workforce. Vernell wrote a Delta Diner song, and we'd serenade our dining guests to the tune of "Nothing Could Be Finer Than to Be in Carolina":

> Nothing could be finer than to eat at Delta Diner in the evening.
> Nothing could be greater than to eat a raw potato at the diner.
> And while you're eating real good food and having a ball,
> You can meet with all your friends and plan the state's fall.
> Nothing could be finer than to eat at Delta Diner in the evening.

We specialized in subversively named entrees, like "Squash the State Casserole." The Delta Diner was open during the first UT shuttle bus strike, when the drivers, represented by the Amalgamated Transit Union, were organizing against stiff owner opposition. We offered to feed all striking shuttle bus drivers and their families for free, and many of them took us up on the offer. They won their contract in February 1972.

The co-op building that housed the Delta Diner burned down on July 4, 1973. I was in San Francisco when my mother sent me a clipping from the *Austin American-Statesman*.

• • • • •

In late March, I traveled to Mexico with Char Pittman, Gary Thiher, Joanie Levine, and Philip Russell. We spent several days in Mexico City enjoying Mexico's rich cultural sites. We visited the National Museum of Anthropology and the Zócolo plaza and saw the work of the great Mexican muralists in the Palacio Nacional and the Museo de Bellas Artes. Joanie and I spent the latter part of Holy Week at a hacienda belonging to the family of an acquaintance of hers. We watched a candlelight procession descend a mountainside to a nearby village in an enactment of Jesus's march to Calvary on the day of his crucifixion.

The Rag, January 31, 1972, p. 15. *Marie Valleroy, artist.*

Ruthie

I met Ruthie Gorton through D. Gorton, her husband. Ruthie and I had seen each other in Mississippi when D. and Jeff were working on the book that was to feature Jeff's narrative and D.'s photography. D., who was from Mississippi, had joined SNCC in 1963 while attending Ole Miss. Not long after, he joined SDS, where he chronicled many meetings with his striking black-and-white photos.

I knew Ruthie Gorton as D.'s wife before women's liberation. The women's movement brought the song out of Ruthie; she became a troubadour

Ruthie Gorton, c. 1970.

songwriter, singing loud and clear and a cappella, without a whit of accompaniment. She came to Austin for several weeks in April.

I helped arrange a number of venues for her, including one on KUT radio. She was mesmerizing, both in content and in her ability to simply close her eyes and sing without an instrument. She sang about stripmining, Vietnam, the Irish struggle for independence, and she sang about women's liberation. She sang at the Delta Diner and performed at a benefit for the striking shuttle bus drivers. Two of her songs became anthems for the Austin women's community. We learned all the words to "This Bird Is Learning How to Fly" and "Crazy Ruthie." I brought Ruthie to my parents' living room, where she sang for them:

> This bird is learning how to fly
> Soaring on the wings of her song

Arkansas

I needed a break from the intensity of New York, Kent State, two arrests in a row, and life without intermission. In retrospect that seems obvious. Communal life in the country beckoned. Perhaps the turn toward the country started with the shift to natural foods, cooking brown rice and vegetables. The first time I tasted tahini oil and tamari soy sauce on sautéed squash, it was simply wonderful. Yogurt was a discovery. We ate brewer's yeast on popcorn and mixed it into orange juice. At Sattva and the Delta Diner, we became accomplished at vegetarian cuisine. Many people I knew chose to leave city life, particularly if they had kids, to go "back to the land." Of course, most had been raised in the city, so it wasn't exactly "going back."

Several friends, including the Minkoffs and the Parduns, went to New Mexico first, but at the beginning of 1971, they headed to the Ozarks, where it was still possible to buy acreage for a song. Robert and Linda Pardun went to Arkansas shortly after their first child was born. They settled in a commune that adjoined the Ozark National Forest, north and east of Russellville, Arkansas. They called it the Ganja Boogie Band Commune. Friends often called it the Doobie Plantation. Bobby and Trudy Minkoff lived there with their toddler, Sadie Grace. Donny and Kathy Gross settled in with a young child, Aaron. Scott Pittman, who had been married to my housemate Char, was there with his brother Wayne. The Doobie Plantation had a large garden, a rustic communal house where meals were prepared and shared, and several smaller homes where people slept. Many of my friends had second children there. The Parduns lived in Arkansas for five years, longer than many others.

I fell in love with Arkansas, with the land, with the pace of communal life. It was the antidote to New York that I needed. A poem I wrote after my first three-day visit included the following lines:

> Remembering the calm that comes from nature's rhythms
> The sustenance from cow's milk, hen's eggs, spring water
> And the company of peaceful, happy people.
> That peace of mind and body was your Ozark gift to us[27]

Two friends from Sattva purchased thirty acres nearby in the valley of the South Fork of the Little Red River, increasing the lure of life in the country. In the summer of 1972, I arrived there to live on that land with Char, Gary Thiher, and Diana Vicars and her daughter, Krissy.

By late June those of us at the South Fork had a floor in our twelve-by-twelve-foot shack, then the sides went up. The shack was small, but it had a loft with a bed for visitors as well as a wood-burning stove. It was the communal area where the meals were cooked and the guitars were played. We pitched tents and built yurts to sleep in. With moonlight, it was easy to find your way back without a kerosene lantern or flashlight. Without moonlight, I was surprised at how easily I could veer off course on the way to my tent.

As residents, we did a lot of coming and going, getting Gary's venerable white truck repaired, paying visits to the larger Doobie Plantation, and making supply runs. We befriended a nearby group of residents from Louisiana who became known as the Louisiana Gang. Two of them worked seasonally as welders on deep-sea oil rigs. I got a puppy from them named "Ti-Shoe," little shoe in Cajun.

Friends like Jim Edwards, Sam Jones, and David Mahler paid visits. Dennis and Judy Fitzgerald came to stay, but I was back in Austin by then. Several women I knew, including Linda Evans and Laurel Wise, camped upstream on the Little Red River. They left on horseback for Las Vegas, Nevada. They were gone when the FBI hiked down the muddy mountain with pictures and questions. I was gone as well. Dennis got his camera out to take photos of the FBI, and they departed quickly.

In Arkansas, the fall announced itself with blazing red leaves on sassafras and maple trees. Winter would place a crust of ice on the creek. Spring would usher in a prodigious population of ticks. We treasured Wendell Berry poems, read books on organic farming, and consulted Frances Moore Lappé's *Diet for a Small Planet* for recipes; we strummed guitars and sang Hank Williams songs. I learned to identify the shape of leafless trees in the winter and the shapes of their leaves in the spring—fat sassafras, distinctive maple, dogwood, black walnut, and witch hazel. I could sit near a brook watching ferns nod toward the current, surprise a blue heron in the pools left behind by the South Fork of the Little Red River when it went dry, marvel at the torrent the river became during the rainy season.

We'd share cowboy coffee, boiled on the wood-burning stove, and Gary Thiher would take delight in picking off ticks and watching them sizzle and pop on the stove top. We had a large army tent for the kitchen, where the dry goods were stored in metal trash cans—beans and rice—and the dishwashing operation was set up to receive water heated on the stove.

The communal meals at the nearby Doobie Plantation began with hands held and the Shaker song "Simple Gifts." The staples there were always rice and beans. Our meals at the South Fork were renowned for their occasional excess after a grocery run. We'd cook beef stroganoff with mushrooms. Char even made an escargot pizza.

We'd fill our ten-gallon container with ice-cold water from the spring box and treat it with a few drops of chlorine. Once, I reached for a copper-colored dipping cup at that spring box before I realized it was a copperhead. We had no electricity, no running water. We used an outhouse and the wood-burning stove. We didn't call it "living off the grid." We called it "back to the land." The locals who had been on the land for generations surely questioned how far back these urban longhairs had to go to find kin who had actually lived on the land.

I remember a dangerous trek back to the South Fork in the winter. We tried to get up an icy incline and finally gave up. With the white truck pulled to the side of the road, we huddled in the cab, using our combined body heat to keep from freezing.

"You'uns could have froze out there," said a local when he heard we spent the night on the road.

We lived communally. Some would say we practiced "intentional living," but we weren't great at articulating our intentions. Gary designed the wonderful octagonal house, and we dug the posts into the ground below the freeze line (eighteen inches) to support the structure. We thought we could live there with our gardens, but the truth was that our efforts were hardly sustainable. We required influxes of money from Austin, from friends, and jobs.

The nature was idyllic. Our relationships weren't always that way. There was drama and a bit of psychodrama. I shared a tent with Alyce Guynn and her son, Geoffrey. He was the same age as Diana's daughter, Krissy. A couple of decades later, Geoffrey and Krissy married. They used a photo of both of them from the South Fork on their wedding invitation. Alyce and her son were only there for about two months. Still, Arkansas made an indelible impression on them. I also shared a tent with a partner, John Muir, who came with a case of rum for rum toddies. But John and rum didn't mix that well. That was a factor in our separation.

Arkansas was a retreat from the heavy politics of the late '60s. We wanted to make a different world with our own hands, free of commercials and commercial acquisitions. We weren't that successful, finding ourselves unable to be self-sustaining in a rural setting. Arkansas was just a temporary way station for me.

California

In the summer of 1973, I made my way out to California again, this time to a house on Mirabel in San Francisco where Alyce was living communally with a group of women. I went to work for Western Girls and Western Men, a temp agency. I had worked for an agency called Kelly Girls in New York, but something about this temp agency's name really got to me. It wasn't Western Girls and Western Boys; it wasn't Western Women and Western Men. Still, I cashed the checks and sent remittances to Arkansas. I remember working as a typist for Kraft Foods in their San Francisco office while the company was celebrating the fortieth anniversary of Miracle Whip. The white spread that went on white bread seemed emblematic of the company.

While I was in California, Austinite Marilyn Buck went on trial there. She had been arrested for illegally purchasing weapons. I visited her in the detention hall where she was being held, talking over a phone and through a glass. Marilyn was the daughter of an Episcopal priest, Louis Buck, a fierce opponent of segregation. My parents had talked about him at dinner when I was in grade school. He picketed St. Andrew's, my elementary school. He was "defrocked," the term my parents used, barred as a priest, for presiding over an interracial marriage. Miscegenation was illegal in Texas until a Supreme Court case overturned the law in 1967.

Marilyn was a bit younger than I, but our paths overlapped. She worked on *The Rag*, helped edit SDS's *New Left Notes*, and was part of a Newsreel film project. She was committed to antiracism work and became allied with the Black Liberation Army. She was eventually given an eighty-year prison sentence for her involvement in armed actions and her participation in freeing Assata Shakur from prison in 1979. While imprisoned, Marilyn got a graduate degree, became an accomplished poet, worked from inside on prison rights, and battled uterine cancer. She was released from prison on July 15, 2010, and died less than three weeks later at the home of friends in New York.

Marilyn had lived in the house my friend Alyce moved into. She had left much of her wardrobe there when she hastily moved out. Marilyn was into fashionable clothes, boots, and dresses. She was quite a bit taller than me, but I wore some of her clothes, trying to look "straight," at my temp job at Kraft.

I hitchhiked back to Austin with two women, Elaine and Amber, and their dog. An older man in a truck stopped for us. "Well, now I've seen everything," he said.

Raising Our Voices: 1973—1979

I FELT I WASN'T SEEN IN THE 1960S, THAT I DIDN'T SEE MYSELF. I was caught like a butterfly, wings pinned, labeled as "Jeff's girlfriend." Women still find it a struggle to forge strong, positive identities independent of relationships. Women's movement work in the '60s was frequently invisible, and even when visible, it was not given equal status to men's work. Until the women's liberation movement blew the lid off.

The first major book about SDS was Kirkpatrick Sale's *SDS: The Rise and Development of the Students for a Democratic Society*, published in 1973. Of the many people Sale interviewed for his book, only a few were women. Helen Garvy's 2001 film about SDS, *Rebels with a Cause*, was a course correction with its inclusion of women's voices.

The first question from many SDS-era friends whom I haven't seen for decades is invariably "How's Jeff?" It's sometimes awkward to see how much shelf life that particular couple identity has had. That question doesn't occur to friends who met me in the '70s. I escaped the chloroform, shook loose the pins, and took flight.

Women's liberation was breaking like a wave around me in New York,

Dick Reavis at a University Freedom Movement rally, April 1967. *Photo by John Avant, John Avant Photographic Archive, Briscoe Center for American History.*

and I regret the years lived with my eyes averted, with my voice on mute, stepping aside instead of forward. Still, I was an example to other women even in the '60s as someone who spoke up. I can see the photographic evidence of me speaking into microphones at rallies.

One of my disciplinary-probation compatriots at UT was Dick Reavis. He became a frequent writer for *Texas Monthly* and authored several books. In our SDS years, he wore overalls and a cloth cap, a SNCC look. He would stand on the UT West Mall fundraising for the Lowndes County Freedom Party of Alabama. In 1965 the party was known for its black panther emblem and was considered to be the place where SNCC began its Black Power identity. Dick's fundraising appeal was blunt: "Every dime buys a bullet."

Dick was a party-to-party kind of guy. I don't mean keg parties. He cycled through organizations and party affiliations, from the Industrial Workers of the World to Marxist-Leninist parties to Mao. Still, he was a perceptive observer. He was back on the UT campus during the mid-1970s and saw me at a union rally. It was the first time the women's band Jubilee performed. He told me, "I remember you quiet. Then I come back to see you standing on the steps of the Tower with a grin on your face belting out a song."

I think Dick got it.

Thirty-First and a Half Street

I returned to Austin from California in the fall of 1973, settling into a house on West Thirty-First and a Half Street with attorney Bobby Nelson. Along with Bobby, my housemates were Richard Halpin, Diana Vicars, John Muir, and two children—Bobby's daughter, Karin, and Diana's daughter, Krissy—who were in elementary school. We made a go at communal life, sharing cooking schedules and chores.

I lived at 614 West Thirty-First and a Half for three years. The house had extraordinary high ceilings, tall windows, and an expansive front porch. My room was the smallest, at the back of the house near the kitchen, and was a good fit for my small footprint of material possessions. After my grandmother's death, I acquired a couple of pieces of antique furniture that further diminished available floor space.

There was an ebb and flow to the housemates. Richard Halpin was there at the beginning, then Martin Wiginton became a housemate and Bobby's partner. Martin built a sprawling dining room table where meals were shared. The house accommodated meetings on everything from women's liberation to protest planning. At first, we all paid rent. Then Bobby purchased the house and undertook some major renovation work to expand the attic into living space and upgrade a backyard building.

As was typical at the time, our house was a community space for political meetings, meals, and parties. Beyond being housemates, Bobby and I were both involved in launching Austin Women Workers and International Women's Day celebrations, particularly in 1974 and 1975. I was acquiring offset-printing skills and wrangled employment at two different printshops, but in my spare time I was helping to launch Fly-By-Night Printing Collective and attending events at the new Bread and Roses Center.

An undercurrent for the first year after my return was the progression of my mother's cancer. After her death, I dealt with grief. I was in a relationship with John when my mother died in 1974. Although we never spoke of the similarities, he had lost his mother to a car crash when he was only eighteen. John was a friend to so many of my friends, a keen intellect, a bright conversationalist, an avid reader, an inspired dancer, and a drinker. I almost had a child with him, but I was able to make a choice—a barely legal one in 1973—to end the pregnancy.

We lived life without margins. We wanted to change the world. Come the revolution, free from the shackles of wage slavery, patriarchy, and racism, we would have meaningful work and equitably share childcare responsibilities and household work. Our concept of revolutionary change was, to put it mildly, naïve.

I helped with the carpooling of the two children who lived with us. A little. Not a lot. We took turns cooking. Both Martin and John were excellent cooks. John's oysters Rockefeller acquired the name "Oysters Dance on Your Grave." It seemed a fitting homage to the protests we planned at the house for Vice President Nelson Rockefeller's 1974 and 1975 Austin visits. Several local posters publicizing the Rockefeller protests called attention to "The Real Rocky Horror Show," including the deaths at Attica prison.

We partied hard and tolerated excess with little understanding and no words for alcoholism and chemical dependency. We talked about dismantling monogamy but discounted emotional vulnerability. It was years before many of us understood that emotional highs and lows had a mental health diagnosis. Bipolar disorder wasn't in our vocabulary. Depression was something you could overcome by an act of will and revolutionary commitment.

Bobby was a feminist attorney, trying to raise a child and earn a living. One of her cases pitted her against the massive legal apparatus of UT, and the weight of that case hung on her shoulders for years. Martin had given up the practice of law to take up the work of radical organizing. Meanwhile, Bobby paid bills as a working lawyer.

Martin was quick with judgment about what we should be doing. He had a huge heart and, at times, a mean temper. He could rage in a way that only loud and large men can. Hungover after a house party marked by lots of alcohol, Martin would find me crushing beer cans to recycle. "You're killing ants when you should be shooting elephants," he'd yell in his thundering voice. His message was that recycling was a waste of time; we needed to smash the state, not beer cans.

Loss

After my mother's diagnosis of inoperable liver cancer, she went through several types of treatment: oral chemotherapy, a chemotherapy applied to the scratched surface of her upper arm, blood transfusions. My sister and her husband gave my parents the gift of travel to Europe. My parents also made trips to Hawaii and Mexico.

I realized how weak my mother had become in 1974. I took her to see *Blazing Saddles* at a movie theater on North Interstate 35, and we ate at a nearby Howard Johnson's. My mother got a kick out of the movie's raunchy, offbeat humor, including the campfire farting that was a long distance from New England propriety. But the fact that she could not open the heavy theater door into the lobby is what stands out in my memory.

In June 1974 her skin took on a jaundiced tone. Liver failure was obvious. Her oncologist, in a cold and clinical manner, said she had only a few more months. She grew increasingly frail. We went on a birthday picnic in September, driving out to the Colorado River off FM 969. We didn't get out of the car.

She became emaciated. Only the hard mass in her liver seemed to grow. She got nauseated easily, so she spent time lying on the living room couch, a pan beside her. Then she spent more time in her bed. Finally, she was so weakened that she couldn't get up to use the portable potty in her bedroom. She wanted to be hospitalized and catheterized.

My parents didn't call and make requests like that to doctors. I remember calling the doctor at his home, my parents watching as though I were breaking long-standing protocols. She wanted to eat a meal at home before we took her to the hospital and wanted black bean soup garnished with slices of boiled egg and lemon wedges.

I went to a small grocery store on Berkman Drive near our house.

I recall standing in the aisle of soups, staring at the Progresso cans, tears streaming down my face, grateful that there weren't many shoppers to witness my breakdown.

My mother was admitted to Holy Cross Hospital on East Nineteenth. As I recall, the rooms were laid out in a circle radiating out from a central nurse's station. Those days seemed to collapse into visits and continued decline. I don't know how many days she spent at Holy Cross. I had a dream that last week of her life that she would die on Sunday. I told my sister, and she booked a flight.

There was a couch in the hospital room. I slept there a few times, and the night before she died, I put a pillow on the floor near her bed and stretched out, listening to her ragged breathing, stirring and sitting up every time there was a lengthy pause. I've been in other rooms like this since. There are now monitors for heartbeats and oxygen flow. She didn't have those in 1974, just nurses coming in and out.

Sunday morning arrived, and I left to catch a few hours of sleep in a bed after my father arrived. She died while he was there, opening her eyes to say, "I love you." When I got back to Holy Cross, my father told me, "I think it was better. I knew her longer." And, of course, he had.

My sister arrived at the hospital shortly after my mother died, before she had been taken from the room. A nurse, relaying what she thought was a message of comfort, said, "Sometimes death is merciful." Nothing seemed merciful about this ordeal.

My sister's family—her husband and three kids, twelve, ten, and eight—came for my mother's funeral. The funeral at All Saints' Church was packed, the coffin draped, not open. My father's sister Jean came to Austin. I remember seeing her put her hand on my father's hand and noticing how much their hands resembled each other. The tall and lean shape of the Embrees, the shape of Embree hands, lingers in my memory. The sister comforting her older brother.

Many of my friends came to the service, and one of them got up as the procession left the church to put a rose on top of my mother's coffin. It was a gesture of affection, out of place with Episcopal protocol. At the back of the church, as we were leaving, the custodian for the Episcopal Seminary of the Southwest, where my mother had worked for many years, got up to greet me. I broke down in sobs then. I was never good at that stiff-upper-lip British bearing that was expected. Too many years growing up in the South had broken all that down. I remember driving my nephews and niece back to my parents' home crying my eyes out. They were darting glances at each other, perhaps wondering about the display of sorrow or the degree to which it was safe to be in the car.

My mother died on October 13, three days before my birthday. And then, ten years later, my father died on my birthday. October became a month marked by grief, remembrance, and celebration.

Something about the first year of grief makes every date without a person in your life hammer a new spike into your heart. That first year after my mother's death, I was caught completely unprepared. I remember staring at a display of Mother's Day cards in a Hallmark store on Congress Avenue, tears brimming over like they had in the soup aisle.

Claiming Space

I enrolled in my first offset-printing class in the fall semester in 1973 at Austin Community College (ACC). Several other women were enrolled in the program. We were learning a skill that had been largely the domain of men. We dove in, ink up to elbows. We learned how to use the copy camera, strip negatives into flats, burn metal plates, attach them to the press, ink up the press, and then watch as paper flew into stacks. We even loved the solvent and the cleaning process that left our fingers stained with ink.

In the spring of 1974, we held meetings at Thirty-First and a Half Street to plan a celebration of International Women's Day on March 8. I was just beginning to gain skills with silk screens, and we needed a negative for a poster. We were using an image by Käthe Kollwitz, a German artist who produced powerful prints of working-class women. Sometimes her images were of women mourning, but this particular one was of two women talking.

The ACC campus housed a number of presses and a large copy camera where negatives were shot for making plates. I was using the copy camera to shoot a negative of the Kollwitz lithograph, hoping I wouldn't be caught doing something that wasn't class related. I pulled the glass cover up and placed the image in the camera bed. Then I began to crank down the camera. I was moving too quickly and had failed to lower the glass cover. The sound of glass shattering brought the head of the department flying into the camera room. I was standing there, my stealth and haste evident, amid splinters of glass. Fortunately, the camera wasn't damaged. I cleaned up the room and paid to replace the glass cover. Somehow, some way, I ended up with the negative, because we were able to silk-screen the image onto posters and shirts.

Despite my clumsiness in the darkroom, I felt that I was coming into my own as an organizer. We felt the exuberance of women reshaping the world, expanding options for women, learning new skills, and claiming space in the process. Just as the women at *The Rag* had literally claimed a corner of the office for counseling, women were opening up space. It had a physical dimension with bookstores and women-run printshops. In other ways, women claimed space as organizers, speakers, writers, and radio show hosts. A women's community blossomed during this period of time and left a lasting mark on Austin.

Austin Women Workers

Bobby Nelson, Ruby Williams, Betty Ann Duke, and I were part of a weekly study group in 1974, reading and talking about feminism. I was always more drawn to action and organizing than I was to studying. Out of our small group we launched an organization, Austin Women Workers. We were no longer students, and our outreach went beyond the confines of campuses. I find our description of the organization to be boldly revolutionary:

> Austin Women Workers is an organization of women from all backgrounds who have come together to analyze and act on those problems in our society which most directly affect our lives. We are all workers although some of us are in the role of unpaid mothers and housekeepers.
>
> We know that the struggle for women's liberation is a revolutionary struggle because the realization of our demands will bring about a basic transformation in our society. We cannot settle for less than the possibility of engaging in meaningful and creative activity: the opportunity to develop those skills which

will enable us to do useful work; adequate compensation for what we do; free, loving care for children; control over the reproductive processes; sexual self-determination for all women and especially for lesbians; the development of personal relationships based on mutual responsibility; and the power to make decisions about all areas of our lives. There will not be a revolution until these changes are made.

We also know that the liberation of women will not occur until all people are free. We do not intend to gain a greater degree of independence at the expense of other oppressed people. Therefore, we struggle against all forms of racism, capitalism, and imperialism. Our most important work is the creation of a society in which every person is provided with the basic necessities of food, clothing, and shelter; every person participates in the decision-making process; and every person is able to expand his or her consciousness to the fullest extent.

Second-wave feminism is often portrayed as reformist white women, middle class and privileged, trying to break through glass ceilings to create a world with more women as CEOs. This was not my experience. Even when we worked to dismantle employment barriers for women as firefighters, bus drivers, emergency medical technicians, and cable splicers for the phone company, we wanted far more than equal compensation. We wanted free and loving care for children, control over our reproductive processes, and sexual self-determination.

In 1974, Austin Women Workers planned a three-day celebration of International Women's Day. It included activities at the Ridgeview Campus of ACC, the UT Student Union, the capitol grounds, the Friends' Meeting House on Washington Square, and Eastwoods Park. Events included a slideshow about women in history, a short film made by Austin women, and two screenings of *Salt of the Earth*. Robin Birdfeather photographed the gathering on the capitol grounds. Vernell and I are singing the labor anthem "Bread and Roses." A friend's daughter is reading the words of the song printed in the International Women's Day program. The photo was included in the 1976 *Cyclar* women's community calendar.

Cheryl Duke, me, and Vernell Pratt, foreground, celebrating International Women's Day in 1974. *Photo by Robin Birdfeather.*

We unearthed women's history that had never been taught to us. We read work by anarchist Emma Goldman, the words of Sojourner Truth and Harriet Tubman, and learned about the long fight for women's suffrage, with its roots in the movement to abolish slavery. We were shocked at what our history lessons had concealed.

We successfully resurrected the celebration of International Women's Day on March 8. In doing so, we learned the history of women garment workers organizing in the mills along the Eastern Seaboard and in the Lower East Side of Manhattan. We learned about the Triangle Shirtwaist fire, in which women perished because they had been locked inside a factory. We learned that the women garment workers held organizing meetings translated into a dozen languages because the immigrant workforce came from so many different countries. Our leaflets recounted this history:

On March 8, 1908, working women crowded the streets of the Lower East Side in New York City, in a demonstration demanding an end to the insufferable conditions imposed upon them by the garment industry. International Women's Day commemorates this demonstration and is celebrated worldwide. Ironically and unfortunately, it has been ignored in this country until recent years.

The following year, in 1975, Austin Women Workers joined forces with other organizations, including the Women's Health Organization and the Radical Student Union, to commemorate International Women's Day with a full day of activities. The program took place at the University Presbyterian Church and included workshops on women in prison, collective living, organizing women workers, women in Cuba, women in Iran, women's bodies, the lesbian world, revolution and culture, and welfare rights. Slideshows and panel discussions covered socialist feminism, women in China, and women in Vietnam. Cultural events scheduled in the evening included a play as well as musical performances by the infamous Soeur Queens and Vivian and Women Working.

Austin Women Workers also worked against prostitution laws, embraced a lesbian caucus, and conducted outreach classes on family law and labor organizing. We created a women's theater group that performed local productions of *Sugar and Spice and Nothing Nice* and *The Independent Female (or, A Man Has His Pride)*.

Each year, Martin and John would place roses and artisan bread on the giant dining room table at Thirty-First and a Half Street to honor International Women's Day.

•   •   •   •   •

Angela Davis's *Women, Race and Class* was first published in 1981, nearly a decade after our small Austin Women Workers study group. Davis takes the lens of history and sharpens the focus to expose the intersections of class, gender, and race as women pursued the right to vote. Davis quotes Belle Kearney, who spoke to the New Orleans convention, on suffrage: "The enfranchisement of women would insure immediate and durable white supremacy, honestly attained; for, upon unquestionable authority, it is stated that 'in every Southern State but one, there are more educated women than all the illiterate voters, white and black, native and foreign, combined.'"[28]

Angela Davis's account of the bald racism and appeal for white supremacy was an eye-opener to me.

Women's Health Organization

The Austin Women's Health Organization (WHO) began in 1974 to educate women about their bodies from a woman's perspective. The organization surveyed women about their experiences with doctors and publicized the need for a woman ob-gyn in Travis County. There were none! My friend Alyce Guynn described the WHO this way: "Our Bible: the Boston Women's Health Collective's *Our Bodies, Ourselves*. Our number one goal: to help women take control over and responsibility for their own bodies. Our method: teach women how to do self-exams, self-exams that extended beyond breast and reached the cervix. Our tool: the plastic speculum."[29]

Nancy Collins illustrated the WHO literature and drew an illustration of a Super Woman brandishing a speculum with the slogan, "At Your Cervix."

Women at the People's Community Clinic advocated for different birthing choices—natural childbirth, birthing centers, and midwife-assisted home births. Organizations began to push for affordable childcare as well. We learned of forced sterilization, particularly affecting women of color, in psychiatric and prison settings and in drug tests.

As that women's liberation movement subsided, the culture wars distilled only two poles in the national discussion of reproduction: pro-choice, pro-life. Third-wave feminists have reset the parameters, beginning a discussion of reproductive justice—with all of its elements—and with particular attention to the reproductive choices and needs of the uninsured and women of color.

Fly-By-Night Printing Collective

I'm sure that the head of the ACC Printing Department didn't know what had hit him. There were a number of women taking printing classes. We managed to talk him into allowing a press mechanic to teach a press repair class in the spring of 1974, using a donated press. Buck Buchanan was the repairman and teacher. He was self-taught, without any academic credentials. That bothered some of the ACC hierarchy. He was well known in Austin as someone who could fix anything that was broken on a press. We spent the spring with that old Multilith 1250, fixing everything we could. Then we asked Buck Buchanan to get it up the stairs to an office on the second floor of a building at 901 West Twenty-Fourth Street. It was quite a feat; he had to use a winch because the machine weighed a zillion pounds.

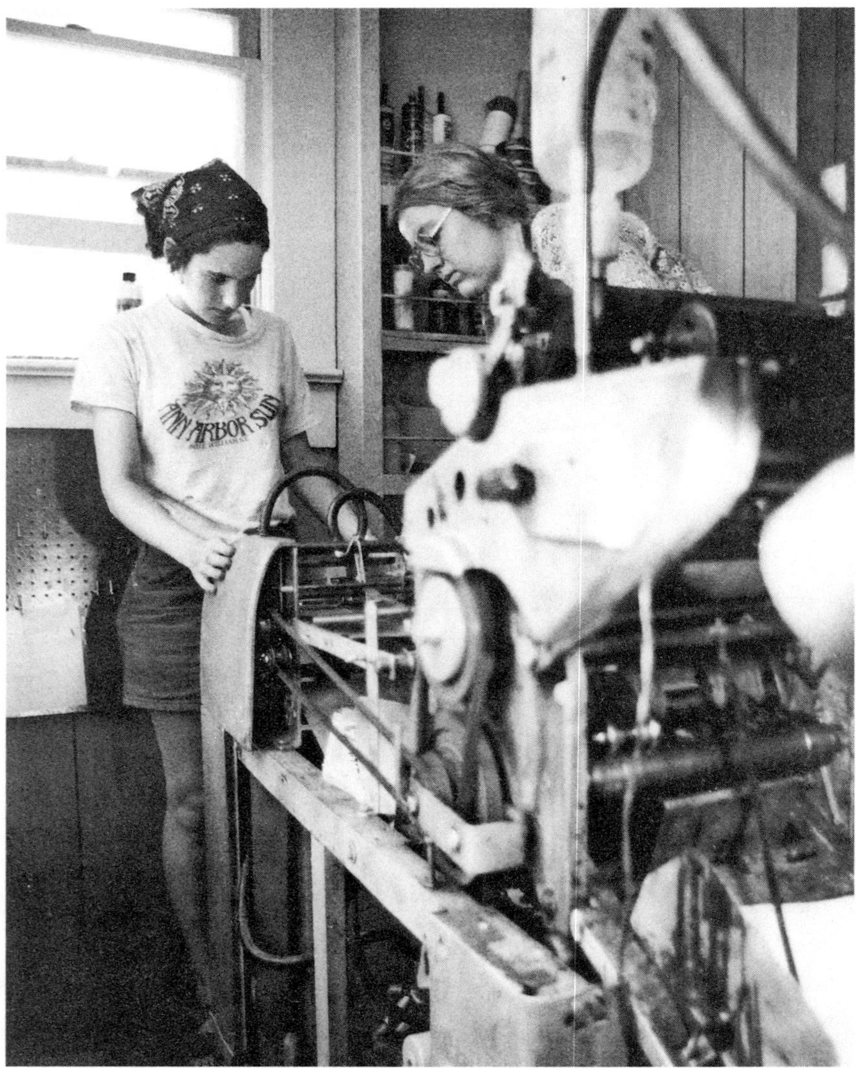

Missy Bondy and Suzanne Gott printing at Fly-By-Night Press, c. 1974. *Photo by Danny Schweers.*

With newly acquired skills, I joined other women to form the Fly-By-Night Printing Collective. Fly-By-Night, the predecessor of Red River Women's Press, began operations in June of 1974 with that rehabilitated press. If the Multilith had a heart, I imagine that it felt like an abandoned stray adopted into a doting, loving family. One of the collective members, a graphic artist, was Rita Starpattern. Our pricing sheet, relying on Rita's wry humor, was called "Offset Reality." We publicized hours of operations, but the collective was primarily a volunteer effort, and most of us had other means of support.

Fly-By-Night didn't provide a steady income stream, and I found a paying job at Ibid Inc., a print and copy shop on Barton Springs Road. Ibid specialized in advertising flyers and bound dissertations. I was working there when my mother died. The owners were kind. With their permission, I used the Ibid press to reprint my father's 1933 poetry book, getting it bound for family gifts for Christmas, the first Christmas without my mother.

My father and I went to Larchmont, New York, that Christmas to be with my sister and her family. He was truly surprised by my gift of his poetry, an homage to his creative youth. My father, the talker, sat stunned into silence with the book open on his lap. As a printer, I took pride in the brown ink on Classic Laid Chatham tan paper. Of course, as a typist, I had retyped all the poems. I paid for the brown hardcover binding with a gold-embossed title. It was worth it to see his reaction.

In 1975, I landed another job as a printer at the Southwest Educational Development Lab. I printed small runs of the lab's curriculum, assembling them with spiral binders. A giant collating machine occupied space in the corner of my basement shop. I tried to show it off to a visitor once without securing the stops on the trays. Paper flew everywhere. It was spectacular, just not in the way I intended. My Chilean friend Renato Espinoza worked as a bilingual curriculum developer at the lab while I was there. He would sometimes visit me in my printing domain.

Fly-By-Night published *The Soeur Queens Songbook* in 1975. The cover and several of the illustrations were by Fly-By-Night artist Nancy Collins. It was saddle stitched, chock full of our favorite songs, with a wonderful lavender cover. I traveled to Antioch, Ohio, for the Socialist Feminist Conference in June 1975 along with several other Austin women. We took the songbook hot off the press.

That fall, Cynthia Roberts and Melita Abrego, Fly-By-Night press operators, printed a large print run of *Cyclar*, a women's community calendar, for the upcoming year. Rita Starpattern and photographer Robin Birdfeather collaborated on the design. The calendar proudly proclaimed, "Put together by women from scratch to finish."

When the Bread and Roses Community Center opened at 2204 San Gabriel, Fly-By-Night relocated. In November 1975, Buck Buchanan, the same press mechanic who had taught us press repair, lowered the machine down the staircase on Twenty-Fourth Street. The press was put on a dolly. Then, surrounded by women printers, it was rolled a couple of blocks down the street to Bread and Roses.

Bread and Roses became a center for activity on multiple fronts. The press was in a small room there. A Puerto Rican artist, Carlos Osorio, had his art supplies set up in the front room. Classes, organizational meetings, and events took place regularly in the living room. David MacBryde, a printer turned shuttle bus driver, lived in the back room.

JoAnn Mulert, a friend of Austinite Marce LaCouture, was nearing the end of a prison sentence for the destruction of draft records in 1969. On Marce's recommendation, I wrote the Federal Bureau of Prisons a letter on Fly-By-Night stationery offering JoAnn a job. The job offer helped satisfy conditions of her parole. JoAnn came to Austin from Alderson prison and joined Fly-By-Night in the fall of 1976. She was a great printer and addition to the collective.

• • • • •

I rented a place of my own in August of 1976, living for two years in a small apartment off Comal Street. It looked like an old motel, with twelve identical cinder-block units arranged on each side of a common driveway. They have all been demolished for UT parking near the baseball stadium. I had a light table that a friend helped me build, an army surplus file cabinet, a kitchen table made from an oilcloth-covered door that sat on cinder-block legs, and a bed that had been in my grandmother's home. I enjoyed my somewhat Spartan experience of a single life with no housemates. I lived there with only one companion, my border collie mix, Ti-Shoe, from the Louisiana Gang in Arkansas. My two years at Comal were still filled with activism during the day but were broken by solitude at night.

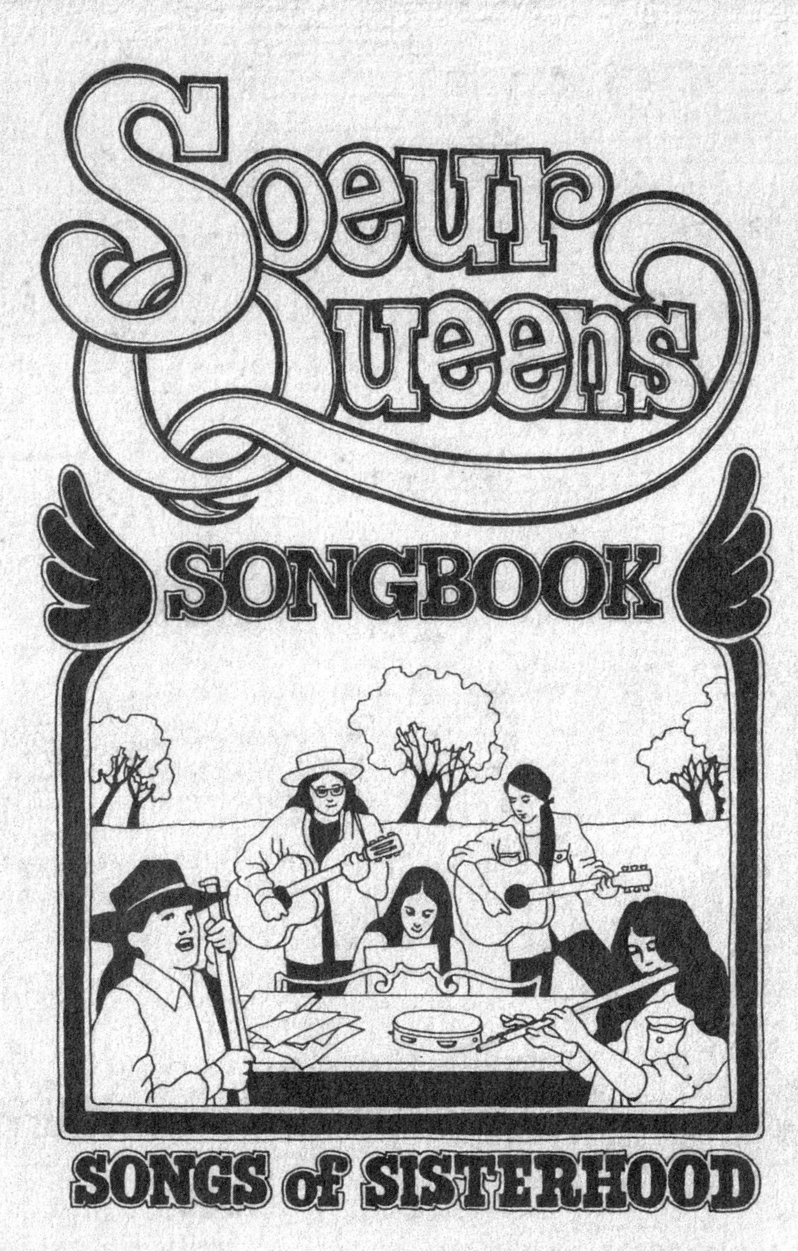

Soeur Queens Songbook, printed by Fly-By-Night Press, 1975. *Nancy Collins, artist.*

Singing solidarity songs for the UT Shuttle bus drivers with Jubilee in 1976. From left, Linda Evans, me, Frances Barton, and Lisa Rogers. *Photo by Alan Pogue.*

Women's Music

In Austin, later to be known as the Live Music Capital of the World, it is not surprising that the women's movement nurtured songwriters and women's music. The poem I wrote about Janis Joplin ended with these words: "we have to find a way to make music." And we did.

The Soeur Queens Songbook borrowed shamelessly from several sources, including Ruthie Gorton ("Crazy Ruthie"), Jimmie Dale Gilmore ("Dallas"), the San Francisco Mime Troupe ("Private Property"), Holly Near ("Hang in There"), Rosalie Sorrels ("Travelin' Lady"), and even Joan Baez ("Prison Trilogy"). It included a number of songs written by local talent, including Vernell Pratt, Lori Hansel, and Diane Goss, as well as our community standards, like the Delta Diner song and "Will the Circle Be Unbroken?"

In 1976, I became part of Jubilee, a women's band. I sang. I wasn't proficient with any instrument, but I loved lyrics. Jubilee began with four women on the UT Tower steps singing songs of solidarity for the UT shuttle bus drivers and the workers at Wallace's Bookstore, both of whom were involved in fights to unionize. Lisa Rogers, Frances Barton, Linda Evans, and I were the earliest version of the band.

We sang union songs and civil rights ballads, "Solidarity Forever" and "We Shall Not Be Moved," and we sang songs from lesbian songwriters like Cris Williamson and Meg Christian, who were just beginning to record with Olivia Records.

Jubilee went on to become a real band, but I faded away as it got more instrumentally serious. Three of the women I sang with on the steps of the UT Tower continued to perform as Jubilee: Frances Barton (piano, accordion, saxophone, vocals), Linda Evans (guitar, harp, vocals), and Lisa Rogers (electric and acoustic guitars, vocals). Marce LaCouture (vocals and percussion), Lynn Keller (bass, flute, vocals), and Christy Wolfarth (drums, vibes, percussion) joined Jubilee in a later incarnation. Benefits, lesbian parties, and community gatherings were the typical gigs at venues like Liberty Lunch, Bread and Roses, Zilker Clubhouse, and more. It created quite a buzz when Jubilee played with other women musicians, Marcia Ball, the Reynolds Sisters, and the All-Person Band, at the Soap Creek Saloon at 707 East Bee Caves Road. The occasion was a February 2, 1977, benefit for Red River Women's Press. I joined in for an arrangement of the

Everly Brothers' "All I Have to Do Is Dream." A couple of tapes survive. Jubilee later morphed into another band, Jubilation.

Lisa Rogers still plays music with the Therapy Sisters, a band that includes Maureen McLean. Their description of the band reveals their offbeat humor: "The Therapy Sisters came together in 1987 as a musical self-help effort that has since turned into an addiction." There are not many instruments that Lisa can't play. Frances Barton's remarkable voice was cultivated in the Czech Brethren Church in Taylor, Texas, where her father was pastor. Frances can still be heard around Austin with the Melancholy Ramblers. Occasionally, she will sing the song I learned with Jubilee, "Amelia Earhart's Last Flight."

> Happy landings to you, Amelia Earhart
> Farewell, first lady of the air.[30]

●　●　●　●　●

In the 1960s, I would never have worn jeans, certainly not shorts, to class. I never read a UT dress code, but it was an internalized expectation. A 1965 issue of the *Daily Texan* has a picture of me demonstrating how to fall to the ground in a nonviolent posture. I am lying on the grass of the West Mall in a fetal position with my hands protecting the back of my neck and skull from potential attack. Wearing a dress, I'm exposing a lot of leg.

We had dressed up for antiwar rallies in 1964—the men in jackets and ties, the women in dresses and low heels. In low heels on the campus of Columbia, I tripped and gashed my chin. Two months later, we were at the 1968 Democratic National Convention. I ran from tear gas and from the police, who were cornering strays and beating them mercilessly. I had switched to pants and running shoes for demonstrations.

We had worn our politics on buttons in the '60s. The diminutive "sds" was a constant accessory for years. I also had a large, red, octagonal "STOP" button with "the war" in small letters. "Part of the Way with LBJ" emerged onto a button in 1964, but I was nineteen and couldn't vote. Buttons printed by the Mobilization to End the War sometimes only proclaimed a protest date; one had my birthday on it. The SNCC button had two hands, a Black hand shaking a white hand.

Daily Texan photo where I demonstrated how to protect your head if you fell, UT West Mall, 1965. *UT Texas Student Publications Photos, Briscoe Center for American History.*

In 1970, the women's movement began to take dress down an increasingly informal path. T-shirts, blue jeans, cutoffs, hiking boots, hair flowing freely, growing freely under arms and on legs. Women disposed of bras and freed their breasts under T-shirts or blue work shirts. One of the most daring accessory items was the tampon, nonchalantly appearing like a pen in the work shirt pocket. My friend Lori Hansel could pull that off. I wasn't bold enough, but I appreciated it when I saw it. Relaxed informality settled into the mainstream.

In the '70s, political statements moved from buttons to silk-screened T-shirts. We began to tie-dye shirts and silk-screen slogans. Our politics could be worn like badges across our chests, alerting everyone, challenging the nonbelievers and emboldening the believers.

Working with Women

By 1975, the women's liberation movement had created many alternative spaces—the space in the *Rag* office claimed by Judy Smith and others for birth control counseling; Red River Women's Press; a peer-counseling center called Womenspace, located in the "Y."

Rita Starpattern, a sister printer, made the creation of space for women a focus of her work—space for women to counsel each other, to learn the printing trade, to create art. I worked with Rita in two of the spaces she helped create, Red River's Women's Press and its predecessor, Fly-By-Night Printing Collective.

The women's community calendar was Rita's first printing project. Rita's research annotated the days. Ads went out and orders came in from around the country. The first run of two thousand sold out. Soon after, Rita was at the center of transforming Fly-By-Night to Red River Women's Press.

At Red River Women's Press we were diverse and intense, lesbian, straight, feminists and activists with many causes, trying to serve a community of social activists and survive as a business. Rita would remind us of our common ground. Her quiet energy sustained us. Sometimes she'd realign us in a meeting using her clever words and bubbling chuckle, a collective chiropractor. Sometimes she simply arched an eyebrow or let out a deep sigh that spoke volumes. She was a trooper. She labored over artwork but also over grant reports, wage reports, tax reports—the tedious stuff that kept us in business.

Rita took skills she had perfected at the press—organizational skills, grant-writing skills, and networking skills—and put them to use building creative space for women in the arts. There she flourished and blossomed and made a lasting impact in the art world, founding Women and Their Work, a visual and performance art gallery on Lavaca Street.

When Women and Their Work approached its thirtieth anniversary in 2007, Rita's friends and colleagues honored her accomplishments with a gallery event. An outreach email described Rita, with her sequence of names, in this way:

> She was born a Murphey, became a Jones by marriage and a Star-pattern by design. Rita Starpattern, founder and first director of Women & Their Work died of cancer in April 1996 at the age of 49. Rita Starpattern was an activist, a feminist and an artist whose inner wanderings were quirky, imaginative, funny and very intelligent. Rita . . . blended all her skills and desires with an entrepreneurial spirit when she undertook the creation of a cultural institution centered on women: Women & Their Work.

Rita's artistic space at Women and Their Work has survived for decades. BookWoman, a women's bookstore space established in 1975 as Common Woman, has survived as well, thanks to the efforts of Susan Post and a women's community that continues to honor its longevity. BookWoman is one of many women's bookstores featured in Kristen Hogan's *The Feminist Bookstore Movement: Lesbian Antiracism and Feminist Accountability*.

Five women created People's History in Texas in 1975, and that nonprofit is still going. Ragstaffer Glenn Scott was one of the founders, as was Melissa Hield, a graduate student at the time. Their first project was to research and publish the 1976 Women in Texas History calendar. People's History in Texas gathered oral histories of four women labor organizers from the 1930s and 1940s to produce a film documentary, *Talkin' Union*. They have continued to be citizen historians. They produced another documentary, *Stand-Ins*, about the 1960 effort to integrate movie theaters near UT. A three-part documentary about *The Rag* grew out of the first *Rag* reunion.

Some of the efforts begun by women morphed into nationally recognized institutions. Women organized in the mid-1970s to support women experiencing sexual and domestic violence. The Austin Rape Crisis Center began in 1974, and the Center for Battered Women began in 1977, the first rape crisis center and first shelter of their kind in Texas. Austin's Safe-Place, now the SAFE Alliance, traces its roots to these beginnings among women advocates.

Women at the People's Free Clinic housed in the Congregational Church became advocates for birthing centers, midwifery, and women's health centers devoted to reproductive choice. Others organized childcare centers like the Open Door, advocated for and helped develop certification standards for childcare, and now train childcare workers in early childhood education programs.

Women active in the Chicanx liberation movements pushed for the creation of Austin's Mexican American Cultural Arts Center. Sisters Lidia and Cynthia Pérez have kept the South American tradition of *peñas* going on Congress Avenue. Since 1981, La Peña has been a space supporting cultural arts and encouraging Latinx and emerging artists.

In 1978, following a visit to Austin by the antigay crusader Anita Bryant,

Pat Cramer helped found the Austin Lesbian/Gay Political Caucus. The group fought discrimination in Austin, effectively grilled political candidates, and provided support to those they endorsed. Any campaign they supported benefitted from their expertise with phone lists, mailings, and call banks. The caucus made its mark on Austin politics by mobilizing volunteers for the candidates they supported.

Velma Roberts founded an Austin chapter of the Welfare Rights Organization in 1969 and went on to found, with Dorothy Turner, the Black Citizens Task Force in 1974. They led community protests at the police station over police murders.

The energy of women founded and sustained activity on multiple fronts. For most of the women who led the way, it was women's liberation that opened the space for their talents.

Red River Women's Press

It was January of 1977 when Fly-By-Night became Red River Women's Press, a women's printing and graphics collective. Several of us held a retreat at Bastrop State Park, hammering out a new vision for a feminist press. A successful musical benefit in February laid the foundation for a move to a larger space. In June 1977, Red River Women's Press opened in a storefront at 908-C West Twelfth Street in the Enfield Shopping Center. Two presses were housed there, the smaller Multilith 1250 and a newly acquired and larger 1850 that could print eleven by seventeen.

We drafted a letter appealing to the community for business and financial support. We detailed a set of needs: a darkroom, improvements to electrical wiring, the purchase and shipping costs for a plate burner, and a paper folder from another women's press.

Our aspirations were bold: a viable, alternative, economic entity— a printshop that would be self-sustaining, an example to women and men of what women can do, a model for worker control, a union shop affiliated with the Industrial Workers of the World, a resource for training, and a community-responsive print facility. Our fundraising appeal was signed by nine women: Marce LaCouture, Kandy Littrell, Barbara Krasne, Lori Hansel, Gail Lewis, Rita Starpattern, Linda Evans, JoAnn Mulert, and me.

Printing at Red River Women's Press, c. 1978. *Photo by Mary Ellen LeBien.*

The Rag, January 25, 1977, cover.

With Rita Starpattern (left) accepting a donation for Red River Women's Press, 1977.

With Rita Starpattern's grant-writing expertise, Red River Women's Press was able to apply for and then administer a Comprehensive Employment and Training Act (CETA) grant. We trained printers Maria Flores, Angelina Mendez, and others. I was able to work full time at the press and to earn a very modest income.

We proudly placed our Industrial Workers of the World union bug on countless print orders—stationery, envelopes, leaflets, pamphlets, and posters (both offset and silk-screened). The shop employed two full-time staff and received CETA funds to train several interns. The movement provided a steady set of customers—law collectives, Brown Berets, the Austin Committee for Human Rights in Chile, Womenspace—as well as walk-in orders.

We silk-screened posters in the basement, where we had the copy camera. We could hang the posters to dry like laundry, with clothespins on two wires. I used my father's tools to drill holes in about one hundred clothespins. In the basement, we screened a poster to benefit the Texas Farmworkers and one that featured a poem JoAnn Mulert had written about the

Puerto Rican nationalist Lolita Lebrón. We silk-screened a poster of Anita Bryant, with a vicious hot-pink face, to publicize a counterprotest of her 1979 antigay event in Austin. We printed many posters in solidarity with Chile and one for the Brown Berets opposing the Town Lake boat races. Our working environment was feminist, but our posters and leaflets were frequently in solidarity with struggles other than women's liberation.

At Red River's West Twelfth Street location, the storefront backed up to a quiet Shoal Creek. Two presses, a Multilith 1250 and a Multilith 1850, paper supplies, typesetter, and light tables were at street level. Our copy camera, darkroom, and silk-screen shop were in the basement. That unobtrusive Shoal Creek flooded on May 25, 1981 (Austin's Memorial Day flood). Floodwaters inundated the basement, submerging the copy camera and rising about ten inches on the presses upstairs. I was working full time at UT, but I arrived to help dig Red River out of the mud.

Red River Women's Press poster protesting Anita Bryant's homophobia, 1978. *Nancy Collins, artist.*

Silt covered everything in the basement. The darkroom had the dank smell of disaster. Expensive boxes of negatives were now soggy, and chemical bottles were covered with muck. The copy camera had been hauled upstairs to the parking lot to be hosed down, not the best protocol for a copy camera. Red River Women's Press survived for a short time but closed later that year. Printing equipment that was still functional was donated to a Chicanx organization.

•　•　•　•　•

About the time the press opened up on Twelfth and Lamar, a battle took place further south on Lamar, at a music venue that Bobby and Martin began. They had recruited a volunteer collective and forged a vision for the new space. What transpired before the opening created deep divisions in the community.

A common throughline was that we thought a collective vision could overcome all things. We weren't careful or intentional with collective aspirations. We failed to spell out the vision, define the responsibilities, and acknowledge the property dynamics. I saw this happen at Thirty-First and a Half Street. The same failures played out in 1977 after I moved out. Bobby had signed the lease and loan papers for the venue in South Austin. The collective believed they had been promised decision-making authority, including the right to dispatch Martin for his authoritarian manner. Picketers were arrested, sides were taken, and divisions persisted.

Several of my friends and acquaintances who were part of the collective were arrested for trespass. I distanced myself from both Bobby and Martin for many years. I reconciled with Martin first. He was living sober with a mutual friend. I was touched that he made sure musician Julie Joyce, who died in a car crash in 1985, was honored in the *Austin American-Statesman* for her contribution to the music scene. When Martin was diagnosed with a terminal illness in 1992, I sang "Joe Hill" to him in the hospital. I reconciled with Bobby a few years later.

Solidarity with Chile

On September 11, 1973—the first 9/11—a military junta bombed the presidential palace in Santiago, Chile. President Salvador Allende died

PROTEST CIA ATROCITIES

in the Americas and around the world

wednesday

november 10th

7:30pm

LBJ Auditorium

William E. Colby, former director of the Central Intelligence Agency,
will be in Austin to defend policies of the C.I.A., Wednesday evening
at the LBJ Auditorium. His presentation is part of an international
conference, open to the public, on "Conflict, Order, and Peace in the
Americas."

ATTEND THE DIALOGUE Wednesday night to protest U.S.-C.I.A. atrocities
and intervention around the world, and to support national liberation
and resistance movements.

Important critics of C.I.A. strategies and U.S. economic domination
of Latin America will also speak at the conference. Among these is
Jacques Chonchol, former Minister of Agriculture with Salvador Allende's
Popular Unity government in Chile, now exiled since the U.S.-C.I.A.-
backed military coup in Chile in 1973.

sponsored at U.T. by New American Movement 

Leaflet calling for the protest of CIA atrocities, November 10, 1976, LBJ Auditorium, sponsored by UT New American Movement.

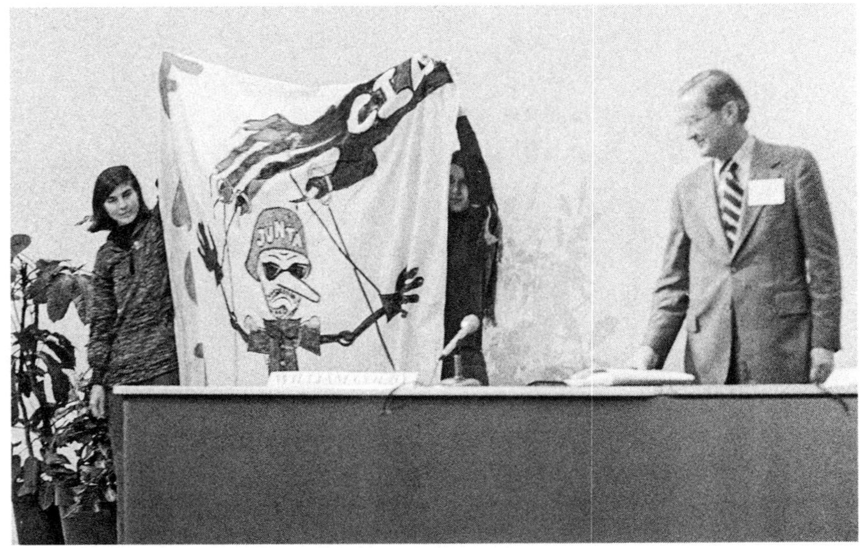

With Lori Hansel holding a banner next to CIA director William Colby, LBJ Auditorium, November 10, 1976. Daily Texan *photo by Howard Fomby, UT Texas Student Publications Photos, Briscoe Center for American History.*

there. Supporters of Allende's democratically elected Popular Unity government were targeted, killed, imprisoned, tortured, and sent into exile around the world.

In Austin, the Latin American Policy Alternatives Group (LAPAG) began a solidarity campaign. They picketed members of the military junta who had been invited to the UT campus. LAPAG mounted efforts to help get Cecilia "Che Che" Ubilla Garcia out of Chile. She had taught me conversational Spanish before the 1967 Chile exchange.

Renato Espinoza, who had come to UT with the exchange program, had returned to Chile with his wife, Loreto. He was imprisoned. A campaign was mounted to get both of the Espinozas out of the country and back to Texas. When they arrived back in Austin, Cam Duncan of LAPAG welcomed the Espinozas. He knew so much about Chile that Renato thought he was a frequent visitor. Cam told him that he had never been there; he had only read about it.

The Austin Committee for Human Rights in Chile, often referred to as

Protesters were removed from the LBJ Auditorium stage and our banner was confiscated, November 10, 1976. Daily Texan *photo by Howard Fomby, UT Texas Student Publications Photos, Briscoe Center for American History.*

the Chile Committee, got its start three years after the coup. It was 1976, only a month after an assassination on the streets of Washington, DC, carried out by intelligence operatives under orders from the head of the military junta, General Augusto Pinochet.

The junta targeted Orlando Letelier. He had been the Chilean ambassador to the United States during the Allende government. After the coup, he became a brilliantly effective ambassador for human rights, urging countries to impose sanctions against the right-wing military junta, which viewed him as a threat. Letelier was working with the DC-based Institute for Policy Studies. He was traveling in a car with a young colleague, Ronni Moffitt, when a bomb placed in their car exploded, killing them both.

Shortly after the assassinations of Letelier and Moffitt, I attended an event at the Bread and Roses community center. Renato's wife, Loreto, announced that the CIA director, William Colby, an architect of the Chilean coup, was coming to UT. "We've got to do something," she said.

So we did. Lori Hansel, Pat Cramer, and I stormed the stage at the

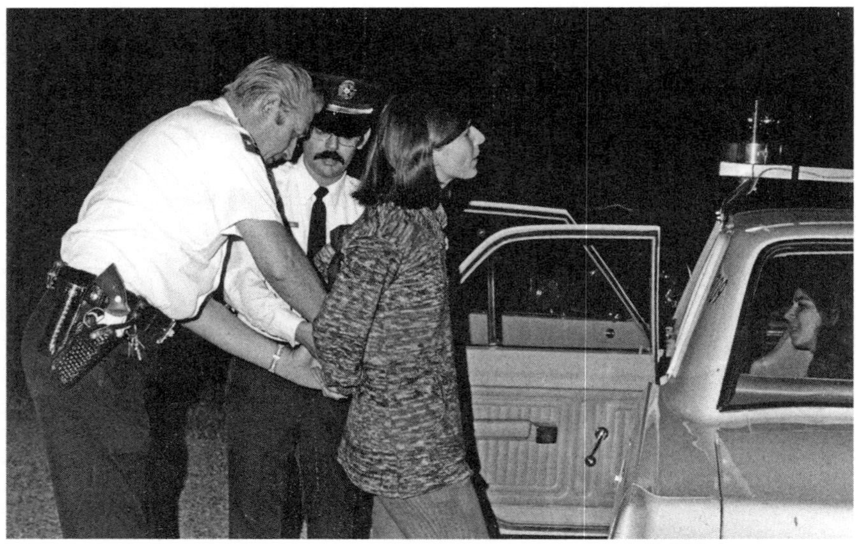

I was arrested for protesting at the UT event featuring CIA director William Colby, November 10, 1976. *Photo by Alan Pogue.*

Colby event and, to Colby's astonishment, unfurled a banner. The banner showed Uncle Sam's arm operating a puppet dictator and said, "U.S. Investment in Latin America." UT cops came flying onto the stage and hauled us away. We were singing "Solidarity Forever" loudly enough to be heard in the auditorium.

After we were removed, about six people at midrow in the middle center stood up, loudly asking for a moment of silence for Orlando Letelier and Ronni Moffitt. They were hauled away as well. Alan Pogue, intrepid *Rag* photographer, got a photo of Lori and me as we were marched into the UT Police car. Malcolm Greenstein, a movement attorney, scrambled to beat us to the city jail. He arranged for a judge to release us through a personal recognizance bond.

We formed the Austin Committee for Human Rights in Chile after this event. The Chile Committee was active from 1977 through 1989, when the first democratic presidential election took place in Chile after the military coup. In 1976, our literature carried this description of the Chile Committee:

Formed after an Austin visit by the late Orlando Letelier, the Committee continues the struggle to regain freedom for all political prisoners in Chile, to force the junta to account fully for all "disappeared" prisoners, and to end the repressive regime that continues to jail and torture the Chilean people. The Committee sponsors films, peñas, presentations, exhibits, letter writing campaigns, boycotts, and other activities designed to educate the public and increase international pressure on the Junta. Regular meetings are held at Bread and Roses Center, 2204 San Gabriel, on the first and third Sundays of every month at 7:30 p.m.

For more than a decade, those of us in the Chile Committee kept a community focus on solidarity with the people of Chile, educating the public about ongoing crimes of the junta, and always bringing attention to US complicity in overthrowing a democratically elected government. We brought speakers, films, musicians, and actors to Austin, organized cultural *peñas* in the tradition of the Chilean Peña de los Parra, put on art shows, and carried out boycott campaigns against Chilean products.

Through the Chile Committee, we became acquainted with the musicians of Inti-Illimani and Quilapayún. Inti-Illimani were in exile in Italy, and Quilapayún were in France. They used their musical talent to serve as ambassadors against the junta until they were able to return to Chile. I have a precious memory of Max Berrú of Inti-Illimani testing the microphone at the Armadillo, singing "Simón Bolívar," and making the walls reverberate. We staged events at the Paramount Theatre, UT's Batts Auditorium, Liberty Lunch, Raul's, and the Armadillo World Headquarters. We got to know many Chileans in this exile community when they came to perform or speak. We'd go to dinner with them, drive them around town, host gatherings.

It seemed as though our work was nonstop, but we always marked the anniversary of the coup, September 11, a day that came to have another sinister meaning in 2001.

My experience with the UT Chile exchange and my years with NACLA predisposed me for this solidarity work. At Red River Women's Press, we

Max Berrú of Inti-Illimani, discussing baseball with my son, Camilo, at Bartholomew Park in Austin. *Photo by Carlos Lowry.*

printed thousands of Chile Committee leaflets and flyers; the large silk-screened posters of the committee all credit the press as the printer.

By the late '70s, progressive political activism assumed and relied on women's full participation. The women's movement was a given. In many ways, the Chile Committee remains the gold standard of shared political work for me. It forged a number of lifelong friendships, as well as one enduring marriage.

Chile would occupy a large part of my heart. I met my husband through this work, and we've made three trips to Chile, the first right after we were married and two more with our children. Familiarity with Latin America would mark their lives as well. Inti-Illimani's Max Berrú stayed at our house several times when the band performed in Austin. When our kids were old enough to play ball at a PONY League park, Max asked to come see our son pitch. Baseball wasn't Max's sport. My husband kept up a running dialogue with him to explain balls, strikes, and why players were running or not running.

Compañero de Mi Vida

Romance crept into my life with a poster design. I was working at Red River Women's Press and didn't see it coming. Renato claimed all the credit as matchmaker.

Renato was a consummate organizer for solidarity, with keen radar for people with Chilean connections and talents that could be put to use. He found both attributes in Carlos Lowry, whom he met at a Latin American film screening on the UT campus. Renato attended Carlos's senior art show at Southwestern University in Georgetown, Texas.

Renato learned that Carlos had grown up in Chile and had been in Santiago during the coup. He knew Carlos had taken a job as a graphic artist in Dallas. Renato asked him for help with a design for the first big event of the Austin Committee for Human Rights in Chile in 1977. It was to be a screening of a movie by Chilean director Patricio Guzmán, *The Battle of Chile: The Fight of an Unarmed People.* The film footage had been smuggled out of Chile.

The fledgling Chile Committee had put its reputation on the line to mark the September anniversary of the military coup. A committee member, Alan Marks, had secured Austin's most prestigious downtown theater, the Paramount, for a movie premiere. We had to fill the theater or lose a huge deposit.

Carlos finished the poster design for *The Battle of Chile* and sent it to Renato on the Greyhound bus. It was beautifully done work, a black-and-white design on strong vellum paper measuring eighteen by twenty-two. Carlos had made two overlays for the colors. He placed crosshair marks at the corners of each layer so that the colors could be perfectly aligned. He included a small mock-up to show the three-color work with ink shades specified.

I was accustomed to the sloppy work of local activists—the kind of artwork that required hours to doctor crooked copy, white-out smudges, and fill in solids before a leaflet would look presentable. Carlos Lowry's work was that of a professionally trained graphic designer.

Later I heard the story of Renato's conversation with Carlos about the layout design. Chileans can practice the art of put-down with great glee. Renato called Carlos in Dallas to let him know that the committee members

Red River Women's Press poster for *The Battle of Chile* showing at the Paramount Theatre, September 10, 1977. *Carlos Lowry, artist.*

had received the design. Carlos asked if they liked it. The conversation, in Spanish, went like this:

> Renato: So, you call yourself an artist?
> Carlos: [*taken aback*] Yes.
> Renato: Well, the committee met and this really isn't up to our standards. That's why I'm asking.
> Carlos: Maybe I could make some changes.
> Renato: No, it's really not what we need. [*Long silence*]

Finally, Renato admitted he was joking. He invited Carlos to come to Austin to help silk-screen the posters. That's what brought Carlos through the doors of the Red River Women's Press storefront. Renato introduced him to me.

"Compañera Alicia," Renato said. That was Renato's typical greeting— the Spanish word for friend and comrade.

"Compañero Renato," I said, getting up to give him the customary embrace and kiss on the right cheek. This greeting had become commonplace in the Chile Committee. Next to Renato was a man with shoulder-length hair. He pushed his glasses up higher on his nose and reached out a hand. His deep-set brown eyes met mine.

"Aquí está Carlos," Renato said. "He's an artist. Un chileno. From Dallas. He did the poster design for *The Battle of Chile*."

"I hope you like it better than Renato did," Carlos said.

After that initial trip, Carlos came to Austin more frequently. He helped silk-screen the *Battle of Chile* posters. And then he came to the movie premiere in September. In the spring of 1978, he moved to Austin, leaving his graphic arts job in Dallas and enrolling in coursework for a teaching certificate. He found an opportunity to be a muralist instead, working with Interart–Public Art.

I fell in love with his talent and with his passion for Chile. We collaborated on leaflets and posters. We quibbled over his penchant for heavy black borders. I would explain how hard they were to print and line up straight on the page.

"It's begging for trouble," I'd tell him. "The rollers will track the ink. You can't get these vertical lines solid black."

Carlos Lowry printing Inti-Illimani posters, Red River Women's Press, April 1978. *Photo by Renato Espinoza.*

But then I'd turn up the ink-jets, move the press wheels away from the borders, and watch with Carlos as hundreds of leaflets spilled into the printer tray. The truth was that I fell in love with Carlos. Sometimes at night, I would sit beside his drafting table at his house watching him work on a poster. He'd absentmindedly say "X-Acto" like a surgeon might say "scalpel." He was entirely in the zone, his eyes fixed on the layout. I admired his skill. He admired my ability to turn his art into posters that found their way all over town.

We collaborated on leaflets that went into stores and onto telephone poles. The large silk-screened posters were sold at events, but ones on cheaper paper were also glued onto dumpsters. Carlos was the artist, but his twin brother, Paul, was my accomplice in putting up posters in the dead of night. Dressed in dark clothes, we'd sponge sweetened condensed milk onto the back of the poster, spread it against the metal dumpster, and then marvel at the staying power—often weeks, sometimes months.

• • • • •

I left my solitary life on Comal Street for one more experiment in communal living, this time on Avenue G. In a large two-story house with a front porch where my dog watched the street from a couch, I moved in with Carlos and several other housemates, including Glenn Scott, Richard Croxdale, Norma Helsper, and Margaret Joyal. Attorney Mark Bennett had a house in the back of the property. A few others came and went. One roommate was Iranian; another was from Pamplona, Spain.

We took turns shopping, cooking dinners, and cleaning. We threw parties that annoyed the elderly next-door neighbor. Carlos and I had separate rooms, but that was more of a technicality than the way we spent our time together. He began to work with Interart–Public Art. I kept working at Red River Women's Press. We both remained active in the Chile Committee.

Gentrification

One of the interns at Red River Women's Press, Angelina Mendez, was very active with the Brown Berets, and the printshop was closely aligned with eastside groups. Everyone in the Chile Committee took part in Brown Beret demonstrations to end the boat races on Town Lake. Brown Berets came to Chile Committee events. When the city proposed a neighborhood revitalization plan, it ignited a powerful East Austin opposition. That coalition work is very relevant today. The city buzzword was "revitalization." The result was gentrification.

In 1979, Carole Keeton McClellan was mayor of Austin. Under her watch, the city issued "Strategies for the Economic Revitalization of Central Austin," a slick publication with a target audience of developers. East Austin groups mobilized to protect the primarily Chicanx neighborhoods threatened by the city's economic development plan.

The groups included the Brown Berets, East Town Lake Citizens, El Centro Chicano, East First Advisory Board, Rainey Street Association, Govalle Association for Survival, and Barrio Unido, as well as staff of the newspaper *La Conciencia.* That long list is a tribute to the depth of community organizing going on at the time.

Carlos illustrated a comic book to accompany an explanation of revitalization. The comic, in both Spanish and English, describes the community impact of the city plans. It explains who would benefit, who would be harmed, and it details an action plan. It captures the spirit of a vibrant Chicanx insurgency.

Sometime later, Carlos and I went to a Carver Museum exhibition on the alliances between African American and Latinx groups in the 1970s. Several articles from *The Rag* were on display, mounted on large panels. We turned a corner and went down a hallway. There was the comic that Carlos had illustrated, a historical artifact credited to my papers at the Briscoe Center, the images enlarged and mounted for display.

It is a testament to what went before. East First Street had not yet been renamed Cesar Chavez. The Austin Convention Center and surrounding hotels were a developer's pipe dream. Juárez-Lincoln University, the Antioch campus, stood at 715 East First. A large mural by artist Raúl Valdez covered the front wall of the university. The building was razed to accommodate an International House of Pancakes. Gilberto Rivera, a Brown Beret activist, captured the demolition of the building and its powerful mural on film.

East Austin has now been penetrated and reshaped by Anglo gentrification. Neighborhood groups still mobilize to protect long-term residents from the onslaught of condos and the displacement caused by rising property taxes and opportunistic developers.

North of the Mexican American Cultural Center and west of Interstate 35 was a neighborhood called Rainey Street. During the yearly film, music, and interactive event called South by Southwest, Rainey Street throbs with activity, drawing tourists like a magnet. Where there were once homes, there are now bars and restaurants.

Comic opposing Austin gentrification plan, 1979. *Carlos Lowry, artist.*

Working Eight to Five: 1979—2004

HOW DOES SOMEONE WHO CALLED FOR SMASHING THE STATE find herself working for it for over two decades? Admittedly, some of our calls for the state's demise were tongue-in-cheek, like the naming of Sattva's "Squash the State Casserole." Still, explanations are in order.

Some might call it a concession for a rebel who had survived for years on lackluster pay from collective endeavors, temporary jobs as a secretary, and a smorgasbord of intermittent employment with Kelly Services, Ibid Inc., Southwest Educational Development Lab, Legal Aid, the Texas Civil Liberties Union, and the *Texas Observer*. It began with a clock. My biological clock's countdown was ringing in my ears. I wanted to have children.

Marriage

Together, Carlos and I left our communal setting on Avenue G for a more traditional one at the beginning of 1980. We moved into a home down the street from my father. The house was one of the stucco-covered cinderblock homes in Delwood 2 that my parents had bought in the '60s for my grandmother and great-aunt to live in.

I wanted children. I wanted to raise them in a committed, long-term relationship that I was hesitant to call marriage. I had tried to explain my feelings on marriage to my mother before her death. "It's a patriarchal institution, a property relationship; I don't feel that we need a legal document." I was involved in a relatively long-term relationship at the time. My mother looked at me as though I were speaking Greek and asked, "Why wouldn't he want to marry you?" I dropped the subject.

When Carlos and I were living together, I used much of the same explanation with my mother-in-law. She would have none of it as well. A few months later, she countered with a different argument. "We are coming to Paul and Cecilia's wedding, and we can't afford to make two trips from Chile." She threw down the gauntlet, so to speak, of practicality.

Reverend Bob Breihan, who would marry us, had Carlos and me come to a counseling session in the Methodist Student Center in 1980. He asked about our parents. I must have answered that my father drank, not that he was an alcoholic. He said, "You know alcoholism is a family disease. The whole family adapts to the disease."

I felt like someone had socked me in the gut. I thought my father's drinking affected him but not me. It was a revelation to think it might have shaped our family dynamics—that we all had a relationship with alcohol. I began at that time to look at literature describing the traits of adult children of alcoholics, shocked to recognize myself in those descriptions.

Carlos's twin brother, Paul, got married in Miami at the end of May in 1980. Carlos and I attended. It was a gala event. The newlyweds and my in-laws flew to Austin for our backyard wedding the following week. Reverend Bob Breihan and Reverend David Lowry, Carlos's father, did the honors. My sister knocked herself out with flower arrangements, table settings, and a several-tiered cake that she made. I wore a dress from a secondhand shop. We went to San Antonio for a honeymoon. It was on a different scale altogether than the Miami wedding a week before. But it stuck.

As we made plans, I felt the loss of my mother acutely. My sister, Alyce, and Loreto stepped up to help. Loreto cooked a giant Crock-Pot of paella for our wedding feast. Many of the guests at the small wedding were part of our Chile Committee inner circle, including David Ray, Gail Vittori, and Sue Higgins. An artist friend of Carlos, Herby Augustin, was there, as was

Carlos's uncle, Don Lowry. It was a small crowd, not well documented with photos. Everyone signed the wedding certificate.

Not many months later, at the People's Free Clinic, I found out I was pregnant. We told everyone. Immediately. Carlos and I went to Chile that Christmas. We went through Cuzco and by bus from Lima to Santiago. With Carlos's parents, we drove on an outing to La Ligua, Chile, after Christmas. I found a spot of blood when I used the bathroom. As we returned to the Lowrys' home, I was cramping, hoping against hope that nothing was really wrong. Back in Valparaíso that night, I began to bleed profusely. Carlos's parents took us to a hospital, where I miscarried. I was devastated. Miscarriage is quite common, but the experience is not often talked about. Nothing prepares you for the loss. The next time I got pregnant, we didn't tell a soul until I was very safely past the first trimester.

Children change your relationship with the world. Our son, Camilo, had just learned to say a few words when we went to a pizza restaurant with a large-screen television. A female gorilla filled the screen. He looked up and shouted, "Mama." Everyone laughed.

The Espinozas were an example to me of how to be in this world, how to have a family life, raise children, maintain friendships, work for a living, and do political work. They showed up as support when I returned from Chile after the miscarriage. When our son was born, Loreto shared her expertise on putting a baby stomach-down across your lap when the baby had colic. They showed up to celebrate our toddlers' birthdays, and even to cheer on one of our children at a high school graduation. When we visited their home near Barton Springs, we were treated to an art gallery of my husband's paintings across the walls of two rooms. They had a million family photos above their piano. I followed suit above our piano. The Espinozas survived the military coup. They supported their daughter through a trauma. They lived with sorrow and cancer. And they did it all with a formidable amount of grace. All the while, the Espinozas kept the story of Chile's democratic promise, repression, and resistance alive in Austin.

For me, making a home for children, working full time, and doing political work became the tapestry of the 1980s. It was a joy; it was a wild scramble for childcare, after-school care, and summer camps. It was a huge lesson in humility, and it provided a different perspective and appreciation of my own parents, particularly my mother, who had taken on the lion's share of home tasks while working. I could not have done this without a partner like Carlos.

Varsity Mural

The Varsity Theatre mural came to life the year Carlos and I married. Carlos put up scaffolding, defying the Texas heat and the determined ants that lived on the scruffy piece of dirt between the wall and sidewalk on West Twenty-Fourth Street at Guadalupe. He used the dark of night at home to project his design onto paper. He perforated the lines. In the day, he taped the newsprint to the wall and bounced a sock full of blue chalk against the paper. The faint blue whisper of his design would appear. It took his artist eyes to decipher the dust prints and transform them into the black-and-white scenes from movies.

The mural was a project of Interart–Public Art, and Carlos was hired by Tom Zigal—who now writes mystery novels—and paid with CETA grant funding. Carlos learned his mural skills from Carlos Osorio, the artist at Bread and Roses. He painted several more Austin murals and assisted another prolific artist, Raúl Valdez, on a few murals.

In the upper left corner Carlos painted a silhouette of Otis, the Varsity custodian, standing on scaffolding. Right after we were married, Otis asked Carlos if we were going to have children.

"Yes," Carlos answered slowly.

"Well, you're laying pipe aren't you?"

We laughed about Otis's way of phrasing it, but we were "laying pipe." In four years' time, there were two flesh-and-blood children: a boy, then a girl. As infants, then toddlers, they commanded much more attention than the mural. But the mural was always part of the family.

For ten years, the mural stood on the Varsity Theatre wall before the building was sold to Tower Records. It was rumored that Tower wanted to replace it. The community rallied the way it might for a kidnap victim. Friends and strangers signed petitions. A neighbor, Sam Griswold, led the charge. City council members and legislators wrote letters. Tower, faced with hundreds of faxed pages of signatures, relented and contacted Carlos to restore the entire mural.

Laura, Camilo, and Carlos posing by Marilyn Monroe, Varsity Theatre Mural, 1990. *Embree family photo.*

Again, the scaffolding went up. The original newsprint transfers were located, and a portion of the design was altered to accommodate architectural changes. The work of restoration began in 1990, this time with some hired artists. But Carlos's attention was required. It was a family affair. The kids are pictured at six and eight in front of the wall. Laura is mugging her precious smile next to Marilyn Monroe. Camilo is pictured, paintbrush in hand, working on Greta Garbo.

Public art doesn't always fare well on public buildings, and survival on privately owned buildings is even harder. When Tower Records left the building, it did not bode well. Taggers struck the mural. In 2011, new building owners repainted many of the movie scenes, moving them higher up and removing the design aspects of floodlights as well as the street-level detail of the Fellini clowns, Marilyn Monroe, Greta Garbo, and Humphrey Bogart.

A block north of the Varsity, Carlos painted another mural to commemorate the Methodist Student Center. The mural featured several scenes, including Sattva serving food, the Ichthus Coffee House, and the center's director, Reverend Bob Breihan, standing with Carl, the center's longtime custodian. A procession of students included my sister as a UT Orange Jacket and Heman Sweatt, the first African American UT law student, whose lawsuit helped dismantle the doctrine of "separate but equal." Carlos's mural did not survive, but we have a picture of our one-year-old son on the scaffolding with his father.

Working Eight to Five

I traded in my relative freedom for a normal workweek and the quotidian life of an eight-to-five state employee. In return, I received a stable paycheck and benefits. In this country, benefits are code for health care, accrued leave, and sick days. In most countries, these are not at the discretion of an employer. When I began working for the state, it didn't occur to me that a state pension was a possibility. That was in a far-distant future.

This trade I made had everything to do with children. I needed health coverage for prenatal, obstetric, and pediatric care for those children, and I wanted to have paid leave. Families still make decisions based on insurance coverage in ways that are unique to this country, but the benefits of benefits were not lost on me.

The University of Texas was the largest employer in Austin. In 1979, I applied for a job in the Spanish and Portuguese Department of UT. I was asked in the job interview if I would stay for a year. Mentally, I crossed my fingers behind my back, and I replied, "Yes." At that interview, I couldn't imagine staying an entire year. I stayed five—most of them working eight to five—with a view of the clock tower on the main mall.

The most stressful part of the job was "adds and drops." All undergraduates had to take a language course. Once enrolled, they would mob the corridor in the building trying to change classes to better suit their schedules. Sometimes there were legitimate work conflicts. Often, an undergraduate would look into our weary UT staff eyes, all of us having gotten up well before 8:00 a.m., and explain that they really couldn't get up that early. Zero sympathy showed on our faces. During adds and drops, anxiety nightmares always interrupted my sleep.

Students rushed to add classes as well as drop them. Since the demand for classes exceeded the allocated budget, the department had to provide staffing justifications to the College of Liberal Arts chain of command. Graduate students taught most of the undergraduate Spanish classes. They might have been writing dissertations on Pablo Neruda, but they were also trying to teach Spanish to freshmen and sophomores who were, in turn, often trying without enthusiasm to meet a language requirement.

In addition to my actual job, I worked with a fledgling union-organizing effort, University Employees Union. It was to grow into the Texas State Employees Union. In September 1981, we held a successful "soup line" on the Tower steps to highlight the university's low wages. We provided free soup and sang union songs. It was a stunt that got media coverage of UT's starvation wages. With several other women employees, we also formed an Eight to Five Organizing Committee to address the specific needs of women, focusing on childcare and publicizing successful organizing efforts among clerical workers in other states. I wrote *Daily Texan* guest viewpoints—one for Secretaries' Day called "Working Women Need Social Justice, Not Flowers and Lunch" and another on International Women's Day. I continued to work with the Chile Committee and mounted a poster for one of our events prominently above my desk.

A professor was diagnosed with a debilitating, and ultimately fatal, disease while I worked there. As it turned out, it was AIDS. It was my first awareness of the disease, before the epidemic began to take down friends.

•　•　•　•　•

Fairly soon at my job, I realized I could take time off work to attend a class. I scheduled an appointment with a liberal arts degree counselor to find out what I needed to finish my BA. The rules allowed me to finish under the degree plan in effect when I abandoned academia in 1967. I set about meeting requirements and using leave time to attend classes during the day. Tuition was still low, but out of my own pocket, and I didn't want to waste a penny. My professor father was delighted.

I took required classes in science and math. Already in my thirties, I couldn't help being an older-than-the-average-student pop-off. In a math class, stumped by a question, I wrote the answer commonly appearing in our textbook: "It is beyond the scope of the text." Fortunately, the math lecturer tolerated my pop-off nature.

I enrolled in a sociology course taught by Gideon Sjoberg, the eccentric professor whom I had known since the '60s. Sjoberg, attired in a dapper suit even in blistering summer heat, would walk every day from his West Campus home to his office, where he kept alarmingly late office hours. His office was filled with papers and books and could have qualified for a feature on *Hoarders*. Sjoberg let me enroll in an independent studies class with him in addition to a regular undergraduate class.

Gideon Sjoberg had eaten my teriyaki at Twelfth Street in Austin. When he was teaching at New York University, he had visited with Jeff and me there. Over the years, I had kept in touch, asking him to coffee at the Student Union. At our last meeting, I found Sjoberg aging into an almost ethereal presence, his skin nearly transparent. As always, he encouraged me to write my story. "It's a unique story. From a woman's perspective," he would argue. I am grateful for that counsel.

I took a folklore class from an iconic American studies professor, Américo Paredes. When I turned in a paper on feminism and witchcraft, Paredes wrote, "Ye Gods" in the margin. Perhaps my identification with witches went a little overboard. He gave me a good grade in the class. I managed to finish my BA in May of 1982 while eight months pregnant.

A photo with my delighted father shows me in graduation robes that obscure my shape but reveal somewhat swollen ankles.

"Gradual" School

I was attracted to a community and regional planning master's program offered in the UT Architecture School. I crammed for the math portion of the GRE and took it in the spring of 1982, literally crammed sideways into a lecture hall chair that didn't accommodate a pregnant belly. Both Sjoberg and Paredes wrote letters of recommendation for my graduate school application.

I was concerned that my near perfect GPA in the '80s would be an insufficient counterweight to my erratic GPA in the '60s, when I was majoring in radical politics. I was accepted and began graduate classes in January 1983 while raising a son who was six months old. I have always called it "gradual" school, a term I first heard used by a friend and Soeur Queen, Del Edwards.

In my work life, I found a wonderful set of colleagues in the Department of Spanish and Portuguese. We tiptoed around academic egos and weathered the occasional infighting that seems to plague most of academia. In this case the divide was Peninsular versus Latin American—Spain and Portugal versus their colonies. The people I worked with—mostly women—supported me through marriage, miscarriage, birth, and death. I count among my blessings a supervisor named Raquel Elizondo who allowed me and another young mother, Susan Luton, to job-share a position. We both maintained health benefits with twenty-hour-a-week employment. And we did a great job splitting up responsibilities with very little face-to-face contact and only rudimentary email.

When I earned a master's degree in community and regional planning from the UT Architecture School in 1987, it was a proud accomplishment. My father didn't live to see it.

My mother could correct grammar and spelling better than my PhD father, but she had never graduated from Shenandoah College. It was a family secret my father disclosed after her death, as though there was some family shame attached. Of course, that would be the attitude of a professor who specialized in overseeing graduate degrees. It was before

My father was so proud when I finally received my undergraduate degree, May 1982.
Photo by Carlos Lowry.

I got a BA, and I had dropped out of the university with an attitude. "If I need a degree, I'll print it," I popped off to my professor father. This wasn't an entirely hollow threat, since I was working as an offset printer.

Just ten years after my mother's death, my father died. In between those markers, I met Carlos, married him, suffered through a miscarriage, graduated with a BA, had a son, got into graduate school, and had a daughter. My mother would have been an outstanding grandmother, but she did not live to see this chapter in my life. My father died when our daughter was just seven months old.

I visited my father the evening before he died. He complained of indigestion. I brewed him peppermint tea. He spoke of a doppelganger, a ghostly presence in the room with him. His foreboding image should have alerted me. I should have known. The next day was my birthday. I walked the half block to his home, my infant daughter in a stroller. The door was unlocked, the house eerily silent, the tea untouched. I parked the stroller with our daughter in the hall, and I found him dead in his bed.

I was working and in graduate school, with two very young children, one still nursing, when I found myself grieving the loss of my father and, surprising to me, again grieving the loss of my mother. They were both gone from my life before I turned forty.

Childcare

We had idyllic years with toddlers, as idyllic as life can be when you are scrambling to work, to get through graduate school, and negotiate childcare. We hosted great, epic birthday parties with our friends. They became birthday parties with our children's friends as our children got older. Neighbors Sam and Patty Griswold had children who were the same ages as ours. The campaigns to move the airport had forged friendships with other neighbors.

A memory, shot through with the adrenaline of an emergency, stands out in my mind. Carlos was out with friends listening to his favorite punk performers. Camilo was two and Laura was an infant. She spiked a fever with an ear infection and her tiny body began to convulse. I called 9-1-1 and remember the patience of the operator. "Take her clothes off, sponge her down with a cool washcloth. Do you live in a house or an apartment?"

"An apartment," I answered. "No, a house." Soon I saw the flashing lights of an ambulance, and EMTs arrived at the door. Within minutes, four neighbors were there to see if they could help. With the cool washcloths and some baby Tylenol, Laura quieted down into a peaceful sleep. The ambulance and EMTs left. It was the instant arrival of neighbors that stood out. The calm of the emergency operator. Later I wondered how I could not answer the simple question, "Do you live in an apartment?"

We had a wonderful friendship circle, concentric rings of friends. Some with kids, some who would never have kids, some from the Chile Committee, some from our neighborhood campaign to move the airport. One friend was an outrageous punk rocker, Gary Floyd, with the band the Dicks. They broke many molds in the early '80s, with Gary as the gender-bending lead singer. Carlos was the loyal fan at performances. The first time I saw Gary, I watched the crowd's reaction when he went to the mic. It was electric. People crowded close, shouting the lyrics Gary had written, like "Rich daddy, I never had one." His memoir features a photo of him, with a Mohawk, holding our infant son, Camilo.

With children came childcare. Arranging for childcare, then after-school programs and summer camps, became a huge undertaking and huge cost. Now, childcare costs exceed college costs in a number of states.

The women's movement had advocated for universal childcare. The Comprehensive Child Development Act passed both houses of Congress only to be vetoed by President Nixon in 1972. The right wing argued that government shouldn't step into the role of parents. Of course, working parents continued to work, and massive changes occurred with workforce participation by women. Childcare costs rose steeply every decade.

That 1972 legislation would have met needs; it would have entitled working families to assistance. The women's movement that had pushed for it would have been permanently aligned with working-class needs. The main outcome would have been to relieve family stress while caring for children. The right wing won. Families lost. Children suffered.

When I was a working mother with toddlers, another major piece of childcare legislation almost passed. It was another lost opportunity. My master's thesis focused on local initiatives to increase childcare access, quality, and affordability. I discovered that other cities had created child-care coordinator positions to document municipal needs and mobilize city departments to respond. Some cities changed zoning provisions, and a few floated municipal bonds to expand childcare sites.

My graduate research, my activism, and my new experience as a working mother all came together with a local childcare action campaign in 1988. In the run-up to city council elections, our coalition sent out a candidate questionnaire and sponsored forums on childcare needs. We asked for a city childcare coordinator. The position was created but hasn't survived.

Through the campaign, I got to know Jackie Goodman, our children's childcare teacher, who later served on the Austin City Council; Jill McRae, who started the Open Door Preschool; and Gale Spear and Sandra Hamilton, who are still teaching childcare providers in the Child Care and Development Department of Austin Community College.

I got to know state childcare advocates at meetings of a United Way of Texas childcare working group. They produced well-researched pamphlets for Texas legislators on employer-assisted childcare, latchkey children, and the Texas childcare crisis. I served briefly on the Texas Employment Commission Advisory Child Care Commission and then the Texas Child Care Development Board, a board begun by Governor Ann Richards to investigate childcare opportunities when the state leased or bought buildings. That board lapsed when Governor George W. Bush failed to appoint anyone to the board.

Childcare needs are overwhelming at certain points in a family's life. Those needs take a back seat as children become eligible for public schools. Then families scramble for after-school and summer-care options. The stress on families is financial, but it takes an emotional toll as well. Without federal leadership and funding, heroic efforts at the local or state level will only provide a patchwork of services. The provision of affordable, quality childcare is as important as universal health care.

• • • • •

Our children went to Maplewood Elementary—where I had attended second grade. It had been segregated then. Our children's classmates were African American, Latinx, and white. The white parents were often older than others, a fact that drew comments from children's peers. "How come your parents are so old?" was a typical question. I served as cochair of the

Parent-Teacher Association one year. My Austin Women Workers friend Ruby Williams was the other cochair. We formed a good interracial partnership for an interracial school.

Our kids played PONY League baseball and softball at Bartholomew Park. It was generally idyllic and also ethnically diverse. Once, though, during a softball game, we heard a popping noise. We saw kids at the other fields ducking under bleachers. We herded our softball girls behind home plate to shield them from the street. One of our coaches was married to an Austin homicide detective. The detective was at the game. He suddenly transformed from dad in the bleachers to cop, racing off toward the danger, stopping cars. No one was hurt by what turned out to be a drive-by shooting by high school students marking the end of the school year. After the game I remember crossing the parking lot with our kids, acutely aware that we had no cover from gunfire. After they were home I went alone to pick up a video at a nearby rental store. I found myself staring at rows of VHS boxes. Every promotional image seemed to feature a gun.

When our children reached middle school and high school, we began to doubt that we had any parenting skills. Nothing can send you into a tailspin the same way that your children can. There were hard times and challenges we hadn't anticipated. Somehow, we are on the other side of most of that.

My mother, with her beautiful singing voice and gentle heart, had managed to survive cancer, work full time, sing in the church choir, raise two girls, keep our home together, and make meals seem effortless. When her father died in Connecticut, I was still in high school. She helped her mother and aunt resettle in Austin, taking on countless errands to support them. She was the kind of grandmother who would pile onto a sled with my sister's children. She died when I was only twenty-nine, before I had any clue about motherhood and its demands.

Move It!

When my parents bought their home in Delwood 2 in 1948, adjacent to the airport, the planes weren't very loud or frequent. As neighborhood kids, we could separate the strands of barbed wire along the fence, slip through, and use the airport as auxiliary yard.

My parents had no idea that Austin would grow fivefold. They could not have imagined that jet traffic would replace propeller traffic, or that flights would become nonstop during the days and nights, with both passenger and freight planes landing and taking off behind their home, rattling windows, and interrupting conversation.

When I say I live near the "old airport," newcomers to Austin don't know what I'm talking about. I'm learning to say "Mueller Development" instead. Recent Austin arrivals have no idea how lengthy and heated the debate about moving the airport was. They haven't heard about the coalition of central and East Austin residents who worked for years to relocate the airport. Even most of the residents of the Mueller Development are unaware of the visionary plan that citizen advocates put forward in 1984. That plan has guided the redevelopment of the seven-hundred-acre airport site.

I became a cochair of Citizens for Airport Relocation (CARE) in 1986. More than fifteen neighborhood associations in central and East Austin were affiliated with CARE. These included J. J. Seabrook, Pecan Springs, Springdale, Ridgetop, Cherrywood, Delwood 2, Wilshire Wood–Delwood 1, Windsor Park, and others.

An electoral effort to move the airport narrowly failed in January 1985. We lobbied city council for a second election that would spell out an alternative location. We kept pressure on the City of Austin to relocate its aviation. Our arguments were (1) that the seven-hundred-acre site was too small to handle projected passenger growth; (2) that it was too dangerous, with a single runway only seven thousand feet long; and (3) that it was too noisy, affecting twenty-seven thousand people who lived within the sixty-five-decibel day-night average noise level. Dangerous noise levels affected ten thousand households, thirty-nine churches, and seven schools.

The intensity of neighborhood battles can leave scars. I was in the thick of a colossal municipal fight that lasted for more than a decade. We went to neighborhood association meetings and candidate forums; we showed up at city hall to testify, wearing "Move It!" shirts and buttons. I became adept at fashioning a three-minute speech, coming in for a landing, so to speak, before the city council buzzer. We worked with neighborhood associations to walk thousands of leaflets door to door each month. We put bumper stickers on our cars.

Rick McCulley, Rick Krivoniak, Sam Griswold, Mark and Joanne Smolen, Mike and Laura Eisenberg, David Van Os, Willie Lewis, Roger Taylor, and so many more worked tirelessly. Memorably, Roger would drive to city hall with a large model airplane in the bed of his pickup and play jet engine noise over speakers.

We built a formidable coalition of central and East Austin residents, and we turned out record numbers to vote in the November 1987 election. I was at a Pecan Springs voting site on the day of the election. The county had underestimated the turnout and had only two voting machines in place. We stood outside the polling place urging people to remain, telling them they could vote if they were in line before the polls closed at 7:00 p.m. We were jubilant in our victory and celebrated the win at Holy Cross Church on East Eleventh.

Only those of us involved can know the sense of betrayal we felt when the city failed to move forward after the 1987 vote. An ally in our fight, State Representative Wilhelmina Delco, sponsored legislation to soundproof affected schools. It was meant to force the city to move forward. The legislation passed and several schools were soundproofed, but the city didn't act. Our "Move It!" yard signs now read "Build It!" Some of us filed lawsuits in state and federal courts. I was a plaintiff in one of those lawsuits.

Four years dragged by before an announcement was made in 1991 that Bergstrom Air Force Base had been recommended for closure. Another year passed before the bonds authorized in 1987 would be reauthorized for use at Bergstrom. Those of us who had fought to move the airport wanted a site that could be zoned appropriately to limit sound pollution. That didn't happen for the Montopolis and Del Valle neighborhoods bordering Bergstrom. It was a bitter pill to swallow, even though almost everyone who was not directly involved with our campaign assumed we were jubilant with the outcome.

Twelve years passed after our electoral victory before Mueller was closed as an aviation facility. The freight activity moved first. In the summer of 1999, the last passenger flight landed at Robert Mueller Airport and passenger service opened at Austin-Bergstrom International Airport. That night, I joined Reverend Sid Hall and a fellow plaintiff from the lawsuit we had filed and finally dropped. We sat in chairs in the parking lot of Trinity United Methodist Church and watched as that final flight came in directly over our heads. The plane then lined its wheels up directly over Ridgetop Elementary, making its descent over Interstate 35. It had been a costly fight, and the result was not the one we had voted for.

For some reason, the jackrabbits we would often see in the adjacent airport property left. I always thought that their giant ears must have gone deaf. There are a few foxes, raccoons, possums, and an occasional skunk. Now I live next to the Mueller greenbelt, not the runway. They built the Dell Children's Medical Center of Central Texas first. They allowed neighbors to tour the hospital before it was open to patients, to see the smaller beds and the child-size entrance to the gift shop. I got up early the day they closed the northbound freeway to bring young patients from Brackenridge Hospital to the new facility. I waved my greetings.

Sometimes I hear neighbors who have just moved into Delwood 2 complain about the commercial activity behind our homes. Sometimes I hear the racket of helicopters as they land or take off from the children's hospital emergency deck. I don't complain.

In ways I did not anticipate, the Mueller Development accelerated gentrification in East Austin. It has provided affordable housing, but not enough of it. It has also added a wonderful greenbelt and several parks that draw a diverse population.

I recently stood in a checkout line with a fellow "Move It!" stalwart, Sam Griswold. We were in an office supply store located on a spot that had been desolate tarmac a few decades earlier. We were cracking jokes. "Didn't this used to be an airport?" Probably very few people in the checkout line knew what we were talking about. It's rare for a city to get an opportunity to transform a seven-hundred-acre site in its midst. That's what Austin achieved through our efforts.

Child Support

My master's degree prepared most of my classmates for jobs in municipal land use planning. I had concentrated on planning for public services. I applied for one city job that I did not get. A friend in the planning department told me that my high-profile role in a campaign to move the airport was not considered an asset. As it turned out, not getting the city job was for the best.

In 1988, I was working for labor lawyer David Van Os when I saw a governor's job bank posting for a temporary planning job in the Texas Attorney General's Child Support Division. My master's thesis had been on municipal planning for childcare. I knew a lot about childcare and nothing about child support. But with a graduate degree in planning, I landed the job as a four-month temp, and I was there for seventeen more years. On my first walkabout in the office building at 210 Barton Springs Road, I saw familiar faces, including attorneys I knew from Travis County Legal Aid and a couple of fellow antiwar activists.

My boss was Raine Lee, a bright, inspirational attorney. She had come to Texas at the invitation of Casey Hoffman when the firebrand attorney general Jim Mattox named Hoffman as IV-D director.

First, I had to learn the acronyms. For those unfamiliar with the alphabet soup of welfare, Title IV-A of the Social Security Act established welfare payments. Title IV-D of that act requires states to establish child support enforcement operations to recoup costs of welfare from an absent parent.

Second, I learned about the interplay of welfare and child support. When I came to work in the program, the average Texas welfare grant was $184 for a family of three, about one-third the amount of an average welfare grant in New York. In a high-grant state, a state paying $300 or more for a family of three, a family can receive both welfare and child support. But in Texas, child support, as added income, can make a family ineligible for welfare, plunging them into a financial tailspin when child support is not regular.

Child support was fairly new to the Texas Attorney General's Office. Jim Mattox was a populist Democrat who ran for attorney general as the "people's lawyer." He had a reputation as a bulldog and a fierce antitrust and consumer-protection advocate. In 1983, just beginning his first term, he made a decision that altered the entire trajectory of the Texas child support program.

Child support had been housed in the Texas welfare agency, still a common practice throughout the nation. A Texas legislative committee, focusing on the program's poor performance, characterized it as a neglected stepchild. Legislators recommended that the Texas Title IV-D functions be moved to another agency, where the program would command more attention. The comptroller respectfully declined. Attorney General Mattox, to the dismay of his close associates, agreed to take it on.

Prevailing wisdom was this: child support was a nest of rattlesnakes, a no-win. Enforcement work rarely made the custodial parent happy, never made the absent parent happy, and the state, although soon to become the nation's second most populous, had a pitiful track record. But Attorney General Mattox was nothing if not stubborn. Furthermore, raised by a single mother, he knew the importance of child support.

Mattox took over the operations of child support on a provisional basis. After two years, the program transferred officially to the attorney general, where it was viewed as law enforcement. Texas developed a statewide standard for services, and with a slew of family lawyers involved, Texas developed standard pleadings that dealt with both support and custody. Many states would rely on a state agency to oversee child support and county welfare agencies to deliver services. Texas escaped this kind of balkanized delivery, making it much easier to set statewide standards and achieve statewide goals.

I was still new to my temporary job when a legislative affairs attorney stumbled upon information that would ultimately transform child support. The state welfare agency was not going to spend some of its appropriation. Retained collections (recouped welfare) and the whopping federal matching funds that state money could draw down were going to go unspent.

This legislative liaison proposed that the attorney general stake a claim on these retained collections in exchange for improved output. It was a chance to vastly increase program resources. It was a planner's dream. My section set to work on a three-year plan. It was a modest document on legal paper delineating costs of adding personnel, equipment, and offices, with one-, two-, and three-year goals to increase program results.

In 1988, 731 field staff in thirty field offices collected just under $100 million for the year. The plan would more than double staffing, with 1,590 deployed in fifty-seven field offices, and it promised huge gains in paternity establishment and a threefold collection increase by the third year.

The most delicate parts of the proposal were the promised results. Field staff convened to hear the three-year-plan presentation. The regional administrators in the field included many big Texas guys, including a former pro football player who had come over from Bob Bullock's comptroller ranks and a quintessential West Texan who flew his private aircraft in for state meetings; the West Texan occasionally opined that he was closer to the capital of New Mexico than to Austin.

The forecasts and promises were laid out. A stony, treacherous silence ensued. Finally, the silence was broken by the voice of a Houston regional manager, a wiry army veteran who had served in Vietnam. "What have you been smoking?"

It was a classic state-office-versus-field-operations moment. Despite the reaction to what were perceived as wildly unattainable goals, the regional administrators were very savvy when it came to resources. They knew they were being given an opportunity to triple staff, even if they had to triple output. They accepted the challenge.

The plan was submitted to the Texas Legislature in October 1988. It laid the groundwork for a remarkable transformation in the Texas Child Support program. I learned a valuable lesson. Public resources plus planning can translate into results. Another lesson learned was about enlisting support from the field.

The Child Support Division collected $18 million the first year it was housed at the Attorney General's Office. By 1990, only six years later, collections totaled $180 million, a tenfold increase. In 2004, the year I left the agency, the program collected $1.6 billion.

I became an expert at national rankings, tracking Texas's improvement from twenty-fifth in the nation in 1983 to the nation's top collector. California, with a much larger population but a balkanized program run through county offices, was collecting less than Texas when I left. As head of strategic planning, I was able to have a front-row seat to transforming a public-sector service relied upon by millions of children.

The next shoe to drop was the election of President Bill Clinton and Vice President Al Gore, sworn into office in 1991. The Personal Responsibility and Work Opportunity Reconciliation Act (PRWORA) passed in 1996. It was more commonly known as welfare reform.

PRWORA was a "bipartisan victory" and a lousy acronym. Its impact on needy families is still a matter of furious debate. But in terms of sheer page count, most of the legislation focused on child support enforcement. It is true that welfare can be avoided if the income of absent parents is reliable. But that assumes a growing economy producing stable jobs, with living wages and benefits. You can't garnish wages for child support if there are no wages; you can't produce reliable child support if wages are intermittent or employers are scrambling to off-load wage earners in favor of contract employees.

I was intrigued by another aspect of the new welfare reform legislation, a mandate to overhaul federal incentives for child support. That was right up my alley of expertise, another planner's dream.

I was dispatched to a series of meetings in Washington, DC, that included an array of stakeholders—representatives from federal, state, and county government; advocates for the rights of children; mothers, fathers, and social and economic policy researchers. I loved it.

Because I knew our state stats and had studied Texas's relative standing among the states, I knew which measures could be easily tracked and how Texas was likely to fare relative to other states. Child support lends itself extremely well to quantifiable output measures: collections, new child support orders, and new paternity establishments. New outcome measures would require the program to scramble to show improvement. It would be a hard sell to the field staff. What wasn't?

After the challenge of overhauling performance measures came the inevitable challenge of explaining them to the field staff. The field did not want an outcome measure pegged to children born to unmarried parents in Texas. "We have no control over that," they argued. But an in-hospital paternity acknowledgement program was getting off the ground, and staff began to see its value. Paternities established in court and those acknowledged in the hospital could both be counted against the births to unmarried parents.

Field staff did not like many of the newly minted outcome measures, but I knew what they would like: collections for both former and current welfare recipients would be given equal weight. That changed everything for Texas.

It required an arduous effort to overhaul the reporting system to capture the new performance measures accurately and down to the field office level.

I learned a lot about business requirements documents, how to involve all of the right stakeholders—field managers, field attorneys, state office staff from training, policy, and information technology. We had to drill the reporting down to the field office level for every single performance measure. In the end, the field staff did what they were always able to do, they delivered. Texas earned the largest share of federal incentives the first year that they were awarded.

After working under the "people's lawyer," Jim Mattox, I worked under three more attorneys general. Democrat Dan Morales was elected as attorney general in 1990 when Mattox ran for governor. Morales was reelected in 1994. The Morales administration split child support field office staff into legal and enforcement chains of command; it took months to put Humpty-Dumpty back together again. Attorney General Morales oversaw a successful $17 billion tobacco settlement. But after he left office, Morales was indicted on several counts. He was charged with fraudulently approving private attorney fees associated with the settlement. He entered into a plea deal and served time in prison.

During the Morales era, the program stuttered through a federal mandate to overhaul the computer system. The contracts for system work were lucrative, and Texas outsourced the work to Andersen Consulting. The new computer system stumbled so badly in its initial rollout that legal filings plummeted. Field staff scrambled for months to make the system work. A million cases, legal filings, income data, financial history, and interfaces with multiple agencies required millions of lines of code. It was complex. Like health care—who knew?

In 2001, I was in transit to the child support office when the 9/11 news began to break. As the magnitude of destruction began to dawn on very somber staff, we managed to hold a scheduled meeting on a systems overhaul. After the meeting, everyone drifted toward available news sources.

John Cornyn, a Republican, had been elected attorney general in 1998. Shortly after he took office, I was told to supervise a former Focus on the Family employee so that he could learn the program. When Cornyn left to fill out the US Senate term of Phil Gramm, the FBI came to question me about that employee. He was going to DC with Senator Cornyn, and they needed to make sure he wasn't a security risk. As someone with a '60s and '70s FBI file, I found it deeply ironic. Greg Abbott, who was elected attorney general in 2002, was the last attorney general I worked for.

I learned my share of acronyms in child support, becoming fluent in the languages of the state Legislative Budget Board, the federal Office of Child Support Enforcement, and field operations. My friendships with remarkable colleagues helped me get through tough days of audits, Sunset Commission reviews, fiscal note requests, and countless reorganizations. And those friendships helped me get through personal hard times as well.

I wrote a poem to read at my retirement party on September 1, 2004. The state fiscal year had just drawn to a close. The poem is filled with the alphabet soup of state government and references the Region Seven field manager, Bill Brown.

FAREWELL

At the end of the fiscal year
All through the state
Field staff is asking
Why reports were so late.
What did we collect?
How many new pats?
Is current support up?
Or did it stay flat?
Now field Ops collects
In a matter of days
What took a whole year
When I came to this place.
We have no paternities
West Texas said.
Only jackrabbits out here
And even those may be wed.
Will I miss the audits?
Will I miss BRDs?
No, but I'll miss the people
Throughout CSD.

To quote from Bill Brown
As he often does say:
It's about feeding children
At the end of the day.[31]

    •   •   •   •   •

Child support was referred to by many in the Attorney General's Office as law enforcement. I was able to use that to my advantage once in the '80s. I was standing in the checkout line at the local HEB grocery store when I noticed that the man I stood behind was none other than "red squad" detective Lieutenant Burt Gerding. He had taken notes at SDS meetings, kept files on us, and driven his unmarked police car past our apartments. He left the Austin Police Department in the '70s, moving on to a private security job. For years, he had enjoyed telling me that he had infrared surveillance photos of several of us skinny-dipping at Hamilton Pool. He had even asked if I wanted to see them. It was time for a bit of payback.

I got his attention. "Burt Gerding, it's Alice," I said. He turned toward me, somewhat startled, and asked what I was doing now. Without missing a beat, I said, "I'm in law enforcement."

The color drained from his face. He was speechless. I savored the moment as I watched him wonder how his world had been so thoroughly upended. Then I told him that I was working in the Attorney General's Office in child support enforcement. We were enforcing laws.

Y2K

The much-heralded millennium finally arrived. Carlos and I walked with our teenage daughter, Laura, along Congress Avenue in downtown Austin on December 31. The wide street had been closed to traffic. Several bandstands were set up, a few blocks separating them. Laura and I bought eye masks adorned with peacock feathers. We looked as though we were at a Mardi Gras ball. We got compliments while hidden in celebratory anonymity.

The federal Office of Child Support Enforcement went through a paroxysm of Y2K phobia. In retrospect, I think the tech companies such as Lockheed Martin and Andersen Consulting had sold the federal government a bill of goods. Every state had to hire consultants to ensure that their computer systems weren't going to implode. Billions of lines of code were scrutinized for potential disaster. Federal auditors came to Texas for a Y2K drill to see if we could handle our caseload of one million with the equivalent of Big Chief writing tablets. I was there as field staff supplied the correct answers and passed the audit with flying colors.

For New Year's Eve, Carlos and I booked a room in the Austin Motel, an old motel that had become a trendy spot on South Congress. On January 1, I had to go in to the state office in southeast Austin at 4:00 a.m. Each field office was required to have skeleton staff on duty, ready to receive our calls.

"Lubbock, do you have electricity? Is your HVAC working? Can you access your computer system? Is caseload data available?"

"Houston, do you have electricity?"

All was well with child support across the Lone Star State.

The century mark ushered in new challenges. Our children left for college. We all acquired college debt via their loans and Parent PLUS loans—in amounts we were unprepared for.

Retiree Activist: 2004—2020

A LARGE ANTIWAR COALITION CAME TOGETHER IN AUSTIN during the run-up to the war in Iraq, turning out thousands to demonstrate at the state capitol. I began to meet with this coalition in 2003 while still working at the Texas Attorney General's Office, but retirement gave me more time and less fear of blowback from bosses.

I found Code Pink through the antiwar coalition. This "Women for Peace" organization is known for its bold agitprop and street theater. Code Pink has both a national and an international presence. You can identify them at congressional hearings by their unfurled banners and pink placards. Code Pink was willing to act up, being clever with costuming and creativity and audaciously disruptive in opposing US wars and occupations.

In Austin, Code Pink women—and one man—showed up over and over again. Code Pink wore black funeral attire, faces veiled, to stand solemnly with a black wreath for the war dead; they marched with caskets for the dead as the numbers mounted; they showed up as "pink police," placing crime scene tape across the doors of military recruiters; they dropped

With Lucia Duncan at the 2009 MLK march in Austin. *Photo by Carlos Lowry.*

Marching with Jim Turpin, left, and an Iraq war veteran at the 2010 MLK march in Austin. *Photo by Carlos Lowry.*

banners from balconies and highway overpasses, rained "Warbucks" dollars down on crowds, and launched antiwar banners on helium balloons in hotel atriums where war proponents spoke. They dropped pink slips from parking garages in front of the federal offices of senators and congressmen who supported the wars in Afghanistan and Iraq.

They joined the San Antonio International Women's Day marches, where Code Pink feathery peace signs were always a big hit. With the best of crafting and glue-gun skill, Code Pink's Heidi Turpin could transform a drab wire with brilliant pink boas—Martha Stewart–level skills put to use against militarism. Still a full-time state employee, I began my transition to retiree activism with Code Pink.

Second Coming of Age

First you come of age, and then you age. That's if you are lucky. My birthday put me on the cutting edge of the baby boom. I found myself on the cutting edge of my generation in another way when my knees wore out. Who knew they had "use by" dates? I had double knee replacement surgery in 2005. It was a lesson in humility and in the benefits of health care coverage.

For five years, cartilage had collapsed, until bone sat upon bone on the inside of both knees. I gamely tried glucosamine, then injections of Hyalgan, a sterile mixture made from rooster combs. But the cartilage didn't regenerate. Mobility ebbed away in increments.

Vioxx quieted the pain for nearly three years, until it was abruptly taken off the market. I had just filled a prescription, paid a thirty-five-dollar copay, and another fifty dollars for my annual prescription copay, when the painkiller was pulled from the market. I was out nearly three dollars a pill when I heard news reports say the drug was dangerous. The bottle sat on my shelf for a long time, a reminder of the coy relationship between the Food and Drug Administration and the pharmaceutical industry.

I found an orthopedic surgeon with lots of experience and hoped he had called his patients about the Vioxx news. The nurse studied my dismal X-rays. On my second visit, she greeted me as the "fifty-nine-year-old with the seventy-nine-year-old knees." After warning me of increased risks for infection and blood clots and recording my desire for bilateral knee replacement, the surgeon agreed to go forward. I was terrified, but I couldn't sit out the rest of my life. As one friend put it, I didn't have a leg to stand on.

People asked why my knees had failed. I began to make up interesting answers: too many picket lines, an injury sustained during the 1968 Chicago street clashes. I don't know what caused both knees to crater. But they did. I had X-rays to prove it.

Since it had become the age of medical privacy restrictions (known as HIPAA) and the era of controversy over "persistent vegetative states," I updated legal documents, permitting my husband to pull various plugs or tubes if necessary. I have a morbid tendency. I imagined that I would try to run from the gurney as they rolled me into surgery. Then I remembered that I couldn't run.

The surgery went well, with experts handling anesthesia, gluing titanium devices into "resurfaced" bones, and closing incisions. I was rolled into recovery, hooked up to catheters, intravenous tubes, and femoral anesthetics. My legs were bound in support hose, plastic devices that filled with air and deflated, blue wraps that circulated cold water from a cooler of ice. But the most exotic contraption was a continuous passive motion machine (CPM), which nurses switched from leg to leg. Resting on the CPM device, my leg was moved back and forth, flexing and extending the joint.

The second day, I was introduced to rehab. Mike arrived to make me stand upon my two tortured joints. He was the first in a series of physical therapists whom I grew to love and hate. I dubbed him Merciless Mike, Malevolent Mike, Malicious Mike. He played along and told me that the only history courses required of physical therapists are about the Spanish Inquisition. Even the surgeon used the term "physical terrorists."

These physical therapists were well trained and universally unimpressed with whining. Their mission was to force motion back into swollen, painful joints. After four days I was released from the hospital with a walker and a CPM machine for our home. It is a long road back to mobility and range of motion, a process guided by physical therapists, not surgeons. Recovery depends upon following the advice of people who speak muscle and tendon. Barbie the Bruiser was a marathon runner. A. V. came to his profession via a horrific traffic collision. Rigo, the pool therapist, worked in the weightless world of water. Rachel, the intern, took careful notes.

If I casually mentioned my fear of walking without a cane in crowds, she would follow behind me, pushing my back or side without warning so that I practiced recovering my balance.

Six weeks after the surgery my vanity was challenged by five-inch vertical scars on my knees (seven inches when bent), but I could walk without a cane. My confidence and endurance grew. I could imagine visiting a museum and staying on my feet for more than an hour, walking Austin's hike-and-bike trail again. I credit the expertise of physical therapists. I had insurance. My copays mushroomed, but I had coverage. My knees were back to picket-line strength.

• • • • •

In August of 2005, our children planned a twenty-fifth wedding anniversary. It was at my friend Bobby Nelson's home. Carlos's mother was there. Even Bob Breihan, who had married us, came with his wife. One of my daughter Laura's friends was impressed when a few women stripped down to their underwear to dunk themselves in Bobby's small pool. We had a great celebration of a quarter century of marriage, even longer if you dated it back, as we did, to our first night together before the Inti-Illimani concert at Armadillo World Headquarters. It's easy to remember the date because the poster hangs on our wall. Saturday, April 23, before the Sunday solidarity event that we had spent the two previous months promoting.

Rag Reunion

We wanted to gather *The Rag*'s community together. But we did more. We succeeded in securing *The Rag*'s place in history. We organized the first reunion for *The Rag* to take place at the end of August in 2005, unfortunately coinciding with Hurricane Katrina. That kept Mary Walsh, a former *Daily Texan* editor, from attending because she was dispatched by her employer, CBS, to the Gulf Coast.

The instigator of the 2005 reunion was Alan Pogue, the Vietnam veteran turned *Rag* photographer, who suggested a photography exhibition. The fact that it was technically the thirty-ninth anniversary of *The Rag*'s founding was a detail that didn't seem to bother anyone.

Alan's partner at the time was Austin attorney D'Ann Johnson. Her home, known as the Old School, was a perfect venue—a tall-ceilinged, historic Greek Revival house on East Eleventh. The Old School accommodated the photography exhibition and a multiday gathering. Alan took a group photo on the beautiful grounds of the historic residence.

Pulling out all the stops, a small planning committee organized a three-day event, a veritable three-ring circus. I made a habit of calling Thorne Dreyer in Houston to give him updates on our discussions. In addition to the photo exhibition, we helped curate an art show at the South Austin Museum of Popular Culture and organized a musical event at Threadgill's, emceed by the artist, musician, and stand-up comic Kerry Awn. Kerry, younger brother of *Rag* founder Dennis Fitzgerald, was a Houston high school student when he drew his first cover for *The Rag*.

People's History in Texas mobilized to capture film interviews in an upstairs room at the Old School. Richard Croxdale and Glenn Scott, who came to the paper in 1974 and stayed until its demise, spearheaded the documentary project. Interviews took place against a background collage of *Rag* covers. A thin brushing of coffee made the collage look like vintage newsprint. Our daughter, Laura, and Lucia Duncan, daughter of former *Space City!* staffers, helped Jim Cullers with filming. The result was a priceless oral history, later edited into a three-part movie.

Ragstaffers arrived from far and wide, including Germany and Canada. The *Austin Chronicle* heralded the events with a cover story, relying on the written memories gathered on a Yahoo! site via Ragstaffer Bill Gordon's contact list. Alan's photos, along with those of Danny Schweers, graced the *Austin Chronicle* cover and the story by Cheryl Smith.

The first night of the reunion, Hunter Ellinger and his partner, Mary Parker, brought a scanner to the Old School to capture photos that reunion-goers had brought with them. As we met during the day at the Old School, I took notes. I loved the camaraderie in the room, the sense of community and purpose. I suggested a blog to keep us in touch into the future. My raison d'être instigated a blog by a former *Rag* writer, Richard Jehn, which morphed into *The Rag Blog* and a sponsoring nonprofit. No doubt fueled by caffeine and the adrenaline rush in the room, I wrote this suggestion in the October 1, 2005, notes I shared: "I have loved some of

With, from left, Thorne Dreyer, Scott Pittman, Jeff Nightbyrd, and Mariann Wizard at a 2005 *Rag* reunion. *Photo by Carlos Lowry.*

the WRITING lately. Even more, I have enjoyed the THINKING behind the writing. Some of what has been written in the Yahoo group could easily be tweaked into ARTICLES aimed at a general public. What if we tried to do a bloggish Online Rag . . ."

The Rag Blog continued, and with it, *The Rag's* lore. Thorne relocated to Austin, reinventing himself after a rough patch in Houston. We incorporated a nonprofit, the New Journalism Project, paying Thorne a modest stipend for editing *The Rag Blog*. Thorne launched another media front. He began to host a weekly interview show, *Rag Radio*, on KOOP Radio, 91.7 FM. Now, four hundred radio shows later, the interviews are being made available online at the Briscoe Center for American History, and Thorne Dreyer is editing a manuscript that will include the show's history and selected transcripts.

The New Journalism Project sponsored events and speakers. Tom Hayden, Mike Davis, Carl Davidson, Bernardine Dohrn, and Bill Ayers, from SDS days, spoke at events and were interviewed on the radio. Some

SDS reunion, Poughkeepsie, New York, 1988. *Photo by D. Gorton.*

of these SDS folks weren't actually talking to each other, but in the hinterlands of Austin, they would all talk with us. We sponsored musical events, annual birthday parties for Thorne, and more.

Part-Timer

Retired from full-time employment, I had more free time, but I worked part-time jobs for the next seven years, directing income to the parent portion of college debt. For ten months I coordinated a food pantry, Micah 6, a collaboration of ten university-area church congregations. It involved heavy lifting. Each week, I'd make a trip to the Capital Area Food Bank in South Austin, picking up cartons of dried food, canned food, frozen food, bread, and pastries. We'd unload them at the University Baptist Church into freezers and onto shelves. We'd also pick up day-old bread and dessert items from Whole Foods. I learned that unhoused people prefer soft, sliced bread to the tough-crusted artisan bread popular among the privileged. It was a demanding job, coordinating volunteers, loading, unloading, cleaning up, serving people on disability, without homes, in need of food. It was light-years from the blazer-jacket and pantyhose days of the Child Support Division.

My longest stint of part-time work was as a bookkeeper for the Center for Maximum Potential Building Systems (CMPBS), a nonprofit so far east on Martin Luther King Jr. that the boulevard was called FM 969. CMPBS was located on thirteen acres that could be idyllic, unless it was desperately hot or cold. Pliny Fisk III was a director of the sustainable-design center. I got the job through a Chile Committee friend, Gail Vittori, Pliny's partner. I said I didn't know much more than Excel, and she responded, "If I can do bookkeeping, so can you."

I learned QuickBooks, billing, and payroll. I handled deposits and accounts receivable. I developed depreciation tables, oversaw annual audits, and more. I had expected to acquire more knowledge about sustainability, but instead I became a nonprofit bookkeeper.

While I was there between 2007 and 2014, the place bustled with interns, and Gail oversaw a slew of LEED projects. I had to look up "LEED" so as not to appear ignorant. Leadership in Energy and Environmental Design consultants like Gail Vittori oversee green building projects. They assess whether the projects conform to a LEED framework for creating healthy, energy-efficient buildings. LEED consultants provide third-party certification that the standards are being met, resulting in one of four rankings: Certified, Silver, Gold, and Platinum.

Gail was a rock star in this world, developing an entire LEED framework specific to hospitals and health facilities. Dell Children's Hospital, located behind our house, became the first hospital in the world to earn LEED Platinum certification from the US Green Building Council. I began to see LEED signs everywhere, particularly in my "backyard," the Mueller greenbelt adjacent to our back fence—even in the Starbucks that is within easy walking distance from my house.

Gail was right about the bookkeeping. My strategic-planning skills required attention to detail. So did payroll and nonprofit tax filings. I learned skills that I could use in other arenas, particularly as a director and treasurer of two nonprofits, the Fort Hood Support Network and the New Journalism Project.

The CMPBS site, or "Max's Pot," as the center is sometimes called, had beautiful mulched paths, massive rainwater cisterns, cacti, and wildflowers. A pathway bordered by a pond and trellis led to my office space. Max's Pot

From left, Lee Forbes, Becky Moeller, Glenn Scott, and me with a Texas State Employees Union banner, at the state capitol, 2015.

also had critters—an albino raccoon with the dexterity to open the outdoor refrigerator, armadillos, snakes. I took a photo of a snake hanging off the trellis in the act of swallowing a small frog from the pond. I saw red foxes. And one day a coral snake made its way into the adjacent building where Gail worked. She was relatively calm about the venomous creature nestled along the wall by her desk. When the weather turned cold, I sat at my computer wearing open-tip gloves so that I could type, my wrists resting on a freezing metal desk. Sometimes the roof leaked. You were never far from nature at the Pot, and I guess that was the point.

No longer tethered to the state, part-time work allowed me to take on political work. I didn't have to worry about the reaction of the Attorney General's Office. I got busy with other pursuits. I also began to assemble archives and found time to reflect on earlier decades of political activism.

I gave more attention to writing. I have, over the years, been part of several writing groups, my participation instigated or organized by my friend Alyce Guynn. For a while, Alyce, attorney Bobby Nelson, and I used prompts to do timed writing together. The subject list was long: collective work, feminism, reproductive choice, clothing, communal living. We brought three perspectives to this work. One of the first writing prompts we used was the word "guilt." I found myself reflecting on the Protestant guilt instilled in me by reciting "We are not worthy so much as to gather up the crumbs under Thy table" from the Book of Common Prayer. Bobby wrote about judicial guilt in courts of law. Alyce, as was typical, broke all the rules. She reflected on "gilt," the gold accent adorning china.

Get It While You Can

I was part of the "Get it while you can" generation. The baby boomers who listened to the throbbing beat behind Janis Joplin as she closed her eyes and sang her heart out. "Get it while you can" meant sex. But it could also mean money. I had a state pension, but I became eligible for Social Security benefits when I turned sixty-two. I could have waited and gotten more. But I wasn't really inclined to wait.

If conservatives had their way, Social Security might be allowed to shrivel up like a tomato vine in a Texas drought, putting the final nail in the coffin of the New Deal. I made an appointment. The lobby of the Social Security office was crowded with squirming babies in strollers, desolate people in wheelchairs making disability claims, and young immigrants applying for Social Security cards in order to work. When my name showed up on a screen in the lobby, I made my way down a corridor of cubicles. A really nice twenty-something young man with earnest eyes helped me with my application.

"This is kind of an erratic earnings history," he ventured. "Is this accurate?" I leaned over to view the screen he was looking at.

"Well, yes," I said. "Those years I was working in a collectively run restaurant." I pointed at the screen. "And there I was going back to school. It took me nineteen years from start to finish to get my BA, and then I went for a master's."

"You were an undergraduate for nineteen years!" he blurted.

"Oh, no," I tried to explain, "I dropped out of college. It was the '60s. We lived communally on as little as possible. We didn't want to be consumers.

Now you call that a 'small carbon footprint.' I went back to school when I had kids and needed insurance."

He turned his attention back to his questions. "So, these amounts look right to you?" I acknowledged that they did. The first decades of my earning history looked erratic and paltry. Later decades showed steady employment and increasing wages.

He did a few calculations, then handed me a paper. "You'll get something in the mail about eight weeks before the first disbursement. Call me if you have questions."

I thanked him and rummaged around in my purse for a leaflet on single-payer health insurance, urging him to post it. "We've really got to build on the Medicare model so that everyone has access to health insurance. Don't you think?"

He stammered, "I really am not supposed to venture opinions while on my job."

"Well, I'm sure you have coffee breaks," I said. "You can put this up in the break room." I made my way out to my bumper-sticker-adorned car. When I turned on the ignition and got the air conditioner to battle the baking-oven heat, I slipped a CD into the player and chose the track I wanted to hear. Janis's voice came on strong and urgent, "Get it while you can."

Generations

Our daughter, Laura, left for El Salvador in 2008. Her haircut was pixie short, a women's liberation symbol tattooed on her left wrist. When she raises her fist, it echoes a fist inside a women's symbol. On her left foot is a tattoo of a design by her father. The image was created by Carlos for the Chile Committee and is emblazoned on T-shirts with the words "¡El pueblo unido jamás será vencido!"—The people united will never be defeated!

She has chosen to tattoo her predisposition for leftist activism onto her body and to follow in her parents' footsteps in many ways. She organized a party at our house the weekend before her departure. The invitation had pictures of both Laura and me. In the first picture, I was skinny and longhaired, speaking into a microphone at a university rally. In the second picture, I weigh more, holding a pink-boa peace symbol and wearing a pink vest and a visor that says "Organize!" It was my chosen Code Pink superpower.

The photos on the flyer show Laura at a table with the Committee in Solidarity with the People of El Salvador (CISPES) in Boston and with a fist raised at another CISPES event. When she came home for those two weeks before leaving for Central America, she wore her height differently, shoulders back—compliments of yoga and self-confidence.

Carlos and I had just been to an event marking the thirty-fifth anniversary of the coup in Chile on September 11. It was a showing of the film *Missing*, about American journalist Charles Horman's disappearance in Chile during the coup. Sissy Spacek plays Joyce Horman, and Jack Lemmon plays Charles's father. I remember the impact that film had in 1982 when it was released.

In the film, Charles Horman had learned too much about US involvement in the coup from speaking with US operatives in Valparaíso. He goes missing, as so many did in Chile—*desaparacidos*. His wife suspects the worst. His father comes to Chile believing that the US embassy could never be connected to his son's death. When I saw that film in the early '80s, I identified with Sissy Spacek. With Laura leaving for El Salvador, I couldn't help but identify with Jack Lemmon as he worried about his child's safety, grappling with his son's decision to put himself in harm's way.

Laura's leaflet announced, "Come Celebrate Alice Embree's Lifetime of Activism and Help Her Daughter Laura Follow in Her Footsteps!" As Laura left for El Salvador in 2008, I was proud of her courage and determination. My heart was also heavy with concern for her safety.

Laura asked me to join a delegation to El Salvador in 2009 at the time of the national election. I was trained, with others, to watch for election fraud. I was certified, given a vest to wear, and dispatched to a small town's schoolyard at the crack of dawn on the Sunday of the election. People were already lining up to vote. I was humbled watching them vote. There were no fancy machines, just cardboard voting stations. Representatives from both parties on the ballot sat at tables where the ballots were counted. We watched the tables as each ballot was counted, wrote down totals, and confirmed that those totals were faxed to the election tribunal. The Frente Faribundo Martí para la Liberación Nacional (FMLN) did not win at every table in that schoolyard, but they won the national election in 2009 and then again in 2014.

Under the Hood

I showed up frequently for Code Pink actions. I got to know Code Pink's organizational skills and staying power best after an army wife, Cindy Thomas, began to join us. With Cindy as the first manager we launched the antiwar coffeehouse Under the Hood in Killeen, Texas, near Fort Hood.

The board included two Vietnam antiwar activists whom I knew: Tom Cleaver, who had worked at Killeen's predecessor coffeehouse, the Oleo Strut, and Jeff Segal, an attorney who had been a defendant in the Oakland Seven conspiracy trial. I served on the board as well, along with Heidi Turpin and Fran Clark from Code Pink. Jim Turpin and many others from Code Pink were stalwart supporters.

Under the Hood stayed open for five years, providing support to several war resisters and offering a place for active-duty GIs and veterans to talk. It was the organizational base for the Right to Heal campaign by the Iraq Veterans Against the War. I was inspired by many there, disappointed by

With Under the Hood director Cindy Thomas, her daughter, and Heidi Turpin at Code Pink's Valentine event on South Congress, Austin, February 2012.

a few. Reaching out to GIs was important work as the wars in Iraq and Afghanistan widened and lengthened in duration, now a longer conflict than the war in Vietnam.

My five-year stint on the board of Under the Hood was valuable to me. I helped paint the walls before the place opened in 2009. With Austin Code Pink and Veterans for Peace members and many participants in the Camp Casey peace community, we held fundraisers and press conferences, stood in vigils in front of the Bell County jail, and wrote successful grant requests to keep the doors open.

After five years on the board, Heidi and I put out an appeal to allied organizations to take on the stewardship of the café. A group of younger allies from around the country began to formulate a plan to take on the board duties. They presented the plan to the existing board, and in an amicable fashion a new board took over. At the time we stepped down in 2014, Under the Hood had lasted as long as its Vietnam-era predecessor in Killeen, the Oleo Strut.

The draft made Vietnam personal to my generation. I've seen how waging war with a volunteer army—an army often answering an economic draft—has been a winning strategy for the Pentagon. I do not mean a winning strategy on the battlefields, but a way to isolate the domestic cost of war. A very small number of military families live with the daily toll of the millennial wars. For most of the population, it is possible to hit the mute button.

Victor Agosto Brizuela

I met Victor Agosto Brizuela in 2008 at a meeting to launch Under the Hood. As a friend of his said, "Victor gives new meaning to the phrase 'still waters run deep.'" His silence was formidable. I began to think it was a language issue. When Carlos accompanied me to the newly opened Under the Hood coffeehouse, I hoped my husband's Spanish would get Victor talking. Something did. They engaged in an animated conversation at a table for more than an hour. On the long ride home from Killeen, I asked Carlos what they had talked about. "The coup in Chile," Carlos said. How many soldiers had I met at Under the Hood who knew anything about the coup that happened decades before they were born? Only Victor.

With Victor Agosto Brizuela, 2009. *Photo by Carlos Lowry.*

Victor was the first war resister that Under the Hood helped to support. He was always quick to explain that he had not served "outside the wire." In other words, he had been relatively safe working IT "inside the wire," not in active combat.

Victor had grown up in Miami, played championship chess in high school, and joined the army, as many young people did after 9/11, because he was stirred by patriotism. Unlike many soldiers in Iraq, he spent his downtime reading. Notably, he read Noam Chomsky's *Hegemony or Survival: America's Quest for Global Dominance.*

Victor was "stop-lossed" close to the end of his contract when he thought he would be getting out. This was a common practice at the time that allowed the military to extend a soldier's contractual obligations. The practice had soldiers returning for second, third, fourth deployments, very different from the Vietnam era.

When Victor was ordered to deploy to Afghanistan, he thought long and hard. In the most succinct message, Victor told his counselor that he would not deploy. "The war is immoral, illegal, and does not make the United States more secure." With this brief comment given to his counselor, he announced his intention to disobey an order. He didn't think he needed a lawyer, but he acquiesced. James Branum handled his defense. Victor's court martial was scheduled for August 5, 2009.

The weekend before Victor's court martial, I wanted to do something supportive. I knew how much Noam Chomsky meant to Victor, and on a whim, I found an email address for Chomsky. With some trepidation about my grammar and punctuation skills, I wrote the distinguished MIT linguist. I told him that Victor was facing a court martial for his refusal to deploy. I said that a message from him would be very meaningful to Victor. I didn't think this busy professor would answer. Within an hour, he did. He wrote Victor an inspired and thoughtful message:

> I have learned, with admiration and respect, of your decision to refuse to deploy to Afghanistan. I was myself involved for many years in resistance to the Indochina wars, and have some sense of the complexity and travail of such a hard decision and the courage it takes to make the right choice and to live with it. . . . I hope you find your own internal peace, and that your honorable choice will inspire others to rethink their duties and responsibilities.[32]

I forwarded the email to Victor and left him a phone message. He called back after he had seen what Chomsky wrote. In his impossibly low voice, with his typical word restraint, he just said, "Wow."

Abuela

Carlos and I became grandparents in 2013. We met our soon-to-be son-in-law in El Salvador. Laura and her husband came to Austin for the birth, and Simón was born in our home with two midwives present in September 2013. The family returned to El Salvador and then relocated to Washington, DC, in 2014. My grandson speaks two languages. His DC public school classes were in both English and Spanish. The family moved to Austin in 2019, and he became a first grader at the elementary school our children attended.

When our grandson was just learning to speak, he was at the front of a DC city bus with his parents. Carlos and I were standing at the back. About a third of the passengers were immigrants, many from Central America, most having moved under the Temporary Protected Status provisions in place for many years. Our grandson saw us near the back door of the bus. "Abuela," he yelled. "Abuela," he yelled again. Passengers looked from him to us and begin to smile and chuckle. I love being his Abuela.

Third Wave

Glenn Scott, my socialist feminist friend, decided in 2015 that we should pitch a panel to a feminist forum at the University of Texas, an intergenerational dialogue. I am not overly enamored with the term "second wave," preferring "women's liberation," but this was pitched as a second-wave and third-wave dialogue.

It was a learning experience. I have stumbled over third-wave terminology: LGBT, LGBTQ, LGBTQA. The new language and designations—lesbian, gay, bisexual, transgender, queer or questioning, and asexual or ally—seem to grow in scope before I can learn them. "Transgender" is used these days to cover all people who do not identify with their assigned gender at birth or with the binary gender system. Gender identity issues are uncharted territory for me. I came into a women's movement that used the word "woman" proudly, correcting anyone who said "girl" and castigating anyone who said "chick." Sexual orientation, as in "same sex," was part of our lexicon.

Terms that young people use as easily as their thumbs type text messages are decades distant from our 1970s-era language of women's liberation and gay liberation. And gender fluidity is, well, fluid. Our meetings in the '70s never began with the question, "How do you identify?" We have a lot to learn.

I tried my best to navigate the trip wires of language in our 2015 workshop. My PowerPoint images of insurgency were enthusiastically welcomed by most of the workshop participants, but one person accused me of erasing the history of transgendered individuals.

I had hoped to convey the '70s struggles with a sense of their glory and accomplishments as well as shortcomings. Women's liberation succeeded on many fronts but failed to create a lasting movement that bridged racial divides and resonated with working-class women. Women of color were leaders, but they often opted to belong to and lead in organizations such as the Brown Berets and the Black Citizens Task Force. I was prepared to speak about lessons we had learned about class, lessons from lesbian activists, lesbian separatists, and women of color. But the comment about transgendered history left me thinking about lessons still to be learned.

After the workshop, one of the Feminist Action Project organizers directed Glenn and me to the refreshments in the foyer of the Gender and Sexuality Center. She stopped suddenly, midsentence, looking out the window, and announced, "There is a huge cow outside."

There was, in fact, a huge and impressive creature—a Texas longhorn—being handled by the Texas Cowboys in the grassy area next to Gregory Gym. It was Bevo, the UT mascot, a steer with massive horns that likely grew longer due to castration. Bevo is usually docile when on public display. I've wondered if he is tranquilized. I suspect if Bevo could speak, he might say, "Whatever."

"I don't think he'd want to be called a cow," I said to myself.

It was an ironic moment in the center devoted to gender and sexuality, but I kept the irony to myself and left with that uncomfortable feeling you get when a learning experience means that you have something to learn.

Tower

I revisited the UT Tower tragedy of August 1, 1966, in 2013 when both Claire Wilson James and Sandra Wilson Thiher came to Austin. Claire had moved away from Austin after the shootings. She found faith and began a career as a teacher in Seventh-day Adventist schools. In 2013 Claire was living in Texarkana.

Sandra and Gary were married and living in Little Rock, Arkansas, raising twins. I had played a small role in that marriage when Sandra returned to Austin on the twentieth anniversary of the shootings in 1986. A group of SDS friends gathered at Scholz Garten. Gary Thiher, although he had been invited, didn't show up. He had become a carpenter and was somewhat of a hermit. I made a run to his house nearby. He never got to Scholz, but he made it to a later event. He and Sandra fell in love. In November of 1986, they got married in Zilker Park. My friend Mariann Wizard decorated the park tables with small picket signs, like "Make Love, Not War!" By then I had two children under the age of five, who walked down the pathway sprinkling rose petals to begin the ceremony.

With mass shootings almost commonplace—from Columbine to Virginia Tech to Sandy Hook—it seemed unbelievable that the 2013 Texas Legislature was considering legislation that would increase the number of guns and make it legal to carry guns on university campuses.

An Austin attorney, Jim Bryce, invited Sandra and Claire to come to Austin to testify at the state legislature. Deeply affected by the shootings, he had kept in touch with many of the victims.

Claire stayed at our home. I left her to go to work one morning and returned to find three television-news vans in front of our home. I had to creep in so as not to disturb ongoing interviews.

As survivors of the massacre, both Claire and Sandra attracted media attention. The day of the legislative hearings, I accompanied Claire as she went through the screening process at the capitol's north entrance. Claire, who conceals very little, explained in advance to the state troopers that she had shrapnel that would trigger the alarm. With my knee replacements, we both made the alarms go off.

Claire and Sandra gave their testimony, as did the local police chief, the UT campus police chief, gun-safety advocates, and a UT graduate student whose friend had been killed at Virginia Tech. The bill passed that session allowed administrators to have discretion over campus carry. That discretion was removed two years later for public colleges and universities.

Jim had arranged a tour of the Tower observation deck. Neither Claire nor Sandra had been to the observation deck since the shooting. We met at the UT Police headquarters, carpooled over in police vehicles, and took the elevator up. I expected to see where Charles Whitman had shot visitors on the stairs and then at the receptionist's desk. I expected to hear how he had aimed his weaponry unimpeded until shots were returned. I knew that he then began to fire through the rainspouts. His range was narrowed, but he was still deadly with his marine-trained sharpshooter skills.

I expected a tour. But what happened was more remarkable. The detective asked us to sit inside. He then asked each of us to recall where we had been during the shootings. The distance of decades collapsed. Tears were shed as each of us recalled that day. It had the feel of a group therapy session for trauma survivors. He also seemed to be processing, as a detective would, a recent crime scene.

After that emotion-filled session, the detective took us outside to the observation deck, explaining where Whitman had stood and where he had fallen after being shot. From the deck, you could see Whitman's vantage point on Twenty-Third and Guadalupe, where Sandra was shot. You could also see Whitman's view of the main mall, where Claire had lain with a baby dead inside her and a fiancé dead beside her.

On the way back to the UT Police headquarters, I rode with the detective, sitting on the hard plastic of the back seat. I thought about how easy it must be to clean when people threw up. He asked, "Have you ever been in a police car before?" He might have known the answer, since he was a detective. I told him, "Yes, but not when I was being taken to my car."

Over the years, the university did its best not to draw attention to the Tower shootings. A director of Admissions Research at UT, Gary M. Lavergne, meticulously documented the events in his book *A Sniper in the Tower: The Charles Whitman Murders*. Claire read that book and wrote to him, saying she thought he had described her accurately. They began to correspond. In 2014, a living memorial took place on the UT campus, with students reading the victims' names in the locations where their lives had been taken. Lavergne came down to the main mall with a bouquet for Claire. In an act of generosity that was of even more importance, Lavergne found where the remains of Claire's baby had been interred. His family donated a headstone for Baby Boy Wilson. Claire was able to visit this grave for the first time in 2014.

Nearly five decades had passed since the massacre when an Austin native, Keith Maitland, began a documentary film project about the events. His movie, *Tower*, was inspired by the stories of humanity he had read—of Rita Starpattern braving bullets to lie by Claire and comfort her with words; of a young man, John Fox (the musician Artly Snuff), battling his fear to run out to rescue Claire. Maitland didn't focus on the killer.

Only Whitman's shoes appear on-screen in Maitland's movie. The documentary focuses on the survivors.

Rita Starpattern, my coworker at Red River Women's Press, had never spoken about the Tower shootings. I didn't know she had been a heroine to my friend Claire. Artly Snuff had rarely spoken of his role in picking Claire up. I was with Claire when she and Artly officially met for the first time.

I couldn't imagine that a filmmaker could deal with this horror through animation. In fact the story was beautifully brought to life, with younger actors speaking the words of survivors. They reenacted scenes that Maitland's crew rendered into animation through a process called rotoscoping. You hear from those who lived through the ordeal as they describe their fear, the sour taste of survivor's guilt, and surprising acts of courage and humanity. The award-winning movie *Tower* premiered at the South by Southwest Film Festival in March of 2016. It has been shown on PBS.

The university finally honored those who had died. On the fiftieth anniversary of the shootings, August 1, 2016, the UT held a poignant memorial to the victims. The Tower clock was stopped, frozen for twenty-four hours at the hour the shootings began. A bagpipe procession led people from the main mall to the turtle pond south of the Tower. The UT president spoke. Claire addressed the gathering, as did US Congressman Lloyd Doggett and many others. A granite monument, donated by a funeral home, was dedicated. It is inscribed with the names of the victims.

Sandra Wilson came to the 2016 memorial as well. She was able to meet Chip Jansen, who had carried her out of Whitman's range. She had only spoken with him by phone. In 1966, Jansen was a young temporary construction worker at the Texas Theater when he saw Sandra fall to the ground. He ran through the alley behind the theater and down Twenty-Third Street to pull her to safety. He was a tall guy. Standing next to her in 2016, he said, "I never realized you were so short." He had only seen her lying down.

Another school shooting, this time at a high school in Parkland, Florida, shocked the nation in 2017. Seventeen lives were lost, many more traumatized. Unbelievably, we have calls to arm teachers, not action to reduce the number of automatic weapons, like the one used by the eighteen-year-old shooter in Florida. The high school students have raised their voices with

"Never again." Articulate and social-media savvy, they have worked to transform their grief into action.

As Margaret Mead said, "Never doubt that a small group of thoughtful, committed citizens can change the world; indeed, it's the only thing that ever has."

Democratic Socialists

In 2014 I agreed to help organize a local chapter of the Democratic Socialists of America (DSA). There were fourteen of us. In March 2015 Bernie Sanders said he would come to Austin if he could speak in a union hall to two hundred people. Danny Fetonte secured the International Brotherhood of Electrical Workers hall, and more than five hundred people showed up. This was before Bernie Sanders officially announced he was running as a presidential candidate in the Democratic Party primary.

The enthusiasm and bold agenda of that campaign provided traction well beyond a candidacy. There are now more than one thousand members in the Austin DSA chapter. DSA has experienced the kind of remarkable growth that SDS did. But the differences are important. It is not a student organization. DSA has a presence on campuses, but it has a far more vibrant chapter life off campus.

These younger activists are energetic, tech savvy, and bold. They know how to nurture and share leadership. They have become very skilled at waging campaigns and winning victories. And, most importantly, they understand that oppression takes many forms that intersect and interact. Only a movement with this kind of intersectional analysis can hope to succeed in a country divided by class, race, gender identity, immigration status, sexual orientation, and more.

I had an organizational home in SDS. I felt the power of chapters in every state. I found a sisterhood within the women's movement, but not an organizational home. For now, DSA is a launching ground for national activity, a multi-issue, multigenerational "big tent" where it is possible to hone strategy and share tactics across the country.

The energy level of younger activists, new to the struggle, is both exhilarating and exhausting. I hope I bring a sense of staying power, a reminder not that we did things better in the '60s and '70s but that movements in our younger years changed the trajectory of our lives, not for a decade or two but for a lifetime. Those movements brought us purpose and camaraderie and created lasting friendships.

I can sense both the continuity and the differences between our insurgency and this current one. We battled for civil rights, for integration, and for voting rights, not fully understanding the tenacity of white supremacy. We were antiwar protesters who came to understand imperialism. We were the New Left, distancing ourselves from a virulent 1950s anticommunism. We looked more to Che Guevara than to Eugene V. Debs. We were inspired by a concept of participatory democracy, not electoral politics. Perhaps that is understandable. When we were eighteen, the voting age was twenty-one. We thought Vietnam could not be repeated; we did not expect that neocons could remake a volunteer military to carry out endless war and occupation without domestic blowback. We felt the exuberance of victory as we gained rights for women. Now we are watching reproductive rights be taken away, state by state, court by court.

It's early in the new incarnation of DSA. These younger activists cut their teeth on the 2008 economic collapse and the Occupy Wall Street movement. They were emboldened by the candidacy of Bernie Sanders, seeing possibility in elections. The Red Scare of the '50s never left its prints on them. They were radicalized by inequality.

They've been inspired by Black Lives Matter and Standing Rock. They are listening to the climate change experts and embracing Extinction Rebellion. They are socialists who campaign for bold domestic programs like the Green New Deal and Medicare for All. They are watching right-wing state legislators and court justices trample women's rights into the dust. For them, Trump's election might have come as a shock, but the kind that jump-starts a heart. Their moment is different, but their enthusiasm rivals anything I saw in the '60s. Their history is being made and is not yet written.

The Rag Turns Fifty

As 2016 approached, the fiftieth anniversary of *The Rag*, we began to think of a second reunion, this time with a book to tell the eleven-year history of the paper.

As editors of the book, Thorne Dreyer, Richard Croxdale, and I made sure that all eleven years were represented, not just the early years. We included one hundred articles from *The Rag*, retyped, with artwork, photos, and contemporary essays. The book, *Celebrating The Rag: Austin's Iconic Underground Newspaper*, is a miracle, as *The Rag* was, of collective will. It relied upon a few paid typists and a slew of volunteers who selected articles and helped proofread final copy. Roger Baker and Phil Prim assembled a digital archive of *The Rag*, with Roger photographing each page in Phil's complete collection. Former Ragstaffer and computer wizard Hunter Ellinger compiled those images, along with a contents table generated by Phil years earlier, into a database that volunteers could search to choose articles to be retyped.

Carlos designed the book but did much more than that. He rescued artwork from photographic images of aging newsprint and rendered cartoons and illustrations into high-contrast black and white. The book looks better than the paper ever did. The graphics are delightful. The irreverent, dope-smoking Fabulous Furry Freak Brothers by Gilbert Shelton, the surreal armadillos of Jim Franklin, the familiar images of muralist Kerry Awn, the playful art of Trudy Minkoff, Marie Valleroy, and Monika Mooney, and the ads that provide a glimpse of pre-metropolis Austin are all there.

We included contemporary content about the beginning, when *The Rag* was the sixth paper in the Underground Press Syndicate. *The Rag's* importance was highlighted by Thorne, who had compiled a substantial bibliography of references to the paper's importance in merging coverage of both radical politics and cultural upheaval. *The Rag*, wrote Laurence Leamer, was "one of a few legendary undergrounds . . . probably the first totally Movement paper. . . . [It was] singularly successful in creating a politically and culturally radical community in Austin."[33]

The contemporary reflections included commentary by Thorne about the Houston connection and the crossover staff with Houston's underground paper, *Space City!* Sharon Shelton-Colangelo wrote about *The Rag* and women's liberation; Glenn Scott highlighted *The Rag's* coverage of local and state union battles; Terry Dubose wrote about the GI resistance covered by *The Rag*. We provided context for *Rag* articles about the University Freedom Movement and the Chuck Wagon arrests and brought to light *The Rag's* relationship with *Roe v. Wade*. We included background on Alan Pogue, the photographer, and Gilbert Shelton and Jim Franklin, the iconic artists. The graphics made it a must-have for any fan of underground comix. The book, timed to be sold at the 2016 reunion, garnered national recognition and many positive reviews. With an index and short statements by many contributors, we made this book a primer on Austin's radical history and countercultural impact over an eleven-year span.

The 2016 *Rag* reunion began with a Gentle Thursday celebration and welcoming event at the Vortex Theater. On Friday, events took place at an Austin Community College campus. A live *Rag Radio* show featured Doug Rossinow, author of *The Politics of Authenticity*. We held breakout sessions on Vietnam and on women's liberation and presented an evening showing of the film documentary on *The Rag*. On Saturday, Kerry Awn again emceed a musical event at Threadgill's, and the following day there was a Sunday brunch. A memorial homage featured photos and words of remembrance for staffers who had passed on.

The second reunion represented a slightly younger demographic compared to the reunion held in 2005. More than a decade had passed. Events were more widely publicized. The UT Departments of History and American Studies sponsored a guest lecture by Doug Rossinow at UT, helping to pay his airfare from Norway, where he was teaching. With the involvement of UT departments and a professor at Austin Community College, more faculty and students turned out for the second reunion in 2016.

With the book, the graphics, the documentary footage, and the photos, it was now easier to make presentations on that era. I presented to history classes on second-wave feminism, and Thorne Dreyer and I spoke to classes on campus and controversy. We joined forces with Austinite Martha Cotera to talk about the insurgencies of the 1960s and 1970s to classes on higher education and American studies. I created a PowerPoint presentation on radical history for Monkeywrench Books and the Austin chapter of DSA. UT history professor Laurie Green assigned the book and had her class conduct oral histories with Austin women activists. The book has had long legs.

Celebrating The Rag adds a new vantage point to the usual accounts of the underground press. In the beginning, *The Rag* and the movement it grew out of deferred to male leadership. A women's movement jarred those foundations loose, and to *The Rag*'s credit, the paper embraced women's liberation. By 1970, when I returned to Austin, Judy Smith, Linda Smith, Bea Durden, Barbara Hines, Pat Cuney, Suzanne Gott, and artist Marie Valleroy were organizing women's liberation front activities, changing *The Rag*'s content and work style, and encouraging women's voices, women's writing, and women's liberation content. I believe the paper's longevity had everything to do with that embrace. Many underground newspapers floundered or split, or in some cases were taken over by women. *Celebrating The Rag* tells that part of the story in a way that has not been told before.

In 2016 I worked on a separate preservation project for *The Rag*. Reveal Digital, a company working to digitize library collections, had included *The Rag* within their Independent Voices alternative press collection. In February 2016, I worked with Peggy Glahn at Reveal Digital to identify missing *Rag* issues and ensure that the collection was complete, all 377 issues.

I got a crash course in the importance of making content available in a digital form. *The Rag* became accessible worldwide without dependence on library microfilm. I learned that many libraries were converting from microform because the film records were unstable and deteriorating. More importantly, digitization allowed for the use of optical character recognition (OCR) software, making the content searchable by text. Reveal Digital is now affiliated with Ithaka, which means *The Rag* is part of the digital library of JSTOR. Ithaka's Independent Voices collection, with searchable text, will provide researchers with online access long after the newsprint crumbles into dust.

The documentary by People's History in Texas, based primarily on oral histories from the 2005 reunion, is an important addition to the historical record of *The Rag*. I have joked that we have a book and a film; now we need a musical.

In late 2019, the New Journalism Project board began to focus on *The Rag*'s Houston cousin, *Space City!*, exploring ways to digitize a collection of that paper. The Houston underground newspaper began publication on June 5, 1969. Of the original six-member collective, three were founders of

The Rag—Thorne Dreyer, Judy Gitlin Fitzgerald, and Dennis Fitzgerald. They were all Houston natives. With Victoria Smith and community organizers Cam Duncan and Sue Mithun Duncan, they launched the Houston paper, all of them moving to Houston and sharing a communal home. *Space City!* published just over one hundred issues and ended publication on August 3, 1972.

By some measures, Houston is now the nation's most diverse city. During the time that *Space City!* was published, the city was marked by Ku Klux Klan bombings and police repression of Black activists. The KKK also targeted *Space City!* That history was reported on the pages of *Space City!* but was not well documented by major media. The newspaper covered the emerging Houston counterculture and the women's movement. Through the efforts of the New Journalism Project, *Space City!* now lives online and is digitally accessible.

Electoral College

Donald Trump did not win a popular-vote victory in 2016. He won through an Electoral College system that harkens back to slavery. It was a system concocted by "founding fathers" with little trust in direct democracy. Electors based on the census count in each state would determine who would be president. In 1790 the census counted the population in five categories: (1) free white males of sixteen years and upward, (2) free white males under sixteen years, (3) free white females, (4) all other free persons, and (5) slaves.

The New England states with small enslaved populations argued that slavery should not be rewarded with increased representation when slaves were excluded from citizenship status. Virginia, the most populous state, with 39 percent of its population enslaved, would have none of that. The concession offered by Virginia's James Madison protected the slaveholding states with this compromise: for the purpose of determining Electoral College representation, slaves would be counted as three-fifths of a person.

My American history classes never taught me that slavery was baked right into the Constitution in this manner. The slaveholding states of Virginia, South Carolina, Georgia, and Maryland made off like bandits in terms of representation—bandits benefitting from human bondage. The

2016 Trump election was the fifth time that the Electoral College delivered a president who did not win the popular vote. What could be a more fitting avenue for a Trump "victory" than a system devised in this manner? Not by any founding mothers but by founding fathers, many of them slave owners.

Sidewalk in July

As a seventy-one-year-old grandmother, I joined a protest on the blistering hot Texas sidewalk in front of US Senator John Cornyn's office. It was July 2017. The sun beat down. About ten people who use wheelchairs were on the sidewalk along with other protesters. We were there because the US Senate was about to vote to "repeal and replace" Obamacare, the Affordable Care Act. All over the country, people were sitting-in at congressional offices, and protesters were getting hauled out of the US Capitol rotunda. The chants were familiar. One of my favorites had a singsong call-and-response: "Tell me what democracy looks like." "This is what democracy looks like."

I thought of the SDS *Port Huron Statement* and its call to participate in

I was arrested in front of Senator John Cornyn's office for protesting the pending repeal of the Affordable Care Act, 2017. *Photo by Carlos Lowry.*

democracy. I thought of the sit-ins in Greensboro, North Carolina, at the lunch counter and the stand-ins to integrate theaters in Austin. Several of us linked arms, blocking the sidewalk.

My picket sign was hanging from my neck by string. I had punched holes and tied string for twenty posters an hour before. My driver's license was in my pocket; I had no purse or phone.

"Put your arms behind you." I was cuffed with those plastic strips they use now. A cop in shorts walked me back to the police car and told me to get in.

Another woman was told to get in as well. She was Sarah Goodfriend. She and her wife had decided that getting arrested was on their bucket list of things they had to do for the resistance. She carried on a conversation with the cop about his knee brace and his health care.

At some point, we were told to change cars. That's when I realized how much I use my hands to get out of a car. My knees weren't that agile. It was impossible to get out. The cop took off the cuffs. I got out, and he put them on again.

I realized how big Austin had gotten since my last arrest, when we disrupted CIA director William Colby's visit. There is no longer a jail in the police station. Now there is a giant county facility. We were processed there. Every piece of my clothing was wet from sweat. It was an icebox inside. My earrings went into a bag. A female cop, with gloved hands, searched inside my bra at the desk, reaching her hands under my shirt.

I mentioned my daily prescription, and that got me sent to the nurse's room near the holding area. I was in my striped jail garb, my pulse racing. My face was red. I was dehydrated. Older than anyone else in the holding area, I suddenly felt my age. The nurse gave me a plastic bottle of Gatorade.

When I joined the others on the hard benches where we sat for hours, a woman who had been brought in on some minor charge took offense. "What did you do to get Gatorade?" I told her. We sat and talked about the Del Valle facility where she hoped to be sent because of its drug recovery program. She showed me her ring that had the Serenity Prayer on it. We said the prayer together. "God grant me . . . the courage to change the things I can . . ."

When we were processed out, I struggled into clothes that were both damp and freezing. I ate a slice of pizza brought by the DSA support group that was waiting outside. Carlos drove me home. Then I followed a routine that was well established from the days of *The Rag*. You organize the demonstration, you go to the demonstration, and then you write about the demonstration. This time, my article was posted to *The Rag Blog*.

Attorney Malcolm Greenstein had arrived at the demonstration before the arrests, even though it was his birthday. He had shown up as well forty-one years earlier, as a movement attorney, when he had gotten me out of jail for standing with a banner onstage with William Colby. For the Cornyn action, I had to pay a fine plus court costs, and I received a deferred dismissal of charges based on my not returning to the scene for one year. The irony did not escape me. I had worked for Attorney General Cornyn and was now barred from the sidewalk in front of his Senate office.

For decades activists have relied upon the largely pro bono services of lawyers who support the causes with their legal expertise. Attorneys Jim Simons, Cam Cunningham, Brady Coleman, and Bobby Nelson were part of the Austin Law Commune, sometimes known as the Twelfth Street Law Office. They were legal lifelines for activists. During May Day 1971, Jim Simons was in the DC courtroom to get me out of jail. Cam Cunningham and Brady Coleman showed up at the jail when we were dressed as witches during the LBJ Library dedication. Malcolm Greenstein has been getting protesters out of jail for decades.

Unprepared for Loss

INEXPERIENCED
January 5, 2018

I'm inexperienced
With snow.
It falls quietly,
Accumulating into drifts,
Silent sentinels
To the passing of the light.
The losses accumulate.

Friends passing.
>Bobby Minkoff
>Loreto Espinoza
>Glenn Scott
>Terry Dubose
>Dennis Fitzgerald.
>We reminisce,
>Post remembrances online,
>Tributes to the vivacious audacity of youth,
>To our shared communities,
>Our families of choice.
>We record memories for their children
>And grandchildren
>As they mourn the passing of their elders.
>We faced down forces of injustice,
>Strengthened by shared solidarity.
>Now we face a relentless adversary.
>Losses mark the passage of time
>In the winter of our lives.

I was unprepared for the loss of so many friends. The year 2018 was particularly harsh. Bobby Minkoff died at the beginning of the year, and Dennis Fitzgerald at the end. For three months, loss was a steady undercurrent in my life. Loreto Espinoza died in August, Glenn Scott in September, and Terry Dubose in October. My posts to *The Rag Blog* were no longer reporting on events. They were remembrances and memorials.

Glenn Scott passed away on September 11, 2018. I was one among a group of women taking shifts at her hospital bedside and helping her family. Her loss affected me deeply. For Glenn's birthday, October 4, 2018, the Austin City Council passed a proclamation declaring it Glenn Scott Day.

Glenn was a founder of DSA, literally there at the founding convention when the group she was in, the New American Movement, merged with the Democratic Socialist Organizing Committee in 1982. She spent decades as a labor organizer, working with municipal and textile workers, teachers, and nurses.

She was battling breast cancer, but when she semiretired from a strenuous stint at organizing with National Nurses United, she stepped into the chapter life of Austin DSA. I had gotten active in 2014. After a particularly brutal DSA meeting in 2015, I was willing to drift away. Glenn would have none of that. She recruited me into a DSA socialist feminist workgroup, and in 2016 we began to fundraise with local activists for reproductive justice and abortion access, building a committee that is five years old as this book goes to press.

Glenn was a socialist feminist to her core, better schooled in theory than I have ever been, with an instinctive ability to recruit, mentor, and raise up voices of younger people. When people gathered at the capitol after the Glenn Scott Day proclamation, many spoke of what she had given them, opening up her home for hearty meals, listening to them when they were down, bringing them soup when they were sick. She unselfishly introduced them to her vast array of contacts that ranged from elected officials to labor and grassroots organizers. She elevated the voices of younger leaders new to politics. Although she often held a megaphone at a rally, she really excelled at being a megaphone to amplify and embolden the voices of others. She understood, as well as anyone I know, that organizing is about building relationships.

Glenn did all of this in Spanish and English. She always sought out allies among people of color, always looked to unions to build coalitions with working people, and always fought the good fight to save public services such as Medicare, Medicaid, Social Security, and public education. She was a natural at it. I was amazed at her stamina. It was the way she dealt with cancer, the way she muscled through chemotherapy sessions and neuropathy. The *Austin Chronicle* headline of September 28, 2018, said it well: "A Comrade in Arms: Glenn Scott Fought for Her Life and for Yours."

2020 Reflections

THE PANDEMIC HAS PROVIDED A NEW LENS ON THE PAST.

I was engaged with the world at the beginning of March 2020. I went to Houston to attend the fiftieth-anniversary celebration of the KPFT Pacifica Radio station on March 1 and met with a small group to promote a project honoring Houston's *Space City!* newspaper. On March 5, I gave the keynote address at the Briscoe Center for the opening of a major exhibition on women, "On with the Fight!" The exhibition included some of the archival material I had donated to the center. Carlos and I attended an International Women's Day exhibition at La Peña on March 8. I attended a DSA Feminist Action Committee meeting on March 10. On March 13, I hosted a *Rag Radio* show on reproductive justice with three guests in a small studio.

Then the world shut down.

We have a house, a yard, a daughter who picks up curbside groceries, and pension income. I put in a raised garden and have been fascinated to see the cucumber curl its slender tendrils around the trellis; the melon plant spend weeks in contemplation before sprawling; the tomato plant shoot

At the opening event for the "On with the Fight!" women's history exhibit, Briscoe Center for American History, March 5, 2020. *Photo by Alan Pogue.*

up, blossom, and bear fruit; the transplanted mint thrive on sturdy stems. Our house and yard, our income, are privileges not parceled out fairly.

The pandemic further exposed the fault lines in the country. It made the need for universal health care glaringly obvious. Like watching a slow-motion train wreck, we saw what a reality-TV-show president couldn't do. There was no leadership, no consistent messaging, no personal protective gear, no rollout of national testing. Just the slow derailment as the number of deaths rose, disproportionately among people of color. Then the murder of George Floyd further exposed the deep fault line of systemic racism with its deadly police violence and incarceration.

At the same time, the Black Lives Matter uprising gave us hope. The pandemic had shattered our sense of normalcy, made us look at what we needed as opposed to what we thought we needed. Many of us stopped driving cars and booking air travel. Fossil fuel profits tanked. Perhaps we can imagine a Green New Deal jobs program as a path out of an economic crater. Perhaps we can imagine.

•   •   •   •   •

I do not want my words to be an ode to nostalgia. I hope they provide a critical lens for present-day activists, a glimpse into the constraints of Jim Crow and the gender roles that we challenged. We made change, but not enough. The fight for social justice requires that generations learn from generations.

Some themes deserve deeper dives than the cord of chronology makes possible. I was transformed by feminism, a term I've never abandoned. My view expanded beyond domestic borders, first because of Vietnam—what the Vietnamese call the American War. Latin America gave me a continental vision. I've been surprised within DSA to find so little attention to global issues other than climate justice. The endless-war cycle doesn't get the attention of Vietnam. That may be the difference between a draft and no draft. The Black Lives Matter marches have ignited the struggle for racial justice. I had not understood how deeply embedded racism was, even when we were lined up, holding hands, singing "We Shall Overcome." We were dismantling the signage of Jim Crow, not grappling with its structural roots.

•   •   •   •   •

My feminist rage can still be tapped. In the raw emotion surrounding the 2017 hearing on Brett Kavanaugh's appointment to the Supreme Court, that 1970s-era anger returned. I was in a meeting when a man interrupted me twice. A deep growl came into my voice as I enunciated each word carefully: "Do not interrupt me." He looked as though he had heard the possessed voice in *The Exorcist*. He stopped talking.

Rebecca Traister's 2018 book *Good and Mad: The Revolutionary Power of Women's Anger* explored the historic fuel of women's rage. Mary Dore's 2014 film *She's Beautiful When She's Angry* chronicled the anger and solidarity of the '70s women's liberation movement. Never underestimate that anger. Robin Morgan called it that "amulet of madness" that women wear around their necks.

Faith

Spiritual grounding and faith are anchors that are neglected, even rejected, in radical politics. Doug Rossinow's *The Politics of Authenticity*, published in 1998, explored decades of activism in Austin, Texas. Its subtitle was *Liberalism, Christianity, and the New Left in America*. Rossinow's focus on Christianity raised some eyebrows among my peers. After all, religion is anathema to many on the left. None other than Karl Marx named it as anathema. The "opiate of the masses," was the phrase I often heard. The full quote was, "Religion is the sigh of the oppressed creature, the heart of a heartless world, and the soul of soulless conditions. It is the *opium* of the people."

Rossinow's book relied upon extensive research and many interviews. As I looked at the dates, I saw that the first people he interviewed, in 1991, were Reverend Bob Breihan and me. I had provided Rossinow with an unpublished essay of mine that described, among other things, my upbringing in the Episcopal Church. At the time that Rossinow interviewed me, he was working on his doctoral dissertation. He expanded his dissertation into a detailed history that recognizes the importance of the New Left in Texas. It adds dimension to a story typically told from an East and West Coast perspective.

I see a clear connection with a community of faith in my formation as an activist. As a teenager, I went with others in my All Saints' Episcopal Church youth group to try to convince a youth group at the Church of the Good Shepherd not to go to a segregated ice rink. We failed. They went.

We snarkily called their church the "Church of the Good Cadillac," a nod to its Tarrytown location. My parents' church, in contrast, had a distinctly intellectual bent, with many professors and their families in the mix. Ritual mixed with academic pedigrees on the hard pews of All Saints'. Beautiful stained glass windows, processions, gifted voices in the choir, genuflecting to the cross, standing, sitting, kneeling—it was how I was brought up. My fellow activist George Vizard IV had carried the cross down the aisle at All Saints', looking as determined as he did on the picket line at Roy's Lounge.

I was confirmed in All Saints' Church, I went to communion, kneeling at the altar. I was never aware that the most prominent window in the church, donated in the 1930s and positioned behind that altar, featured an image of Confederate general Robert E. Lee. A Black congregant and others made their concerns known, and the window was removed and replaced in 2018. The stained glass replacement now features abolitionist clergyman Absalom Jones and seminarian Jonathan Daniels, a civil rights activist killed in Alabama while shielding a young Black woman from gunfire. The new window is a sign of progress but a grim reminder that I grew up with the backdrop of Jim Crow as a literal backdrop behind the cross in my church.

When we first took our children to Trinity United Methodist Church in 1989, we found an older congregation that enthusiastically embraced newcomers. In 1992, that congregation voted to become a Reconciling congregation. It was the first Methodist church in Austin to take this step, openly welcoming lesbian, gay, bisexual transgender, and queer (LGBTQ) participation and advocating for LGBTQ rights in the Methodist Church. Trinity became a home to many who felt unwelcome in other churches.

Reverend Sid Hall III has been arrested protesting the Methodist policy on same-sex marriage. Several years ago, Trinity became co-affiliated with another denomination that allowed same-sex marriages. The Methodist Reconciling Network has grown by leaps and bounds in the last quarter century. In 1992, when Trinity voted to become Reconciling, it was a small congregation, not a progressive powerhouse, a reminder that change often has humble origins.

I've needed to connect with faith lately, to reflect with others on hope. It pushes the mute button on cable news, connects me with the life and death journeys of others seated on the Methodist padded chairs, arranged in a circle. I need a sense of peace that "passeth all understanding" to get me through anger and despair.

For many months I worked with an interfaith coalition, the Austin Sanctuary Network, that provides sanctuary for immigrants within two churches and mobilizes against draconian immigration policies. The network is made up primarily of communities of faith, but it also includes organizations—unions and others—with no religious affiliation. The network has continued to provide both sanctuary and sustenance.

My husband is the son of two Methodist missionaries, David Lowry and

From left, with Marina Vasquez, Stephanie Molnar, Keely Wahi, and Anita Privett of Trinity United Methodist Church at an immigrant rights rally at the state capitol, August 30, 2018. Janet Cook is behind the banner.

Mary Sue Lowry. David was a pastor and Mary Sue was a pediatrician. The Lowrys left for rural Southern Chile when Carlos and his twin brother were almost two. They raised their children to embrace Chilean culture and the Spanish language. The Lowry kids were sated on religion at a young age and didn't follow their parents' path into regular church attendance. They were, however, molded by a moral code.

Carlos's parents became effective human rights advocates after the military coup in Chile. They took risks to march with mothers of the disappeared on International Women's Day and to officiate at funerals for leftists, who could not be buried in Catholic ceremonies because the government had decreed them to be suicides.

My mother-in-law set up a comprehensive program for health in Temuco, a place with services from physicians and psychological caregivers—doctors, social workers, and psychiatrists all in one place. She organized support groups for the families of the disappeared and imprisoned. In 1991, I attended an afternoon gathering—called an *once* in Chile—at her health center. It was a celebration for a political prisoner in the southern region who had finally been released from prison.

The example of my in-laws is one of many ways that faith and political action have merged. In El Salvador, Archbishop Óscar Romero is revered for his embrace of liberation theology, for speaking out against poverty and social injustice. He is honored for the price he paid for these messages. He was assassinated while giving mass on March 24, 1980. Pope Francis declared him a martyr in 2015. The pope visited Romero's tomb—as I have done—in the basement of the cathedral in San Salvador.

The radicals of the 1960s and 1970s depended—no matter how much they might have objected to religion—on the generosity of communities of faith. The North American Congress on Latin America had church support and an official address at the Interchurch Center, 475 Riverside, in New York City, the location we irreverently referred to as the "God Box." I received funds from the United Ministries in Higher Education to organize the 1970 Texas Media Conference.

In Austin, the basement of the Congregational Church at 408 West Twenty-Third was the location for our first women's liberation skit in August of 1970. That same church basement housed the People's Free Clinic for years. The University Presbyterian Church made its space available for a day-long 1975 International Women's Day event. The vegetarian restaurant Sattva was first housed at the Hillel Foundation and then at the Methodist Student Center.

I doubt that *The Rag* could have survived or that a women's community could have incubated without the generosity of several faith leaders and church-funded locations. Frank Wright, who directed the University YMCA for thirteen years in its location at 2200 Guadalupe, was fearless in his advocacy of desegregation. That site was where organizers of the stand-ins mobilized, successfully integrating university-area movie theaters. The building was damaged when a white supremacist planted a bomb in the adjacent alley. That "Y" was also the home of *The Rag* from 1968 until the building was torn down in 1970.

A second "Y," upstairs at 2330 Guadalupe, became the next home of *The Rag*. Alice Kresensky Cunningham, known as "Cris" Cunningham, was the director at that location from 1973 to 1981, allowing not only *The Rag* but also birth control counseling, abortion referrals, draft counseling, Womenspace, Middle Earth, and many other organizations a space to operate. She was a quiet, graceful presence, part of a faith-based social justice ministry. She died at the age of eighty-one in 2017. She helped sustain a raucous movement. She generously mentored many and shared her skills at grant writing with nonprofit start-ups.

Last, but not least, was Reverend Bob Breihan, who presided over the Methodist Student Center. He died in 2017 at the age of ninety-two. I wrote a tribute to Bob Breihan for *The Rag Blog* on the occasion of his ninetieth birthday bash, and the following memorial after his death:

> Bob Breihan will be remembered by those of us fortunate enough to know him in the '60s and '70s as the director of the Methodist Student Center, a vibrant home to peace and social justice advocacy and a multitude of cultural events. The Center housed Ichthus Coffee House, Sattva Restaurant, and the Latin American Policy Alternatives Group (LAPAG). Bob Breihan, an ardent defender of civil, human, and gender rights, provided both draft and birth control counseling.[34]

I am in need of faith. I need to be reminded to forgive and to be forgiven. I need to be able to push the "reset" button to move forward. I need quiet, contemplative time. Perhaps I could fulfill this need with some solitary practice, but it is helpful to be in the company of others.

"We Shall Overcome," the anthem of the '60s civil rights movement, was an expression of faith. "Lift Every Voice and Sing" is a stirring hymn often called the Black National Anthem. The sentiment expressed in the song "Joe Hill" is one of transcendence. The famous Industrial Workers of the World organizer was put to death in Utah, but the song says he never died. Wherever folks are striking and organizing, Joe Hill's spirit lives on.

I love many of the songs written by the "Wobblies." They are often set to the tunes of hymns sung by the Salvation Army. The Wobblies competed with the Salvation Army for attention on the streets in the early 1900s. "The Preacher and the Slave" is one of the Wobbly songs, written by organizer Joe Hill. I used to hum it around my longhaired preacher father-in-law.

> Longhaired preachers come out every night
> Try to tell you what's wrong and what's right
> When you ask them 'bout something to eat
> They will answer with voices so sweet,
> You will eat, bye and bye,
> In the glorious land above the sky
> Work and pray, live on hay;
> You'll get pie in the sky when you die.[35]

I still love that song, with its critique of preachers. But I have known many courageous faith leaders who acted upon the simple message "Do unto others as you would have them do unto you." They didn't tell people to wait for their heavenly reward.

Child Support Revisited

I've had a decade and a half to reflect on child support. It is a program that has long enjoyed bipartisan support. Republicans, in particular, have viewed the program as a means of recouping public benefits. Texas Democrats have benefitted from the program's self-financing mechanisms. Almost everyone has agreed that supporting children with the income of absent parents is a laudable goal.

Anyone with a divorce decree, anyone with dependent children and no support from an absent parent can now receive child support services in Texas. But services were not always universal. At its inception, child support was joined at the hip to the provision of welfare payments. It was launched as a companion to the Aid to Families with Dependent Children program. That's where the origin story gets murky.

Welfare payments were never adequate, particularly in Texas, as a path out of poverty. Welfare recipients were often the victims of political and cultural shaming. "If only the fathers were contributing . . ." The blame fell on deadbeat dads and unmarried mothers. In reality, entitlement to payments meant that the father couldn't be in the home. If he was, the recipient could be punished for welfare fraud and made to pay back assistance. So the very mechanism of welfare contributed to growing numbers of single parents who were subsequently shamed.

When the Clinton administration "reformed" welfare, the move was lauded as a bipartisan stroke of genius. The benefits were to be temporary, with work requirements—the Temporary Assistance to Needy Families program. The time limits, work requirements, and increased state control over eligibility mean that fewer families benefit under the newer program.

The Clinton overhaul vastly increased the punitive aspects of child support enforcement. Although measures were in place for wage garnishment and seizure of tax refunds, the 1996 federal legislation required state legislation to seize property, take licenses, and revoke passports. All employers were required to report new hires to a federal database to make wage garnishment more efficient. There was a doubling down in the ability to punish absent parents, usually poor parents, for nonpayment, even sending them to jail.

In the twenty-twenty light of a COVID-19 pandemic, everything looks different. The stabilization funds that were given to families didn't require a test for income eligibility; they didn't require that recipients pay back assistance; they didn't require proof of personal responsibility; they didn't require employment. They were given as a response to a need. They didn't go as far as presidential primary candidate Andrew Yang had suggested. The stabilization payments weren't universal basic income. But for many struggling families, they were at least income.

In the light of a national pandemic response, a great deal seems possible that didn't seem possible before. In light of the national response to the murder of George Floyd, the racial disparities and inadequacies of the current welfare system look different. The highly punitive measures of child support look different. The program I worked for is another system that needs to be reimagined and reconstructed. Supporting children is a laudable goal. It can be done without shaming families and punishing parents.

Vietnam Revisited

In April 2017 the manager of Austin's public television station, KLRU, contacted me about an upcoming documentary by Ken Burns. The epic, eighteen-hour documentary on Vietnam was slated to air later in the year. I was invited to a screening at the end of April, and told they wanted "protesters" to participate in a "town hall" taping in early May. The town hall would promote the documentary with local content. I suggested contacting Vietnam veterans who had been active in the antiwar movement after they returned from deployment.

The segment of the Burns documentary screened in the LBJ Library Auditorium played to a full house. Both of Lyndon Johnson's daughters were there; Lyndon Johnson's granddaughter, a KLRU board member, introduced Ken Burns. The film segment was only thirty-six minutes of the full eighteen hours. I found them excruciating.

I had learned from antiwar activist Tom Hayden's writings that the Pentagon budget included millions of dollars aimed at reshaping the Vietnam War narrative. I had the eerie feeling that I was in the midst of that shape-shifting effort. In large measure, in that auditorium, it was also the remaking of LBJ's legacy.

I was reminded of a visit two years earlier to the LBJ Museum exhibition on Vietnam. I laughed out loud when I saw a *Rag* cover with a photo of an antiwar demonstration. The photo was a May 1971 demonstration. The caption didn't reveal it, but it was a protest at the dedication of the LBJ Library. It was specific to the building we were in. There was no mention that "War Criminal" had been spray-painted on the face of the museum several days before the picture was taken. Nothing was said about the library hexing that took place or the scale of the antiwar mobilization that occurred while the dignitaries gathered.

The snippet of documentary I saw in that LBJ Library made the architects of the war seem blameless. Johnson's role was cast as tragedy, lamenting the quagmire he inherited, the way it interfered with his domestic agenda. The audience celebrated the heroism of POWs, the courage of soldiers who had to return to a divided country. As is so often the case, so *very* little was said about the Vietnamese. It is the original sin of omission in the domestic conversation about Vietnam.

I tried like hell to wrap my thoughts around the war again. I remembered my first demonstration, recorded by a police surveillance photo in 1965. We were standing—so young and earnest—at the Texas Capitol steps. I had a kerchief tying back my hair. I remembered printing the picket signs in the crafts room on the third floor of the UT Student Union.

"U Thant, Pope Paul, Senators Gore, Morse, and Greuning ask for negotiations in Vietnam. So do we!"

"The Congress shall have the power to declare war—U.S. Constitution."

"We demand immediate cease-fire and negotiations in Vietnam."

I have a photo taken by the United Press International that captures a vigil later that same year at the entrance to the LBJ Ranch. Again, I look solemn and earnest. Alan Pogue photographed me in 1970 standing near Episcopal priest Frank Doremus, a family friend, my face aged with anguish. It was days after the National Guard shot into the crowd at Kent State, and the protest was enormous.

How did we discover the lies? Why did we feel betrayed by our country? How did we finally come to believe, as Daniel Ellsberg says in the documentary *Hearts and Minds*, that "we weren't *on* the wrong side, we *were* the wrong side"?

We were the well-financed military machine of an imperial power, raining down bombs, committing atrocities, burning villages, napalming children, and defoliating forests with toxic Agent Orange, leaving genetic deformities in Vietnam and slowly poisoning many US veterans.

By the war's end, seven million tons of bombs had been dropped on Vietnam, Laos, and Cambodia—more than twice the amount of bombs dropped on Europe and Asia in World War II. Bomb craters in rice fields, unexploded ordnance, forests without leaves, genetic abnormalities, children with napalm scars, adults with lost limbs, hospitals and schools in ruins. That the Vietnamese never wanted to bring horror to our soil is remarkable, certainly in the new millennium, when terrorism marks our national psyche.

KLRU put on a town hall in 2016 that was filmed for local content to accompany the Ken Burns movie. I was billed as a "boomer protester." My friend Terry Dubose, who had been an organizer for Vietnam Veterans Against the War, was there, along with three other veterans, two of them twins who had served in the marines. There were several high school students; one had just signed up for military service.

What do you say on a small stage under lights where a casual exchange is scheduled? How do you explain to the high school students onstage that the Vietnamese were fighting a war of national liberation, intent on unifying their country and expelling foreign invaders?

How do you answer the broadcast journalist when she says, "We never talked about the war." We did nothing but talk about the war for eleven years.

When she asks, "What did we learn?" and answers her own question, "We learned we needed to listen to vets, to honor their service."

I learned to listen to veterans, but I also learned that veterans had to talk with veterans, the same way that women had to talk with women to understand their own narrative, to process their pain, to imagine their lives in new ways.

I learned that my country was financing 78 percent of the French colonial fight in 1954! The United States didn't just step into the French boots after their loss at Dien Bien Phu. We bought those boots.

I learned that Secretary of State John Foster Dulles and his brother CIA director Allen Dulles had no intention of allowing the free elections demanded by the 1954 Geneva Accords to unify the partitioned country. Walt Rostow said, "Ho Chi Minh couldn't be elected dogcatcher." Daniel Ellsberg responded in *Hearts and Minds*, "*Dead* Ho Chi Minh could have been elected president."

I learned that five presidents allowed this war to grow and metastasize, to escalate in intensity and deadliness. I learned how the steady drumbeat of war let Lockheed and Boeing build warplanes and sell their wares to Congress. RAND was promulgating military rationales; DuPont was manufacturing napalm. It was a bonanza, and we still reap the results. We began to see this military excess as the tanks developed for overseas military use were deployed against domestic protesters in Ferguson, Missouri, and then in many other cities.

The United States spends as much on the military as the next eight nations combined. And, with no trace of irony, the pundits blame violence in this society on video games. The marine sniper who admits he was very good at his job also admits he couldn't talk about the war—even with his marine twin brother—for fifteen years!

President Dwight Eisenhower is often praised for warning against the "military-industrial complex," but he was telling the Dulles brothers, "Full steam ahead so long as it doesn't blow back in my face." While they were teaching me the civics lessons of American exceptionalism in grade school, the Dulles brothers were taking out elected governments in Iran (1953) and Guatemala (1954); they were determined to take down Ho Chi Minh but could not.

The blood of three million Vietnamese stains the hands of Truman, Eisenhower, Kennedy, Johnson, and Nixon. And the man scuttling the peace effort at the end of 1968, Henry Kissinger, colluded in the assassination of the Chilean general who would have supported democracy in Chile, clearing the path for a barbaric military regime.

I don't believe that Ken Burns's lengthy documentary addresses what I learned reading *I. F. Stone's Weekly*, or in the teach-ins, at the SDS meetings, and on the streets. What we learned was documented by other filmmakers, in *Hearts and Minds* (1974), *Rebels with a Cause* (2001), *Sir! No Sir!* (2005). They capture the anguish, the mounting sense of rage, the courage of the antiwar movement as it built from earnest to angry, from protest to resistance. It was a long journey from the civics lessons of the 1950s to the belief that we *were* the wrong side, that imperialism was our biggest export.

The soul-shattering legacy of the war in Vietnam that Martin Luther King Jr. warned of in 1967 still haunts us as a nation.

America

Our daughter has a T-shirt that announces, "Mi Patria es America"—My country is America. On the shirt, the country is shown as the continent, transcending national borders. Heroes of popular struggles dot the map, from Rosa Parks in North America, to Archbishop Óscar Romero in the narrow waist of Central America, to Chilean singer Víctor Jara in the Southern Cone.

America is not Trump's slogan "Make America Great Again." We are the continent America. More than eight thousand miles separate the Alaskan

Inuit from the Mapuche of Chile and Argentina. The long spine of mountains from the Rockies to the Andes knows no borders. The American Cordillera connects us North and South.

I began to view the world through an international lens because of Vietnam. With Vietnam, different truths became self-evident. We unlearned lessons, stumbled over evidence of complicity in coups and colonialism. When I traveled to Chile in 1967, I was careful to say, "Yo soy norteamericana." Not "Yo soy americana." Working with NACLA, our span of interest was intercontinental. We were North Americans studying US policy in Latin America so that we could prevent the next Vietnam on our continent.

Chile's brutal coup got personal through my friendship with Chilean exiles. In the 1980s, we became aware that the United States was backing right-wing death squads in Central America. We demonstrated with the Committee in Solidarity with the People of El Salvador. We supported the Sandinistas in Nicaragua and the FMLN in El Salvador.

Chile had nationalized the country's major resource, its copper. In Guatemala, Jacobo Árbenz wanted United Fruit Company's unfarmed land to go to landless peasants. With globalization, we have seen national sovereignty collapse under the weight of trade laws and treaties written in corporate boardrooms. The treaties codify the rights of mining and petroleum companies to *future and unrealized* profits. In international tribunals, the quality of air and water never gets equal time. Even *anticipated* profits trump environmental concerns. Profits talk. Corporate wealth can whisper and be heard.

What is the antidote? Building cross-border solidarity. We need to link the struggle for clean water for Flint, Michigan, to El Salvador. We need to understand that the immigrants whom Trump denigrates are fleeing countries that the United States has destabilized for decades. We need to build upon a new understanding of "America."

The New Insurgency

We experienced an unprecedented wave of insurgency as a reaction to President Trump's election and agenda. He didn't use a dog whistle to signal his racist intent, he used a bullhorn, demonizing nations. He never failed to denigrate women. The activism in response had many roots: Black Lives Matter, the Bernie Sanders 2020 presidential campaign, the Me Too movement. The women's march on January 21, 2017, was an outpouring beyond anyone's expectation, bubbling up from those who felt disenfranchised.

In the aftermath of George Floyd's murder, as well as Breonna Taylor's in her bed, and Ahmaud Arbery's death at the hands of vigilantes, the Black Lives Matter movement spread across the nation, into small towns and giant cities, and then across the globe. It was seismic and swift, an awakening by a younger generation that gets diversity. Four hundred years after slavery came to this continent, white people must reckon with racism, with the privilege and prejudices of systemic white supremacy.

The large footprint left by the activists of the '60s and '70s may finally be eclipsed. We forged community, but it was fractured by differences and betrayals. Some of our work has survived for decades. Other efforts have disappeared. I hope our shortcomings can be the compost nutrient for current struggles. I hope that some of us can pass solidarity from one generation to another.

Marge Piercy wrote a description of the effort that is required to move forward that has always resonated with me. It is in her poem "To be of use":

> I love people who harness themselves, an ox to a heavy cart,
> who pull like water buffalo, with massive patience[36]

I do love those people—and there are many—who have never forsaken that heady dream that we can make the world a better place, that we can democratically, as peacefully as we are allowed, build a better world that benefits the many and not the few.

Marge Piercy reminds us that we must care for each other as we move forward. In her poem "The spring offensive of the snail," she advises us to remember "to sing and make soup" and to "bury old quarrels behind the garage for compost."

There will be victories and defeats, but what lasts is the community forged in the struggle. This is one thing that I wish to convey to younger activists.

•   •   •   •   •

A braid's strands take their turns on top as they meld into a stronger, interwoven rope of hair. The different strands of my life—family, political passions, creativity, and work—have also taken turns, coming into prominence, slipping out of view, gathering strength over time. I find tenacity to be a virtue.

In the midst of the new insurgency, I've felt the power of being part of a national organization again, something I have missed. I've had a front seat to the chapter life of DSA, a group busting at the seams with new members in the wake of the Trump presidency. It is exhilarating to raise funds for abortion access in Austin and to know that DSA chapters across the country are amplifying our local effort tenfold.

It has given me hope to be around youthful energy and zeal, young people who believe that transformation is possible. A feminist action committee and a queer coalition have emboldened new voices. The organization is still a work in progress. I'm still amazed when I hear a meeting cochair describe the concept of "stepping back," amazed to watch men make a serious effort not to dominate dialogue. What a refreshing departure from the movement days when women rarely had speaking parts.

DSA's embrace of "intersectionality" is a breath of fresh air to me. By 1968, we called ourselves radicals and revolutionaries. We recognized different types of oppression. But too often, this engendered interminable discussions in small rooms. Dominated by men, these arguments were over the "primary contradiction." Was it racism, imperialism, or class?

Theory outweighed action in those rooms, and the hierarchy of oppression usually omitted gender, an oppression with personal resonance. Like counting angels on the head of a pin, the arguments didn't broaden participation. Instead, the ferocity of advancing the "correct" position always seemed to be an incubator for sectarianism.

In 1989, Kimberlé Crenshaw introduced the term "intersectionality" in her paper "Demarginalizing the Intersection of Race and Sex." Crenshaw, an attorney, argued that it was impossible to understand the oppression of Black women by independently considering race and gender oppression; the interaction of oppression must be understood. Intersectionality is one of the lessons I have learned from DSA.

Black and White

I grew up in the Austin of the 1950s. Like a postcard from the Jim Crow South, my early memories are captured in Black and white. Austin touts its progressive reputation now: "the blue dot in a sea of red." Of course, almost every big Texas city—Houston, Dallas, San Antonio, El Paso—votes Democrat, not just Austin; and Houston is perhaps the most diverse large city in the country.

UT professor Eric Tang used the scalpel of statistics to peel away Austin's progressive veneer. His research showed Austin to be the only rapidly growing city in the nation with a shrinking African American population. Historic African American neighborhoods have succumbed to new condos. African American residents have been displaced to surrounding suburbs. Rising land costs and staggering property taxes have seen to that.

The Austin Justice Coalition campaigns today against police shootings of unarmed people of color. It is the voice of Black Lives Matter in Austin. Its predecessors in the Black Citizens Task Force paved the way, leading demonstrations on the sidewalk in front of the Austin Police Department.

Before Black Lives Matter became a national movement, Velma Roberts and Dorothy Turner led the way, with the Black Citizens Task Force marking every incident—choke holds, smotherings, and shots fired at unarmed men. Larry Eugene Jackson Jr. died in 2013 in Austin, unarmed and fleeing from an officer who shot him in the back of the neck. Rayshard Brooks died in Atlanta in 2020, shot in the back as he fled. Cell phone cameras can amplify the anguish now. Social media connects that anguish across state lines in a way that was not possible when Velma and Dorothy demonstrated at the Austin Police Department. These women aren't here to witness their legacy take hold with a new generation. But they are surely here in spirit.

The Brown Berets marched against police terror in the 1970s. Paul Hernandez was badly beaten by Austin police at a 1983 anti-Klan rally. He spent years using a wheelchair before his death in 2020. After President Trump's Muslim ban was announced, the Muslim and immigrant communities came together in Austin for a "No Ban, No Wall" demonstration. Paul was there with other Brown Berets. "We didn't cross the border," he said. "The border crossed us."

• • • • •

This is my homage to an earlier time of insurgency. I could not let these experiences fade like vapor, never to be found in the new world of a searchable past. Red River Women's Press, the Piccadilly sit-in, and the hexing of the LBJ Library are stories that cry out to be told. The audacity of George Vizard, the moral conviction of the Espinozas, the courage of Rita Starpattern, the tenacity of Glenn Scott. I want their voices to live on.

I am grateful to have had a front seat to today's insurgency. When I am around younger activists, I realize how many lessons I still have to learn. The definition of a lifelong commitment is that it lasts a lifetime. Thus, I learn the new concepts, like intersectionality. I don't talk about segregation when I'm invited into a classroom; I talk about Jim Crow laws and white supremacy. I try to give the flavor of the women's liberation movement, not the paler rendition of second-wave feminists. When I call myself a socialist feminist today, it has a resonance with many younger women.

I have found a community of optimistic young people who believe that the world can be transformed. They give me hope. With them, I've been able to raise my voice in chants. With them, I can add my voice to the rousing choruses of "Bread and Roses" and "Solidarity Forever." These verses from "Solidarity Forever" were written in 1915, but they stand the test of time:

> They have taken untold millions
> That they never toiled to earn
> But without our brain and muscle
> Not a single wheel could turn
> We will break their haughty power
> Gain our freedom when we learn
> That the union makes us strong
>
> In our hands is placed a power
> Greater than their hoarded gold
> Greater than the might of armies
> Magnified a thousand-fold
> We can bring to birth a new world
> On the ashes of the old
> For the union makes us strong[37]

Epilogue

A YEAR HAS PASSED IN PANDEMIC ISOLATION. AS PEERS ARE vaccinated, hope stirs that we may interact more freely. In this year, we have witnessed the resilience of health care workers, the brilliance of scientists, the strength of community. And we have witnessed catastrophic failures in leadership. We have seen the fragility of our ecosystem. In Texas in early 2021, many were affected by the loss of heat, potable water, and the power that supplies connection to the outside world. We witnessed the fragility of democracy, easily prey to lies and the rage fomented by those lies. At the same time, there was Georgia, resilient in the face of voter suppression, a lesson for so many states, including Texas.

My activism took place via Zoom over the past year. I worked with the Texas Alliance for Retired Americans (TARA), a union affiliate, to educate voters about voting by mail. At every turn, Texas elected officials countered our efforts to safeguard democratic participation. Judicial decisions expanding vote by mail were appealed and overturned. County officials were admonished when they opened twenty-four-hour voting sites and attempted to expand drop boxes for mail-in voters.

My husband and I were retired. We could isolate. Our children could work from home. Our grandson's life was disrupted, his social environment shrank, his team sports put on hold, but technology allowed him to see teachers and classmates virtually.

George Floyd's murder exposed structural racism and ignited a generational uprising. It spread across the country into small towns, big cities, and across the globe. It made the disparities in our justice system and in pandemic health outcomes highly visible.

We are forced to see with new eyes what should be self-evident. Health care is a human right, one we must continue to fight for. Despite the heroism of health care workers, the COVID-19 death toll in this country has been catastrophic. Our broken health care system, leaving so many without access, has exposed our healthcare vulnerabilities.

Our lives are intertwined, but our divisions are so easily exploited in an age of social media. Solidarity works. Divisions are deadly.

Government can deploy vaccines and dispatch needed relief. Government can be accountable to the needs of people. On the other hand, leaders beholden to private interests, who dismantle oversight, can leave you huddled without heat in your home, melting snow to flush toilets.

We do not succeed with false patriotism. We need both movements and organization. We need the steady voice of unions as advocates for the working class, the steady voices of Georgia's John Lewis and then Stacey Abrams against voting suppression. We need the diversity and insistence of younger voices. We must learn our history of dissent and insurgency in order to understand our strength. We must always seek to unite our struggles for justice.

A government's response to popular needs requires vigilant advocates and voices for social justice. We must understand that we do not hand off our democracy every electoral cycle. We participate in democracy as we build a culture of solidarity.

Acknowledgments

I AM GRATEFUL FOR ALL THE WOMEN AND MEN MOVED TO action in the '60s and '70s, determined to right the wrongs of racial and gender injustice and end a war. We did not know it then, but we changed the arc of history. Many of us continued to be engaged in fights for social justice and have now lived long enough to see a younger generation step boldly forward to meet today's challenges.

Stories cry out for telling. Fortunately, the Briscoe Center embraces those stories, the archives, the oral histories, the photographs, and my own story told in this book. I was moved to write it down, to add a storyline that embraced the New Left and women's liberation, a woman's perspective to history often told by men. I hope this book reflects the Austin audacity I know and love. I hope it pays tribute to the rich community of resistance and solidarity that is still alive and well in Texas.

I owe a great deal to two women in my pre-pandemic writing group, Alyce Guynn and Sharon Shelton. They listened to and read this book as it progressed. They were midwives to words, urging me on. Julia Mickenberg, friend and professor, lent her critical eye to this work, version by version. Another writer, Kathleen Orillion, used her screenwriter skills to help hone the flow of words. My nephew Thomas LeBien and novelist friend Tom Zigal shared publishing expertise.

Photographers Alan Pogue, John Avant, D. Gorton, Robin Birdfeather, and Stanley Farrar graciously permitted their work to be included as did artists Nancy Simons, Trudy Stern, Carlos Lowry, and Marie Valeroy. I am so grateful for their talent, their documentary photography, and their artistic skill.

When Don Carleton, executive director of the Briscoe Center, decided to publish this manuscript, it graduated to the care of Holly Taylor, head of publications at the Briscoe Center. My work was greatly enhanced by her attention to detail. I have only met Holly in person once, in March 2020, before the pandemic shut down the world we had known. From her home, Holly coordinated the project's path to publication, by overseeing editing, rewrites, design, and more. Alison Beck, director of special projects at the Briscoe Center, managed photo acquisition, making several trips to my porch to pick up material. Hal Richardson and Caitlin Brenner at the Briscoe Center scanned many of the images. Abby Webber did a skillful job with the copy editing, and designer Derek George made everything look great.

Friends made this effort possible with their words of encouragement. And my family grounded me. Carlos Lowry, my partner, perfected his pandemic cooking skills when I was working long hours. Our children, Camilo and Laura, reminded me of every reason we have to make a world worthy of our children and grandchildren.

Notes

1. Kevin Brass, *Austin Chronicle*, February 12, 2010.

2. Manumission societies advocated that owners free slaves; abolitionists advocated that the government abolish slavery.

3. Alice Embree, *Looking Glass* (Austin, TX: New Journalism Project, 2018), 13.

4. Lois Steele and Jack Fulton, "(You Oughta Go-ta) North Dakota," 1958.

5. Thorne Dreyer, Alice Embree, and Richard Croxdale, eds., *Celebrating The Rag: Austin's Iconic Underground Newspaper* (Austin, TX: New Journalism Project), 283.

6. Abe Peck, *Uncovering the Sixties: The Life and Times of the Underground Press* (New York: Pantheon Books, 1985), 58.

7. The following section was originally published in a slightly different form in *Celebrating The Rag*, ed. Dryer, Embree, and Croxdale, 66–68. Reprinted with permission.

8. Marge Piercy, *Sleeping with Cats: A Memoir* (New York: HarperCollins, 2002), 193.

9. Piercy, 194.

10. Fred Rosen, "NACLA at 50: Looking Forward, Looking Back," *NACLA Report on the Americas* 50, no. 3 (2018), 219–228.

11. Rosen, 219–228.

12. Thomas McKelvey Cleaver, "The Oleo Strut Coffeehouse and the G.I. Anti-war Movement," *The Rag Blog*, July 28, 2008, http://theragblog.blogspot .com/2008/07/under-hood-anti-war-gi-coffeehouse-in.html.

13. Paco Ignacio Taibo II, *'68* (New York: Seven Stories Press, 2004), 121.

14. Margaret Randall, *I Never Left Home: Poet, Feminist, Revolutionary* (Durham, NC: Duke University Press, 2020).

15. Hoffman wrote, "All this brought us together and when Jeff, who is Alice's man, said 'Alice says I have a tendency to snub you,' I knew we could work together." Abbie Hoffman, *Woodstock Nation* (New York: Vintage Books, 1969), 130.

16. New York Liberation News Service, "YIP Myth Becomes Reality," *Los Angeles Free Press* 6, no. 284 (December 26, 1969–January 1, 1970), 2.

17. Peck, *Uncovering the Sixties*, 214–215.

18. Robin Morgan, "Goodbye to All That," *Rat*, February 9–23, 1970, 6–7.

19. "*The Rag*: Part 2" (People's History in Texas, 2016), documentary film, http://peopleshistoryintexas.org/documentaries/the-rag-austin -underground-press-1966-1977/.

20. Sarah Weddington, inside cover blurb, in *Celebrating The Rag*, ed. Dreyer, Embree, and Croxdale.

21. The final three paragraphs of this section were originally published in a slightly different form in *Celebrating The Rag*, ed. Dryer, Embree, and Croxdale, 282. Reprinted with permission.

22. Beverly Burr, "History of Student Activism at the University of Texas at Austin" (master's thesis, University of Texas at Austin, Spring 1988), 44.

23. Alice Embree, "Janis," *The Rag*, October 12, 1970, 20. Reprinted in Embree, *Looking Glass*, 27–28.

24. *The Rag*, October 12, 1970, 20.

25. "Embree delivered a jeremiad on her contemporaries," Rossinow wrote. Doug Rossinow, *The Politics of Authenticity: Liberalism, Christianity, and the New Left in America* (New York: Columbia University Press, 1998), 289.

26. Alice Embree, "People's Music," *The Rag*, August 9, 1971, 6.

27. Embree, *Looking Glass*, 29–30.

28. Angela Y. Davis, *Women, Race and Class* (New York: Random House, 1983), 125.

29. Alyce Guynn, "Women's Health Organization: 2nd Post," *Collective Impressions* (blog), June 19, 2016, https://collectiveimpressions.wordpress .com/2016/06/19/womens-health-organization-2/.

30. Red River Dave McEnery, "Amelia Earhart," 1939.

31. Embree, *Looking Glass*, 68–69.

32. Noam Chomsky, personal communication, August 2, 2009.

33. Laurence Leamer, *The Paper Revolutionaries: The Rise of the Underground Press* (New York: Simon and Schuster, 1972).

34. Alice Embree, "Rev. Bob Breihan (1925–2017) Was a Courageous Fighter for Social Justice," *The Rag Blog*, November 13, 2017, http://www.theragblog .com/alice-embree-metro-rev-bob-breihan-1925-2017-was-a-prominent -fighter-for-social-justice/.

35. Joe Hill, "The Preacher and the Slave," *Little Red Songbook* (Industrial Workers of the World, 1911).

36. Marge Piercy, *To Be of Use* (New York: Doubleday, 1973), 49.

37. Ralph H. Chaplin, "Solidarity Forever," *Little Red Songbook* (Industrial Workers of the World, 1915).

Bibliography

Selected Sources

Burr, Beverly. "History of Student Activism at the University of Texas at Austin."
Master's thesis, University of Texas at Austin, Spring 1988.

Cleaver, Thomas McKelvey. "The Oleo Strut Coffeehouse and the G.I. Antiwar
Movement." *The Rag Blog*, July 28, 2008. http://theragblog.blogspot.com
/2008/07/under-hood-anti-war-gi-coffeehouse-in.html.

Davis, Angela Y. *Women, Race and Class*. New York: Random House, 1983.

Dreyer, Thorne, Alice Embree, and Richard Croxdale, eds. *Celebrating The
Rag: Austin's Iconic Underground Newspaper*. Austin, TX: New Journalism
Project, 2016.

Embree, Alice. "Alice Kresensky Cunningham (July 14, 1935–June 23, 2017)."
The Rag Blog, July 10, 2017. http://www.theragblog.com/alice-embree-metro
-alice-kresensky-cunningham-july-14-1935-june-23-2017/.

———. "Celebrating the Life of Terry J. Dubose." *The Rag
Blog*, November 20, 2018. http://www.theragblog.com/
alice-embree-celebrating-the-life-of-terry-j-dubose/.

———. "A Chile-Texas Connection." *Texas Observer*, June 1, 1984, 15–16.

———. "Compañero Renato Espinoza." *Texas Observer*, June 15, 2007, 31–32.

———. "Give Us Bread, But Give Us Roses." *The Rag Blog*, September 17, 2018.
http://www.theragblog.com/alice-embree-give-us-bread-but-give-us-roses/.

———. "Honoring the Enduring Courage and Generosity of Rev. Bob Breihan."

The Rag Blog, January 7, 2015. http://www.theragblog.com/alice-embree-metro-honoring-the-enduring-courage-and-generosity-of-rev-bob-breihan/.

———. "Janis." *The Rag*, October 12, 1970, 20.

———. *Looking Glass*. Austin, TX: New Journalism Project, 2018.

———. "Media Images 1: Madison Avenue Brainwashing." In *Sisterhood Is Powerful: An Anthology of Writings from the Women's Liberation Movement*, edited by Robin Morgan, 175–191. New York: Random House, 1970.

———. "The Murder of George J. Vizard IV." In *Celebrating The Rag: Austin's Iconic Underground Newspaper*, ed. Thorne Dreyer, Alice Embree, and Richard Croxdale, 66–68. Austin, TX: New Journalism Project, 2016.

———. "People's Music." *The Rag*, August 9, 1971, 6.

———. "Pollution Smothers: *Tom Smothers* vs. Smog of CBS." *Rat*, September 24, 1969, 14.

———. "Remembering Dennis Fitzgerald: Underground Journalist and Veteran Activist." *The Rag Blog*, December 17, 2018. http://www.theragblog.com/alice-embree-dennis-fitzgerald-underground-journalist-and-veteran-activist-dead-at-74-in-canada/.

———. "Remembering Judy Smith." *The Rag Blog*, January 14, 2014. http://www.theragblog.com/alice-embree-and-phil-primm-remembering-judy-smith/.

———. "Rev. Bob Breihan (1925–2017) Was a Courageous Fighter for Social Justice." *The Rag Blog*, November 13, 2017. http://www.theragblog.com/alice-embree-metro-rev-bob-breihan-1925-2017-was-a-prominent-fighter-for-social-justice/.

———. "The Urban Removal Masquerade. *Rat*, May 17–30, 1968, 4.

———. "Working Women Need Social Justice, Not Flowers and Lunch." *Daily Texan*, April 21, 1982, 4.

Ferlinghetti, Lawrence. *A Coney Island of the Mind*. New York: New Directions, 1958.

Hoffman, Abbie. *Woodstock Nation*. New York: Vintage Books, 1969.

Lavergne, Gary M. *A Sniper in the Tower: The Charles Whitman Murders*. Denton: University of North Texas Press, 1997.

Morgan, Robin. "Goodbye to All That." *Rat*, February 9–23, 1970, 6–7.

New York Liberation News Service. "YIP Myth Becomes Reality." *Los Angeles Free Press* 6, no. 284 (December 26, 1969–January 1, 1970): 2.

Pardun, Robert. *Prairie Radical: A Journey through the Sixties*. Los Gatos, CA: Shire Press, 2001.

Peck, Abe. *Uncovering the Sixties: The Life and Times of the Underground Press*. New York: Pantheon Books, 1985.

Piercy, Marge. *Sleeping with Cats: A Memoir*. New York: HarperCollins, 2002.

———. *To Be of Use*. New York: Doubleday, 1973.

Randall, Margaret. *I Never Left Home: Poet, Feminist, Revolutionary*. Durham, NC: Duke University Press, 2020.

Rosen, Fred. "NACLA at 50: Looking Forward, Looking Back." *NACLA Report on the Americas* 50, no. 3 (2018), 219–228.

Rossinow, Doug. *The Politics of Authenticity: Liberalism, Christianity, and the New Left in America*. New York: Columbia University Press, 1998.

Sale, Kirkpatrick. *SDS: The Rise and Development of the Students for a Democratic Society*. New York: Random House, 1973.

Taibo, Paco Ignacio, II. *'68*. New York: Seven Stories Press, 2004.

Annotated Resources

Coates, Ta-Nehisi. *We Were Eight Years in Power: An American Tragedy*. New York: One World, 2017.

Coates's book made me realize that Obama's presidency evoked a backlash because of its competency. Obama challenged the narrative of white supremacy, as Reconstruction had before. I learned very little about Reconstruction in Texas schools. "Carpetbaggers and incompetents," I was told. The lies run deep, and Coates's book exposes so many of them.

Davis, Angela Y. *Women, Race and Class*. New York: Random House, 1983.

Davis's book was a revelation to me. I'd had a simplistic view that women's suffrage had been built upon an abolitionist experience. Davis exposes the fault line of white supremacy, particularly during the suffrage fight in the South.

Gates, Henry Louis, Jr. *Colored People: A Memoir*. New York: Alfred A. Knopf, 1994.

Gates writes with such love about his close-knit West Virginia community in *Colored People*. It calls to mind both the courage and the sacrifice of breaking the color lines of segregation the way Saundra Kirk did in Austin.

Traister, Rebecca. *Good and Mad: The Revolutionary Power of Women's Anger*. New York: Simon and Schuster, 2018.

Traister has written a brilliant book about women's rage, although I found it strange that there was no nod to the film *She's Beautiful When She's Angry*. We were, and are, both beautiful and angry.

Wilkerson, Isabel. *The Warmth of Other Suns: The Epic Story of America's Great Migration*. New York: Random House, 2010.

Wilkerson opened a window for me into the African American migration out of the South, the forces driving it, the destinations determined by railroad lines, the fact that the cruelty of lynching and Jim Crow laws pushed as hard as northern industrial jobs pulled.

Index